A FOREST
OF YOUR OWN

A FOREST
OF YOUR OWN

The Pacific Northwest
Handbook of Ecological Forestry

KIRK HANSON and **SETH ZUCKERMAN**
Northwest Natural Resource Group
Foreword by Jerry F. Franklin

SKIPSTONE

*To my parents, who instilled in me their love and awe
of the natural world, and the humble joy of being a steward.*

—Kirk Hanson

*To Jen and Nick, who have walked miles with me
in the forest and share my joy in trees.*

—Seth Zuckerman

Published by Skipstone, an imprint of Mountaineers Books—an independent, nonprofit publisher

Skipstone and its colophon are registered trademarks of The Mountaineers organization.

Printed in China
27 26 25 24   1 2 3 4 5

Design: Jen Grable
Illustrator: Elara Tanguy
Maps on pages 26 and 182 by Sam Castro
Photo on page 35 courtesy University of Washington Libraries, Special Collections, Darius Kinsey, photographer, D. Kinsey63D
Front cover photographs: *Fir Seedling* (Photo by SimonSkafar/iStock); *Partial timber harvest* (Photo by Matthew Freeman-Gleason); *Townsend's Warbler* (Photo by CavanImages/iStock); *Sparse tree crowns* (Photo by Matthew Freeman-Gleason)
Back cover photograph: *Using a clinometer app on a smartphone* (Photo by Alexandra Dolk)

Excerpt from the poem "At the End of the Fiscal Year" by Jerry Martien on page 117 included by permission of the poet.

Library of Congress Cataloging-in-Publication Data is on file for this title at https://lccn.loc.gov/2023037085. LC ebook record available at https://lccn.loc.gov/2023037086.

Printed on FSC®-certified materials

MIX
Paper from responsible sources
FSC® C188448

ISBN (paperback): 978-1-68051-636-4
ISBN (ebook): 978-1-68051-637-1

Skipstone books may be purchased for corporate, educational, or other promotional sales, and our authors are available for a wide range of events. For information on special discounts or booking an author, contact our customer service at 800.553.4453 or mbooks@mountaineersbooks.org.

Skipstone
1001 SW Klickitat Way, Suite 201, Seattle, Washington 98134
206.223.6303 | www.skipstonebooks.org | www.mountaineersbooks.org

LIVE LIFE. MAKE RIPPLES.

CONTENTS

PART III:
Stewardship in Action

PART IV:
The Bigger Picture

FOREWORD

The book you hold in your hands provides wonderful guidance for folks who have decided to get into the very rewarding activity of managing a forest property. It covers the spectrum of issues that need consideration and does so in a very personal and accessible fashion.

What sets *A Forest of Your Own* apart from other books I've seen is Kirk and Seth's emphasis on managing forest properties using ecological principles. Forest management guides generally emphasize wood production because of its economic importance. This book is about managing forests for the *multiplicity of values* that they provide—wildlife, watershed protection, recreation, inspiration, and carbon storage—as well as wood. This broader perspective involves managing a forest in a very different way than as a short-rotation industrial plantation.

Ecological forest management aims to steward forests in ways that maintain their ecological integrity or completeness, which is what makes them capable of providing so many benefits simultaneously. In recent decades, we have really begun to learn how to put this into practice. It involves a different philosophy than simply managing some trees to try to maximize wood production or return on capital. A very basic example is recognizing the importance of dead wood in creating a healthy forest! Kirk and Seth provide the reader with a great introduction to both the philosophy and practice of ecological forestry.

Climate and other environmental changes, including the increased danger and extent of wildfires, are putting forests at serious risk of deterioration or even loss. Managing forests in ways that maintain their ecological integrity is more important in the twenty-first century than it has ever been. This book will help you do that.

Jerry F. Franklin
Professor Emeritus
University of Washington

INTRODUCTION

BY SETH ZUCKERMAN

I cut my teeth in forestry during the late 1980s and '90s, a time known on the West Coast for the Timber Wars. Hardly more than a century after lumberjacks first arrived in the region, it had become inescapably clear that timber harvest was decimating the few remaining ancient forests. Environmental activists raised the alarm: apart from small preserves in state and national parks, the grandeur of western forests was at risk, along with the habitat they provided for creatures ranging from spotted owls to steelhead trout and slender salamanders. On the other side of this concern for old-growth forests, loggers and millworkers saw a threat to their livelihoods, and the forest industry sensed a threat to its bottom line. Battle lines were drawn.

You could see the conflict in any town on the coast, from Fort Bragg, California, to Bellingham, Washington, expressed in a counterpoint of bumper stickers: a clenched fist shouting, "Earth First!" on a Subaru station wagon, and "Earth First—we'll log the other planets later" on a Ford F-150. The wittiest ones always seemed to come from the logging side: "Spotted owl tastes like chicken," and my personal favorite, "Hug a logger—you'll never go back to trees."

But among the wide selection of slogans, I never found one that resonated with me enough to put it on my own car. Trees are a renewable resource, and can provide the raw materials for roofs over our heads and chairs under our butts—with much less environmental impact than steel, concrete, or plastic. And yet, the old-growth forests were irreplaceable on any human time scale. I could walk among these towering trees and feel both small and at peace, moved in a way that transcended what I felt when I hiked through a meadow or younger forest. To cut the last of these magnificent forests was to waste a legacy that our generation had been put temporarily in charge of. So, how to distinguish good, thoughtful logging from rapacious liquidation of our natural heritage? I wanted to make clear that I understood the need to harvest some timber, but I also appreciated

OPPOSITE: *Foresters at work near Silverdale, Washington*

the other jobs a tree can do besides becoming a two-by-four.

The answer I came up with, which I wrote out in block letters on a sheet of waterproof paper and taped onto the back of my VW bug, was "CUT TREES, NOT FORESTS." In a sense, the work I've done in forestry ever since has been an exploration of how to translate that idea into action.

Over time, that quest led me to embrace an approach—developed by luminary scientists such as Jerry Franklin of the University of Washington and Norm Johnson of Oregon State University—called ecological forestry. From this perspective, the forest isn't just a wood factory or the equivalent of a cornfield with taller plants; it's a whole system entrusted to its current human stewards, who are tasked with looking after it until the time comes to hand it off to the next caretakers. In the meantime, we may harvest what the forest can spare while still maintaining its integrity—all of its parts and the intricate connections between them. When our turn is done, the forest passes on to the next team of stewards—either by sale or inheritance for private forests or by turnover of staff or leadership in the case of corporate and public forests. Either way, the forest will likely outlive anyone who is looking after it at the moment.

In 2017, I found a perch from which to advocate this approach at Northwest Natural Resource Group (NNRG), a Seattle-based nonprofit that has been promoting better stewardship of Oregon and Washington forests since 1992. Before joining NNRG, I spent most of the previous two decades writing about forests, salmon, energy, and other aspects of the North-west's resource economy, getting a chance to see what innovations were being tried from Northern California all the way to the Alaskan panhandle. Then came the chance to be part of a team that was spreading the good word and demonstrating its impact on the ground. That's where I met Kirk Hanson, NNRG's director of forestry, who has led the organization's on-the-ground work with landowners for many years. From workshops to management plans, site visits with landowners, and demonstrations of how to use a chainsaw, Kirk has been teaching people how to care for their forests for more than twenty years—first with the Washington Department of Natural Resources, and since 2006 with NNRG. It was with Kirk that I hatched the idea for the book you hold in your hands, and we have created it together, as a way to collect and pass along what we have learned about the stewardship of forests.

IF YOU LIVE IN THE NORTHWEST, FORESTS ARE likely in your blood, or at least in the view out your window. They are the signature feature of our landscape, like volcanoes in Iceland, grasslands in Kansas, and cacti in the Southwest. This book will help you understand forests and learn how to take care of them. If you own a forest—or even a patch of trees in your backyard—this book will give you information that you can immediately put to use. If you are thinking about buying a piece of forested land, this book will help you identify what to look for so that the forest you own will meet your combination of goals, means, and desires. Even if you don't fall into either of those categories, all of us

Northwesterners have a stake in the forests that are managed on our behalf by the state and federal governments. Quite a few of us are constituents of county and municipal forests as well. We don't expect every reader of this book to have their own forest—in fact, only one of us (Kirk) owns more than an acre of woods. We use the phrase *your forest* in this book to mean whatever forest you have in mind or is near to your heart.

Like the care of any patch of ground that we want to coax to a particular use—tomato bed, pea patch, rose garden—forestry requires an understanding of how the myriad factors of soil, sun, water, and beneficial species come together to produce the plant community we desire. But compared to those crops and gardens, forests are unique in their longevity. If you sow tomatoes, however well or badly your plants produce, you'll likely get a chance to try again next year. But forests call upon us to think across longer time scales, to consider the next custodians of these woods, and to enrich the variety of options those custodians can choose from when it is their turn as stewards. Broadening that spectrum of future choices is especially important as climate change accelerates and shifts the very conditions that made forests possible.

What's more, forests are diverse, interconnected communities of fungi, soil microbes, invertebrates, birds, mammals, amphibians, and yes, trees. Many of those connections have just come to light in the last few decades, as scientists have developed tools to track the flow of nutrients and water through the intricate web of life that lies beneath the soil and have learned to ascend into the forest canopy with climbing gear. A basic premise of ecological forestry is that all of those parts contribute in some way to the health of the forest as a whole. As conservationist Aldo Leopold wrote, "To keep every cog and wheel is the first precaution of intelligent tinkering."

In this book, we will show you the many cogs and wheels that whir together in a Northwest forest and drive it forward into the future. As intricate and awe-inspiring as the processes at work in the forest are, they aren't that complicated—just ignored as we go about our busy human lives, which unfold at a pace that must look frenetic from the standpoint of a six-hundred-year-old cedar tree. The processes all take place in a context that is at once economic, historical, and ecological—economic because the value of Northwest trees in commerce has determined much of the trajectory of these forests since the mid-nineteenth century; historical because the forests we see today are the product of the epochs-long path they have traveled; and ecological because it is the combination of climate, soil, flora, and fauna that shapes the potential of each forest. That's the essence of Part I.

With an understanding of this context, you will be able to see deeper into your forest. In Part II, we'll discuss how to find forestland for sale and how to get to know your forest better by looking more closely at the canopy, the understory, and the roads and streams running through the woods. You'll look for threats such as signs of insect infestation, tree diseases, and invasive species. Once you are armed with those observations, we'll equip you to make a more detailed inventory of your forest that will provide information and ideas you can fold

Maidenhair fern (Adiantum pedatum) *has been used by Indigenous peoples for millennia in basket making and as a medicinal.*

into a management plan. Since forests are such long-lived systems, it pays to take the time to become familiar with your forest and make a plan for how you will manage it over the years to come.

In Part III, we'll explain how to put those intentions into practice for your forest or backyard woodland. We'll describe how you can establish a new stand of trees and protect it from deer that would eat it or from the salmonberry or salal that would engulf it. Once the seedlings turn into saplings, controlling their density becomes the next important task, and we'll show you different ways to keep them

not too crowded but not too sparse either. You'll learn about ways to improve the timber value of your forest, protect it from catastrophic fire, and make it more useful to wildlife. Where the previous chapters answered the why and the what, these chapters lay out the how. We'll help you distinguish, too, between projects you can take on yourself and those that will require you to enlist the help of skilled and better-equipped professionals.

This section also delves into the many rewards of forest ownership and how to reap them—from the more obscure, such as floral greens, mushrooms, and medicinal plants, to the more obvious, such as timber harvest and trail construction.

Finally, in Part IV, we'll conclude by looking at forests for the long haul. We'll talk about the satisfaction that can come from dedicating your land to conservation purposes through agreements that restrict what you and succeeding owners can do with the forest. These agreements can be designed for a wide spectrum of purposes: to protect songbird or salmon habitat, to store more carbon in the forest so it isn't in the atmosphere aggravating climate change, or simply to safeguard your favorite patch of woods from urban development in perpetuity.

Thinking about the future also means recalibrating our expectations in light of climate change. By the end of this century, a tree planted today will experience a climate that is quite different from the weather patterns that prevailed in the 1900s. Anticipating that change calls on forest stewards

to think adaptively, with an eye toward resiliency. The longevity of trees also means that a forest's current owners need to think about how to hand it off to its next caretakers, whether it be family members or purchasers. The forest is a living system that could outlast you and even your grandchildren . . . and there's a line to walk between not only making clear your goals and guardrails but also trusting the next generation to rise to the challenges of the future.

THE PACIFIC NORTHWEST IS AN OUTSTANDING place to raise a forest. The trees in this region are amazing—unsurpassed in the quality of their wood, their grandeur at full age, and their longevity. Connecting with these forests—not just as hikers, skiers, or mountain bikers, but as stewards who care for a patch of northwestern woods—is an adventure that we have found deeply satisfying, and we are excited to share it with you.

NEXT SPREAD: *A maturing forest in the Oregon Coast Range*

PART I

The Need for
Ecological Forestry

CHAPTER 1

What Is Ecological Forestry, and Why Does It Matter?

BY SETH ZUCKERMAN

Ecological forestry seems like it ought to be a redundancy, like soil-based farming or love-based marriage. If there's anything we've learned about forests in recent decades, it's that forests are more than just crowds of trees, just as oceans are more than big ponds of salt water dotted with schools of fish. As a result, any reasonable strategy to care for or manage a forest must take its interconnectedness into account. That is the core meaning of *ecological*—considering the trees as part of a holistic system in which the countless component parts affect and even depend on one another. We encounter all kinds of interactions in a forest, starting with the most basic: species nibbling on one another or eating each other whole. They sometimes compete for light, water, and nutrients, while in other cases, they cooperate and share resources. They parasitize one another, and nest or take shelter in nooks and crannies of habitat that other species have created. Ultimately, a crew of decomposers swoops in to consume them in death.

In this way, the distinct species add up to a greater whole, like the instruments in a symphony. If you think of forest managers as the conductors of that symphony, ecological forestry means paying attention to the strings, woodwinds, brass, and percussion all with equal concern. Imagine if you were the conductor, and you focused only on the strings section: the composition would sound pretty dissonant, and the concert hall would empty out in short order. But enlist

OPPOSITE: *Autumn larches*

all the instruments, and you can create a thing of beauty. That's the framework we adopt in this book: to care for the forest as an organic whole, taking our cues from natural processes already at work. Our goal is to influence those processes so they provide the forest and ourselves with what we need, recognizing that there is still much for us to learn about how the forest functions.

The rewards of this approach are as diverse as the forest itself. Forests give so much to humanity, starting with their role in providing clean, reliable water. From roots to canopy, they protect the soil and keep it from eroding and thereby muddying the streams that flow through the woods. Forest soils and even the tree crowns absorb some of the rain that falls on the landscape and slow its release into the streams below, reducing the magnitude of floods in the wet season and extending runoff later into the summer. Finally, they moderate the temperature of creeks and rivers that traverse the forest both by shading them and through evapotranspiration (the evaporation of water exhaled through the trees' leaves and needles), keeping the water cool for salmon, salamanders, and other cold-water-loving creatures. The watersheds that supply many cities' drinking water, including Seattle, Tacoma, Bellingham, and Portland, are all covered in well-managed forests, which protect the quality of the water for those municipalities.

Care about wildlife? Forests shelter innumerable species of mammals, birds, and amphibians, not to mention less charismatic creatures such as insects and mollusks, as well as life-forms yet unknown to science. Some of those animals find the food, cover,

or habitat they need only in forests that have reached a certain age—perhaps they need to excavate their nests in dead trees of a certain minimum size, or build their nests in a tree that has developed the complexity and broken tops that only occur in older forests. Others need the accumulation of downed logs that hold moisture through the summer or provide shelter against predators. In Chapter 5's guided walk through the woods, we'll get into more detail about attracting and sustaining wildlife in your forest.

Ecological forestry doesn't ignore the timber that can be harvested from the forest. As the timber industry is fond of saying, wood is one of the most environmentally sound construction materials—an assertion we agree with, so long as the wood comes from well-managed forests. In many cases, the harvest of timber will be the most valuable source of income that the forest generates, making the harvest of trees crucial to maintaining the land in its forested condition and paying for its upkeep. The key is to start by asking how much timber the forest can afford to give, not how much its human stewards wish to take.

If you think about the trajectory of a forest from a carpet of ankle-high seedlings to a majestic, cathedral-like grove of ancient giants, the number of trees per acre drops drastically over the centuries. Starting with seedlings that might be anywhere from two to ten feet apart, totaling in the high hundreds to mid-thousands per acre, a typical northwestern forest will thin itself to a few dozen trees per acre, spaced twenty to forty feet apart, by the time it is a couple hundred years old. As a first approximation, the majority of the trees that die over the

Edible oyster mushrooms (Pleurotus ostreatus) *are commonly found growing on hardwoods, especially red alder.*

years can be harvested without affecting the development of a mature forest (depending on the particulars of how to extract them from the woods, which we will cover in Chapter 14 and beyond). But the choice of which trees to take, how many, and when needs to be made with consideration of the forest as a whole, not simply the value of the timber or how to get the greatest economic return. As University of Washington professor Jerry Franklin says, "A general principle of ecological management is that you don't ever try to maximize anything—any time you do that, you're going to begin to marginalize other values." Another way to frame this is that in ecological forestry, you come to a potential timber harvest with the question of "What would be the condition of the forest after this harvest?" instead of "How much timber can we cut?" As it happens, this approach will also support a steady sup-

ply of timber and jobs rather than a boom-and-bust economy.

Of course, timber isn't the only product that can be harvested from the forest. The Northwest has a thriving industry in greens that are used in wreaths and floral arrangements, from salal and ferns for bouquets to fir boughs used in seasonal wreaths. Mushroom pickers and truffle hunters gather the bounty of edible fungi and sell them at top dollar to gourmet consumers (or sauté them for an epicurean omelet of their own). Salal berries can be made into jam, huckleberries are delicious in pies or oatmeal, and there's even a nascent trade in maple syrup made from the sap of the Northwest's own bigleaf maple. Since forests provide cover to elk and deer, and safeguard the quality of water in salmon's spawning streams, you could arguably count those wild foods among the bounty of the forest.

Forests also store carbon, keeping it out of the atmosphere where it would warm the climate. Oregon forests, for instance, contain more than one hundred times as much carbon as the state emits every year through the combustion of fossil fuels. (This figure accounts for all biomass in the forest, both living and dead, including roots and downed wood, but not the carbon contained in organic compounds that are part of the soil.) Every year, that state's forests accumulate another thirty-two weeks' worth of fossil fuel emissions—more than half of what is given off by all the fossil fuel use in Oregon. In Washington, forests store sixty-three times the annual fossil fuel emissions and accumulate about one-fifth as much additional carbon each year as the state emits from the combustion of fossil fuels. As impressive as those numbers sound, the carbon storage by both states' forests falls well short of their capacity. We'll talk more in Chapter 21 about the ways carbon accumulation in forests can be tracked and even monetized; but for now, just bear in mind that carbon is one of the strengths of Northwest forests.

Finally, a practitioner of ecological forestry takes into account the value of their forest to the human spirit. Whether it is for hiking, mountain biking, or quiet contemplation from within or from afar, the forest has long held a place of reverence in people's hearts. In Shakespeare's *As You Like It*, the duke finds in the Forest of Arden "tongues in trees, books in the running brooks, / Sermons in stones, and good in everything." Scottish novelist Robert Louis Stevenson noted that the "emanation from the old trees ... so wonderfully changes and renews a weary spirit." The forest, he said, is a "great moral spa ... the best place in the world to bring an old sorrow that has been a long while your friend and enemy." And that's without even citing the usual suspects of John Muir, Henry David Thoreau, or Theodore Roosevelt. In the social context of forest stewardship, the forest's importance as a source of solace and renewal is not to be underestimated.

FROM WATER TO CARBON, SPIRITUALITY TO timber, the forest has a lot to offer, and ecological forestry concerns itself with all of those parts. We used to think of caring for a forest mainly as maintaining its *integrity*, but with the acceleration of climate change, there is another quality that we need to consider: *resilience*. As global warming continues, simply keeping forest conditions within the realm of what has worked for the last hundred years isn't enough. We have to think about enabling the forest to adapt to the changing conditions it will experience over the next decades of a warming climate. For now, at least, it doesn't mean radical changes, but it does mean thinking beyond what contributed to integrity and stability in the face of a twentieth-century disturbance regime. Instead we must think about what will sustain a functional ecosystem when it experiences unforeseen heat waves, droughts, insect outbreaks, and wildfires. We'll get into this at greater length in Chapter 22; but for now, just note that an ecological forestry approach has to consider not only where the puck is but also where the puck is headed. Otherwise, the forest will be pucked.

Thinning underway at the Nisqually Community Forest near Ashford, Washington

It's worth mentioning that advocates for a holistic approach to forest stewardship use a variety of different labels; *ecological forestry* is just one of many terms. In the 1990s, it was common to speak of *sustainable forestry*—practices that could be maintained indefinitely without degrading the quality of the forest. But that term's popularity faded, partly from overuse and partly because a timber-industry-backed trademark, the Sustainable Forestry Initiative (SFI), began to use it. With the capital for robust marketing campaigns, SFI influenced the public's understanding of "sustainability" as it applies to timber.

Other terms that have gained currency at various times in the last couple of decades include *restoration forestry, ecoforestry* (also the name of nonprofit organizations in the United States and Canada), and *regenerative forestry*, which speaks to both the impact on human communities that depend on the forest and the regeneration of the living systems in the forest itself. All of those terms are, at the very least, allied with ecological forestry, if not synonymous with it, so we won't spend time delineating the finer distinctions between them. Instead, know that these labels coexist within the larger realm of frameworks that prioritize the health and vitality of the forest as a whole over short-term financial goals.

Our advocacy of ecological forestry places us at odds with two other approaches, which we believe to be misguided. It will come as no surprise that we prefer not to think of the forest simply as a financial asset, to be harvested whenever and however it will result in the highest return on investment. That may be good business in the short run, but it isn't good forestry, and we believe that across the broad range of

Why Hyphenate Douglas-fir?

In the taxonomy of trees, Douglas-fir (of the genus *Pseudotsuga*, meaning "false hemlock") doesn't count as a true fir (in the genus *Abies*) because of the little bracts, sometimes said to resemble mouse tails, that stick out between the scales on its cones. If it were written *Douglas fir*, that would imply to botanists that it is a kind of fir, and botanists are a sticklish sort.

possibilities afforded by forestland, it yields inferior results. Thus, we part ways with the majority of industrial timber ownerships, which are guided by a sense of fiduciary duty to maximize profit for their investors and by a strong preference for short-term profits over long-term returns.

At the same time, we also take issue with the diametrically opposite school of thought, which contends that Northwest forests have suffered too much abuse during the last century and a half of lumbering and should simply be allowed to rest and heal themselves. It is understandable that people may have arrived at this conclusion after seeing the effects of thoughtless logging—vast clear-cuts, often right up to the edges of streams, followed by monocultures of young Douglas-fir that are never allowed to get beyond age forty. But it will take

active stewardship to restore those forests to health—thoughtful care that this book will explain how to practice. A forest of uniformly spaced thirty-year-old Douglas-fir will recover its ecological functions and the complexity (and thus richness) of its habitat more quickly if it is managed toward that end rather than simply neglected. What's more, its continued maturation and development will be more reliable with active management, since a dense and homogeneous forest is more vulnerable to insect outbreaks, disease, and wildfire. It's important to note that we advocate this approach only on forests that have already been logged and crisscrossed with roads. Forests that have never known an axe or saw are so rare—and have so much to tell us about the ecology of forests in the absence of human disruption—that they should not be logged.

As it happens, ecological forestry is also a sensible strategy for local economies. If we focus on increasing the complexity of forests and rebuilding their integrity, they will in turn be able to contribute to the prosperity and livelihoods of the surrounding human communities. Over time, this will provide a more stable, secure, and enriching foundation for the wood products industry than either the lock-it-up or the cut-it-all-down-ASAP schools of thought.

In the next two chapters, we will survey the Northwest forest landscape—first, the kinds of forest ecosystems that thrive here, and then the historical context that got us to this point.

CHAPTER 2

The Northwest Forest Landscape: Forest Zones and Types

BY KIRK HANSON

I grew up in a very different environment than the one I've lived and worked in for the past thirty years. I was born in Minnesota in a belt of hardwood forests that stretch across the Midwest states, a forest composed of red and white oak, sugar maple, birch, and the occasional pine. Although my family lived on the outer rind of the suburbs north of the Twin Cities, we also owned eighty acres of forestland in the St. Croix River Valley a couple hours farther north. Over the first twenty years of my life, my family frequently traveled to "The Woods," as we called it, and tinkered with the hardwood forest.

My parents were of the Aldo Leopold school of conservation—if you're a careful steward of the land, the land will support you. They spent countless days planting white pine in the understory of the second-generation hardwoods, protecting the seedlings from deer browse, and eventually thinning the oaks and maples to make way for the return of the pine as it gradually eclipsed the forest canopy. We cut endless cords of firewood from the diseased red oak as it slowly expired to a root fungus that was epidemic throughout the forest. We filled water jugs from natural springs that seeped through the porous, sandy soils. Not being hunters ourselves, my dad leased the annual hunting rights to our property for the value of the annual land taxes. We cross-country skied, hiked, camped, picnicked, played, and developed an awe and appreciation for nature. Later, my dad took oak logs to a local mill and had them turned into lumber from which he made various items, including a set of heirloom-quality Craftsman-style living room furniture for my family.

An eastside ponderosa pine forest after thinning and prescribed burn

White pine was the original old growth across much of the Midwest before it was logged off to feed a growing nation—a prelude to the future of forests in the Pacific Northwest. Before my parents sold a conservation easement on their land to the Minnesota Land Trust, the crowns of the white pine they had planted for decades were just beginning to emerge from the canopy of hardwoods, effectively restoring this original old-growth species to their plot of land. My parents eventually sold the family forest to another private owner when they moved west to live near me and reinvested in forestland near Black Diamond, Washington.

When I moved west more than twenty-five years ago, it felt like an existential imperative that I acquire my own forestland into which I could send down roots, make sense of this world, and pursue the endless fascination of tinkering in the woods. In 1995, my sweetie and I purchased our first tract of land, what I now refer to as our homestead property, just south of Oakville, Washington. I had just enough college tuition money left over after graduating to make the down payment on the land—something unheard of today. Like a forced savings plan, we put every spare penny we earned into paying it off.

Our Oakville forest sits at the northern terminus of the Willapa Hills, a massive series of ancient submarine clay ripples. If you scramble down the deeply incised seasonal stream drainages on the north side of the hills, you will find a horizon of sedimentary soil choked with seashells—evidence of the era when these antediluvian marine terraces were submerged beneath salt water. Over eons of subduction, the Juan de Fuca Plate ground its way beneath the North American Plate, shoving the current shoreline up out of the ocean, exposing the marine terraces, and setting into motion the ecological succession that led to some of the most biomass-dense forests our planet has ever known, second only to the redwood forests of Northern California.

The old growth is long gone. My family's Black Diamond and Oakville forests and a third forest we recently purchased near Bucoda, Washington, now support a third generation of trees composed largely of young Douglas-fir and red alder. Ghosts of the former old growth still linger in the shadows of our woods in the form of massive stumps and downed logs, but these have nearly faded to nothingness and require a keen eye to find. Restoring the structure, habitat, and character of the old-growth forests of the Pacific Northwest is one of my family's missions, and in so doing we will generate periodic dividend checks by thinning trees from the two-hundred-acre forest investment we've made. However, to quote a common saying in the world of restoration ecology, "The desired future condition is not the past." My family is not endeavoring to manage our forest back to a historical condition. Instead, by looking to historical and current old-growth forests as examples, we're using principles of ecological forestry to manage our forests forward. Forward into a new climate that may not support the same assemblages of plant species that existed historically. And forward into a condition that we hope will provide a sustained supply of high-quality forest products and a

rich panoply of ecosystem services such as wildlife habitat, carbon sequestration, and biodiversity.

With this book, Seth and I provide ideas, principles, and examples of management practices that we believe can help restore older forest functions and characteristics to forests across the Pacific Northwest. These ideas come from our combined fifty-plus years of forest management experience and the wisdom we have gleaned from a community of forest practitioners who are working to advance the science and application of ecological forest management. Seth's and my experience is primarily rooted west of the Cascade Range. As a result, this book focuses largely on this region and the Douglas-fir forest type. However, the principles of ecological forest management that we describe in this book can be applied to many different forest types, including forests east of the Cascades, and are relevant in both the wetter and drier parts of the Pacific Northwest, from the Olympics to the upper Klamath basin.

FOREST ZONES

In the Pacific Northwest, a tremendous diversity of climate, elevation, and soils creates a mosaic of *forest zones* where different combinations of trees thrive, and some zones where forests don't grow at all, like the sagebrush steppe of the interior (see Figure 2-1). From the Sitka spruce forests of the Olympic coast, to the Douglas-fir, western hemlock, and Pacific silver fir forests that dominate the west side of the Cascade Range, to the pine-dominant forests that grow in the drier environment east of the Cascades, each forest zone is different and

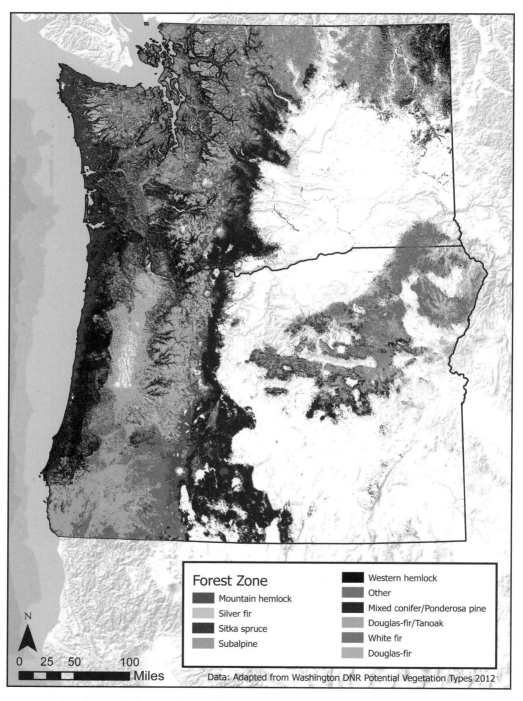

Forest Zone

Mountain hemlock
Silver fir
Sitka spruce
Subalpine
Western hemlock
Other
Mixed conifer/Ponderosa pine
Douglas-fir/Tanoak
White fir
Douglas-fir

N

0   25   50   100
Miles

Data: Adapted from Washington DNR Potential Vegetation Types 2012

Figure 2-1. Forest zones of Oregon and Washington

supports a unique community of plant species. The actual *forest type* on your land is an outcome not only of the environmental factors that create a forest zone but also the history of the land and its use—such as the fire history, previous logging or forest management, or whether your land was cleared for farming. Understanding the inherent environmental factors of your site, the land use history, and the potential effects of climate change will help you determine how to care for your forest now and in the future.

In the early 1970s, two forest ecologists with the United States Forest Service, Jerry Franklin and C. T. Dyrness, developed a system for classifying forest vegetation across the Pacific Northwest, which later became colloquially known as the "Franklin and Dyrness forest zones," and was described in their book *Natural Vegetation of Oregon and Washington* published by Oregon State University Press. Their system of classification is based on the species of trees that will achieve dominance on a particular site given sufficient time, influenced by regional elevation, temperature, and rainfall. Due to the Cascade Range that intercepts moisture flowing inland from the Pacific Ocean, the Pacific Northwest can handily be divided into two primary ecosystems: the mesic, or wet, forest ecosystem throughout most of the west side, and the dry, fire-dependent forest ecosystem across most of the east side of the Cascade Range. Since the Franklin and Dyrness vegetation system came out in the 1970s, newer vegetation maps and typing systems have been developed and continue to be updated, including Landfire Biophysical Settings, Terrestrial Ecological

Systems of the United States, and Bailey's ecoregions.

It is useful to know the forest vegetation zone a particular forest occurs within, as each zone has similar biophysical conditions, plant communities, pathways of forest development, and historical disturbance regimes. Table 2-1 summarizes nine major forest vegetation zones across Oregon and Washington. Within each of these broad vegetation zones, smaller forest zones are present where, given unique soil and microclimatic conditions, other tree species are more likely to achieve dominance, such as the Oregon white oak savannas of the southern Puget Sound and Willamette Valley or the mixed conifer zones of southwestern Oregon.

DISTURBANCE AND FOREST SUCCESSION

Forests grow on an ecological continuum that follows cycles of birth, growth, death, and rebirth, all of which are playing out simultaneously within any stand of trees. The forest before you may have been planted following logging, it may have naturally regenerated following a major natural disturbance like a fire or windstorm, or it may be in one phase of a centuries-long process of ongoing change. To fully understand your forest, you need to understand its life history and the complex processes of forest development that have shaped its current composition and character.

All forests are shaped by natural disturbance. There are many *natural disturbance events* that can either reset a site back to zero (no living trees at all) or alter the conditions of the site enough to stimulate the natural regeneration of a new cohort of trees. The 1980 eruption of Mount St. Helens may be the most dramatic example of a natural disturbance event, where the trees within the blast zone were entirely killed by the force of the eruption. A wind disturbance or an ice storm is a more moderate example, as not all of the trees are blown down and a lot of *legacy structures* remain, such as both live and dead trees, along with a lot of

Table 2-1: Pacific Northwest Vegetation Zones

VEGETATION ZONE	PHYSIOGRAPHIC REGION	ELEVATION (FT.)*	RAINFALL (IN.)*
Sitka spruce (*Picea sitchensis*)	West side, coastal	0–2,000	80–120
Western hemlock (*Tsuga heterophylla*)	West side, lower elevation	0–3,200	60–120
Douglas-fir (*Pseudotsuga menziesii*)	West side, lower elevation; east side, higher elevation	0–3,500	14–60
Douglas-fir (*Pseudotsuga menziesii*) and **tanoak** (*Lithocarpus densiflorus*)	Southwest Oregon	0–3,500	40–100
Silver fir (*Abies amabilis*)	West and east side, higher montane	3,000–5,000	40–60
Mountain hemlock (*Tsuga mertensiana*)	West side, higher montane	4,000–5,500	60–100
Subalpine fir (*Abies lasiocarpa*)	West and east side, higher montane	5,000–6,000	60–100
Ponderosa pine (*Pinus ponderosa*)	East side, mid-elevation	2,000–6,500	14–30
Grand fir (*Abies grandis*) and **white fir** (*Abies concolor*)	East side, low montane	3,000–5,000	20–100

*The listed elevations and rainfall amounts are generalizations and can vary widely across the range of each tree species.

The silver fir zone is found above the Douglas-fir and western hemlock zones in the Cascade and Olympic ranges.

downed dead wood that feeds an elaborate nutrient cycle. Even a severe fire that kills most of the trees still leaves a substantial legacy of dead wood, vertical and horizontal alike, as well as a dispersed mosaic of surviving trees and other vegetation. Going even further back, the original disturbance from which many Northwest forests were born was the retreat of the glaciers at the end of the last ice age.

Other common natural disturbance events include landslides, disease, insects, and drought. Certainly, humans are another common source of disturbance, with land clearing for agriculture or development, logging, and other purposes. Indigenous human populations also have a long history of using natural disturbance agents, such as fire, to alter the species composition in a manner that yields innumerable valuable forest products.

Along with the patchy distribution of living and dead trees that endure natural disturbance events, there are often countless diverse species of tree seedlings in the understory that, combined, set the stage for the next generation of forest—depending on the nature of the disturbance. From any of these disturbance events begins a chain of sequences referred to as forest development. Forest development is often defined as the process by which the biology and structure of a forest evolves over time.

Often, forest development begins with a site becoming rapidly colonized by a *pioneer species*. A pioneer species is any tree, shrub, or other plant that can thrive under the difficult conditions of a newly disturbed site. Pioneer species that prefer wetter sites include red alder and salmonberry. Ones that prefer drier sites include Douglas-fir, ceanothus, and even the highly invasive Himalayan blackberry. These species tend to seed into a disturbed site at a high density, aggressively outcompete most other species, and typically form a monocultural stand of trees or shrubs. If the pioneering species are trees, they often quickly form a dense canopy, and the developing stand enters a *competitive exclusion phase* where individual trees compete with each other for increasingly limited resources such as sunlight and soil moisture. If the pioneering species are shrubs and tree seedlings take root at the same time, those seedlings may eventually grow taller than the shrubs and shade them out of existence. (Alternatively, the shrubs may be so successful at hoarding moisture and sunlight that the tree seedlings may perish in the shade of the shrubs, and the site may remain a brushfield until some other disturbance makes way for new tree seedlings.)

As trees begin to develop on a site, some will grow taller than others and dominate the canopy. Many of the less dominant trees may gradually succumb to *competition-based mortality* as they fail to adequately compete for limited resources, particularly sunlight. Many stands can remain in this competitive condition for decades before they gradually thin themselves, opening their canopy and creating opportunities for other tree and plant species to enter the stand. Given enough time, and the absence of additional disturbance events, these formerly homogeneous stands gradually gain species and structural diversity.

When trees succumb to competition-based mortality or other mortality agents, such as disease and storm damage, they become snags (dead trees) that are valuable to numerous species of wildlife—the older the stand, the larger the snags, and the greater their value. As trees fall in the

Forests laid flat by the eruption of Mount St. Helens

Figure 2-2. Beginning in the aftermath of a fire or disease outbreak which left numerous snags, this forest was founded by pioneer species that initiated a new stand. As they grew from saplings to poles, the stand passed through the competitive exclusion stage. Eventually, the canopy began to break up, allowing a new cohort of seedlings to take root in a process known as understory re-initiation. Finally, the forest enters the structural diversification stage, in which a multi-storied canopy provides complex habitat for a wide array of wildlife.

forest, they add ever-larger downed logs to the forest floor that can provide habitat for hundreds of species of insects, which in turn support an intricate food chain. As gaps form in the forest canopy due to disease or windstorms, they create opportunities for other species of trees and shrubs to enter the forest. In areas where the canopy remains dense, more shade-tolerant trees—such as western redcedar or western hemlock—may establish themselves and begin their long journey to eventually eclipse the dominant but less shade-tolerant pioneering trees. This process may continue for hundreds of years until some of the first generation trees reach an age and size that is commonly referred to as "old growth"—that is, of course, unless a major natural disturbance event, such as fire, resets the stand, leaving behind legacy structures and providing the conditions in which an entirely new generation

of forest takes life, and starts the process all over again (see Figure 2-2).

For thousands of years this process of forest development has played out across the Pacific Northwest landscape. The mosaic of forest types range from newly regenerating forests with relatively simple stand structures to ancient, complex, multi-canopied forests noted for massive conifers and hardwoods and an extraordinary range of biodiversity that includes many as yet undiscovered plant, fungi, lichen, insect, and other species.

In this chapter we laid out the ecological processes that create the character and composition of forests in the Pacific Northwest. In the next chapter, we will look at forests on a temporal scale—from the establishment of forests in our region, through the influence of early humans, and to the contemporary land ownership demographics that shape the forested landscape we see today.

CHAPTER 3

How Did We Get Here? A Brief History of Northwest Forests

BY SETH ZUCKERMAN

A history of Northwest forests could plausibly begin with the emergence of their most widespread tree species, the Douglas-fir, which has existed in more or less its current form since the early Tertiary Period, about 50 million years ago. But it is probably more useful to pick up the narrative as the last ice age waned and glaciers began receding from the Cascade Range, the Wallowa and Klamath Mountains, and the lowlands of Puget Sound.

Massive rivers of ice had flowed south from what is now Canada, having developed in the high country after centuries of snowfall accumulated over one winter to the next. As the ice meandered downslope, it scraped up everything in its path, erasing whatever plant communities had occupied the land. Even land that remained ice-free—farther south or at lower elevations—was shaped by the cooling, drying impact of the glaciers.

So when Earth began its most recent postglacial warming some 12,000 years ago, the forests that we think of as iconic to the Northwest had not yet begun to develop in most of what was to become Oregon and Washington. Based on analysis of pollen deposited in lake sediments from the Willamette Valley to northwestern Washington, Douglas-fir and western redcedar were rare in the south and nonexistent elsewhere, likely because it was too cold and dry for them. Instead, pine and spruce prevailed. In some areas, trees were scarce compared with herbaceous plants.

Older trees lend structure to the forest and complexity to the habitat it provides.

Simultaneously, first peoples began to appear in the archeological record. Each culture has its origin stories for the forest and their habitation of this land, which are theirs to tell. For a sampling of these perspectives on the ancient past of Pacific Northwest forests, check out the books in the Resources section. The story as told by pollen and other preserved plant remains shows that over the next several millennia, the species mix shifted. In the Puget lowlands, which had been covered in ice, red alder played an important pioneer role in restoring the soil's fertility, and was widespread until displaced by western redcedar. Farther south, in the Willamette Valley near present-day Eugene, pine gave way to Douglas-fir, while western hemlock maintained a steady but minor presence. East of the Cascade Range, sagebrush savannas turned to pine forests, mixed first with alder, and later with western hemlock, Douglas-fir, and larch.

When European settlers first arrived, they found vast, magnificent forests that appeared to them to be trackless wilderness. Perhaps because of their prejudice against the Indigenous peoples who were already living here, they missed the impact of Native forest stewardship in shaping the forests they saw. They didn't realize that clearings had been created by intentional burning so that grasses and berries could thrive, to the benefit of both humans and wildlife. Indigenous peoples had also used burning to keep forests open and not too dense in the drier, more fire-prone parts of the region. The pioneers saw majestic oak groves without recognizing that they were well-tended acorn orchards. More than a century after they were abandoned, First

Nations village sites in British Columbia still have a greater diversity of trees and other species in their proximity, especially seed-bearing plants.

Not long after Europeans first arrived, though, they began looking at the forest through a different lens. Rather than harvesting a small portion of the forest's bounty as the Indigenous inhabitants had done—for instance, by splitting planks off the sides of living cedar trees, peeling strips of bark for clothing, or pruning spruce roots to weave watertight hats—the European approach was to cut the trees down and run them through a sawmill. (In fact, in the early days of white settlement, they sometimes just girdled and burned the trees to clear land for farming.) It was arduous work with nineteenth-century technology, particularly given the tremendous size of the old-growth trees they encountered. But early settlers saw the forest solely as an economic resource for industrial production.

In this pursuit, they were aided by US federal policies. In order to encourage the American settlement of the West, the federal government gave away millions of acres to railroads, timber companies, and homesteaders, scant years after seizing that land from the American Indian tribes, sometimes without even the benefit of a treaty negotiated under duress. Railroad companies were given alternating one-by-one-mile squares of public land, in a twenty- to fifty-mile-wide checkerboard pattern, along the tracks they laid. Homesteaders could claim up to 160 acres per person for farming, but that offer required the claimants to occupy and make improvements to the land for five years before they could own it free and clear.

In 1878, the lesser-known Timber and Stone Act was passed, allowing anyone to claim 160 acres of unfarmable land for $2.50 an acre. Although this legislation was nominally intended to spread land ownership to smallholders, in practice it was used by timber companies to build mammoth forest empires as they hired local citizens to claim tracts of forest and then sell them to the company.

THE EARLY DAYS OF LOGGING

Once the land was privatized, timber companies set about logging it. At first, the forests seemed inexhaustible, and there was no thought of what would come next after these trees were felled and fed to the mill. The gargantuan trees required ingenuity and hard work to turn into lumber. Equipped only with hand tools, loggers often needed a full day or more to fell an old-growth tree. Not for nothing were the two-man crosscut saws they used known as misery whips. The trunks of some trees, particularly western redcedar, swelled as they neared the ground, so lumberjacks hacked notches into the trunk, set up scaffolding planks known as springboards, and cut the tree several feet up so they could saw through its narrower girth. This era bequeathed to us sepia-toned images of families picnicking on the mammoth stumps left behind, and the Pacific Northwest incarnation of giant lumberjack Paul Bunyan and his blue ox, Babe.

Landing the tree on the ground was just the beginning of its journey to the mill. Workers then chopped off its branches and sawed the trunk into pieces short enough to move. In the early days, this meant yoking them to oxen, sometimes on "corduroy roads" built of logs laid crosswise to the

These loggers had just cut five 32-foot logs from this western redcedar in Washington (1916).

direction of travel, to keep hooves and logs alike from sinking into the forest soil. In steeper terrain, they used the stream network as log highways: they'd roll logs into a creek, build a temporary reservoir called a splash dam, and then open its sluice gates, sending the logs downstream, borne on the unleashed flood. Ah, the good old days! This technique ravaged fish habitat and riparian vegetation, and reflected that early frontier attitude toward forest management: extract the resource by any means necessary.

Since then, technological change has been a constant. Steam donkeys—self-propelled motorized winches—were introduced to drag logs to steel tracks where they could be loaded onto railcars that transported them to the mill. Then, in the 1930s, tracked vehicles, a peacetime spin-off of technology developed for military tanks, made their appearance. These vehicles were able to cut roads through the forest and drag logs to a landing where they could be loaded onto trucks. Gasoline-powered chainsaws were originally designed to mimic the two-man saw, but after World War II, they were retooled to be handled by a single logger and became widespread . That suite of technologies is memorialized in Ken Kesey's 1964 novel, *Sometimes a Great Notion*, later adapted into a movie starring Paul Newman as tough-minded logger Hank Stamper.

But technology has moved on from the Stamper family's cat skinners (tractor drivers) and choker setters (who wrapped wire rope around logs so they could be pulled from the woods). Over the last three decades, logging has become even more mechanized with the advent of self-propelled logging machines such as the feller buncher and harvester, in which operators sit in a cab and control saws and hydraulic arms to turn trees into logs. Arguably, more logging jobs have been lost to highly efficient machines than to regulations that protect endangered species.

While technological evolution may be the most visible change in the practice of forestry, our shifting perspectives on the purpose of a forest have arguably affected it even more profoundly. The first Euro-American settlers saw the Northwest's primeval forests simply as a resource to be extracted, heedless of what came next for the land. Starting around 1900, thinkers such as Gifford Pinchot, the first head of the US Forest Service, advocated for a forest reserve system that would provide a sustained yield of timber, based in the European practice of scientific forestry. By the 1930s, large private landowners also started to think about the woods that might grow back to take the place of the old-growth forests that had sparked the industry. The Lumber Code, passed as part of the New Deal in 1934, required timber companies to prepare plans for reforestation after logging. Three years later, Weyerhaeuser Timber Company ran advertisements with the then-radical idea that "Timber is a Crop" and opened its first seedling nursery the following year. In 1941, the company dedicated its first "tree farm" on 120,000 acres of cut-over land in Grays Harbor County, Washington, proposing that it could raise and eventually harvest a new crop of trees after cutting the old-growth forests. Weyerhaeuser thus renounced the short-term cut-and-run mentality of the first timber barons in favor of a longer-term perspective that included future harvests as well, even though it still saw forests only through the lens of the timber they could produce.

The idea that trees were a crop came to dominate forestry roughly from the 1940s through the 1980s. While this notion did represent progress compared to the log-it-and-leave-it approach, viewing the forest purely as a field of row crops had some undesirable side effects. Driven by market demand for Douglas-fir, second-growth forests were planted solely with that one species, and it was only by happenstance that other species sprouted in the clear-cuts—if seed blew in from adjoining tracts, or if hardwood species such as bigleaf maple or Oregon myrtle grew back from their stumps. As the postwar era of the twentieth century wore on, the same engineering mindset that led to the Green Revolution was applied to forestry, in what was variously called "high-yield" or "intensive" forestry. The forest industry, research universities, state forestry departments, and the US Forest Service conducted breeding experiments to produce faster-growing cultivars, and tested the application of urea fertilizer to forests to make trees grow fatter and taller. Borrowing the same practices a farmer might use in a cornfield, they used herbicides to kill off any plants they didn't consider to be crop trees, such as red alder, salal, salmonberry, and (farther south) manzanita.

FORESTS: NOT JUST FOR TIMBER

But by the 1990s, the limitations of this approach were showing. The impacts on water quality from extensive roadbuilding, logging right down to the streambank, and

In the late twentieth century, old cedars came to be prized for another value: wildlife habitat.

herbicide runoff had begun to provoke citizen opposition. The public was asking for forests to provide more than just timber and employment in the forest industry: they wanted clean water and healthy habitat as well. Salmon runs were declining, partly due to habitat degradation. In Washington State in 1974, nineteen American Indian tribes had won in federal court when they sued to enforce their treaty rights to fish on an equal footing with the non-Native inhabitants. In 1980, a second decision, known as Boldt II, held that their fishing rights implied a right to protect the upstream habitat the salmon needed if there were to be fish in the river to catch. As the 1990s drew to a close, several runs of salmon and steelhead trout were listed under federal and state endangered species laws.

The attitude that forests were just a means to wood production was being challenged on land as well. Field and laboratory experiments were starting to document the role of old-growth in the life cycles of scores of forest species, which would be lost if the forests were managed as fiber plantations to be cut while still young (for a tree). Based on this research, the 1990 listing of the northern spotted owl as a threatened species halted the logging of the old-growth forests that the owl inhabited, and was followed by the listing of the marbled murrelet (a seabird that nests in coastal old-growth forests) two years later. All of these reflected a new societal expectation: that forests were meant to provide habitat as well as timber.

Those species listings were milestones in the Timber Wars, which rocked the region in the 1980s and 1990s, as activists sought to protect roadless areas and old-growth refugia from the saw, primarily on public land because that's where nearly all of the remaining primeval forest—less than 20 percent of its original extent—was found. The ripples of the Timber Wars and their resolution through the 1994 Northwest Forest Plan—which protected most old-growth forest on federal public land—changed the basic ground rules for forestry on private and municipal forests as well. Endangered

and threatened species provisions affect forest management throughout the Northwest. They shape forest practice rules and influence the plans of forest stewards who need to watch out for vulnerable species if they should happen to take up residence in their woods. These provisions also prompted researchers to try and develop new systems of forest management that reconcile society's need for timber and other wood products with its desire for other services that forests can provide, such as wildlife habitat, clean water, and recreation. Indeed, the ecological forestry approach that we describe in this book grows out of these conceptual innovations. More recently, forests have come to be valued for carbon sequestration as well.

As societal expectations of the forest have changed, the economic drivers of forestry operations have been shifting, too. For decades, forest products companies owned not only the most productive tracts of forestland but also lumber mills, and managed these operations as a single enterprise. That began to change in the mid-1970s, when federal policy incentivized pension funds to buy timberlands as a way of diversifying their investments. Then, between 1999 and 2006, four of the largest industrial forestland owners in the US restructured as real estate investment trusts to reduce their investors' exposure to federal taxation.

While these changes fattened the financial bottom line, they had severe implications for much of the industrial forest. Its fate is now steered by decision-makers who see it as an asset whose profit must be maximized, regardless of the forest ecosystem or community well-being. A firm

Forest Ownership in Washington: 19.3 Million Acres

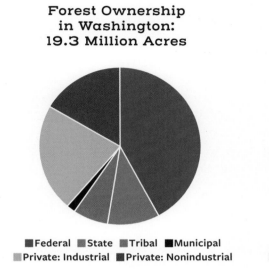

■Federal ■State ■Tribal ■Municipal
■Private: Industrial ■Private: Nonindustrial

Forest Ownership in Oregon: 29.7 Million Acres

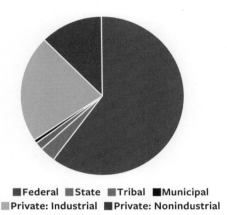

■Federal ■State ■Tribal ■Municipal
■Private: Industrial ■Private: Nonindustrial

Figure 3-1. The public owns most of the forestland in both Oregon and Washington. Of the privately held forests, nonindustrial owners control slightly less than half, for a total of nearly 7 million acres in the two states.

that manages portfolios of timberland in Colombia, Brazil, Poland, and Oregon may optimize its returns by harvesting a couple hundred thousand Northwest acres over twenty years, and then letting the land rest for another twenty. For towns that depend on timber from those tracts to employ local loggers and supply local mills, those wildly fluctuating harvest levels are seriously destabilizing. But capital doesn't care.

As forestland became a fully financialized asset, another impact was on the rotation, or the age at which a forest stand is clear-cut and replanted. Early tree farms on the west side of the Cascade Range aimed to cut trees when they were eighty to one hundred years old, a cycle that roughly maximized the forest's average productivity over its lifetime. But as investment managers moved into the driver's seat, the pressure for quick returns led them to clear-cut

sooner. Economists devalue, or discount, future earnings compared to cash in hand, because that money can be invested elsewhere. At an 8 percent "discount rate," earning a dollar ten years hence is worth only forty-three cents today. Those ratios lead financial managers to harvest trees as soon as they are merchantable and their growth slows down at all. What's more, liquidating older trees in an investment portfolio means higher cash returns, which looks better to investors.

Across the industrial forest landscape, the result has been a continual shortening of the rotation age, to the point where it now hovers between thirty-five and forty years on good tree-growing ground on the west side. This strategy is stuffed full of side effects. These forests never grow old enough to provide complex forest habitat for most birds or other forest creatures; they are more flammable and vulnerable to being completely killed in a wildfire; they sequester less carbon than if they were allowed to age a few more decades; and they are thirstier than older trees, soaking up more water from the soil and thus leaving less summertime flow in streams for fish and amphibians.

Fortunately for the ecosystems of the Pacific Northwest, not all forestland is subject to these pressures. (Nevertheless, even land that is currently exempt from them has likely been shaped by economically driven harvesting at some point in its history.) While the forest industry and associated investment bodies own a majority of private forestland in Oregon and Washington, nonindustrial private forest (NIPF) owners control about 43 percent of Washington's private forestland and 36 percent of Oregon's—at 6.9 million acres, an area larger than Massachusetts (see Figure 3-1). That share includes several hundred thousand family forest owners, as well as land owned by conservation groups, more and more of whom are engaged in active forest stew-

ardship. Beyond those sectors, other forest owners such as municipalities (half a million acres), American Indian tribes (1.8 million acres), and state departments of natural resources (2.95 million acres) control nearly 11 percent of the two states' forestland and manage them for numerous goals besides financial return. Finally, a few industrial owners, such as Starker Forests, Inc. in Oregon, practice forestry with a long-term orientation that puts the forest first.

It is this variety of owners and public managers who inspired us to write this book. Each forest owner has their own set of reasons for owning forestland and their own objectives they hope to achieve with it. Those objectives may or may not include financial return, but what all of those owners have in common is that financial return is almost never the *only* factor motivating them. Ecological forestry, with its focus on achieving multiple goals on a parcel of forestland, is an ideal approach for these diversely motivated forest owners.

OPPOSITE: *In a forest near Rickreall, Oregon*

PART II

Understanding
Your Forest

CHAPTER 4

Shopping for a Forest

BY KIRK HANSON

Throughout this book, I certainly don't hide my opinion that owning or managing a forest is one of the greatest expressions of earth stewardship. I wholeheartedly encourage you to go out and acquire your own tract of forestland and put your conservation ethic into practice. As my mom always says, "Land is a good investment because they're not making any more of it."

My family owns a tad over two hundred acres of forestland that we manage as much as a legacy investment as we do for conservation benefits and recreation. Our forests in Washington carry on the tradition of land stewardship that my parents started in Minnesota—providing firewood for our home, recreational activities like camping and hiking, and homes for all creatures great and small. We've done what good farmers do—we invested in good soil. As a result, the opportunity to manage these lands as a natural capital endowment for ourselves and future generations is hard to ignore.

I'm confident that, with good management, within the next ten to fifteen years we should be able to generate, conservatively, $40,000 of gross logging revenue each year from our land, while continuing to increase both timber volume and value ... and do this indefinitely. After deducting the costs of logging and land stewardship (at least half of the gross revenue), that obviously doesn't provide a salary to live on, nor does it even cover annual tuition at a land-grant college these days. However, it is a good basis for a retirement fund, and it will certainly help sustain our health and well-being.

Along with a periodic dividend, my family gains incalculable value from all of the other benefits a forest provides. What other investment can you walk through, breathe in, repair your spirit, or practice a stewardship ethic with (a practice I feel all humans are inherently compelled toward)? My bias as a forester notwithstanding, sharing the value of forest stewardship from generation

Forest light near Hood Canal, Washington

to generation is one of the best gifts we can bestow on humanity. A stewardship ethic breeds compassion for life—all life in its many forms and manifestations—and compassion is a virtue our world sorely needs.

WHY OWN A FOREST?

The path of a forest steward is a very personal one, yet there are many values that unite us in this shared ethic. Many of us have a personal connection with forests, one that may even stem back to childhood experiences. When you ask yourself what you love, appreciate, or value about a forest, what comes to mind?

Do you value forests for their . . .

- Biodiversity, fish and wildlife habitat, and other **conservation values**?
- Beauty, grace, majesty, or similar **aesthetic, recreational, or spiritual values**?
- Ability to produce clean air and water, sequester carbon, and other **ecosystem services**?
- Valuable forest products, ability to provide stable, long-term income, and other **economic values**?
- **Legacy value**, and the role they play in your family's livelihood and multi-generational estate?

You may have other values or may articulate yours differently. Owning a forest need not be a daunting task even if you have no prior forest management experience. Across the Pacific Northwest, there is a bevy of private and public financial, educational, and technical assistance programs that can help forest owners and managers understand how to better manage their land and offset the costs of forest restoration activities, as we will discuss later in this book. Further, forestland that is managed, at least in part, in a manner that periodically produces merchantable timber qualifies for the lowest property tax rate of any land use type. Lastly, there is a community of *consulting foresters* who can work with you to develop a long-term management plan for your forest, and implement any number of forest conservation and timber management activities.

THE SEARCH FOR LAND

I don't like shopping. At all. But shopping for land is quite a different experience. It's fun to see what's for sale, what current forestland prices are, and how those prices change based on location. How is the land being marketed? What are the sizes of forested parcels for sale? How was the land managed previously, and what shape is the forest in? The internet is a perfect enabler, and a quick search for "forest land for sale Washington" (or Oregon) immediately returns multiple real estate websites that include rural, undeveloped land. These sites have become more sophisticated over the years, and many of the forestland listings now include stand maps and rudimentary descriptions of the forest or timber. This makes armchair real estate prospecting fun and informative, but also possibly misleading. The potential for scams or illegitimate sales raises the importance of working with an agent who can help buyers find legitimate listings and can arrange safe opportunities to view the land in person.

The value of daydreaming about owning land only lasts so long, and then you have

Sparse tree crowns may suggest stressed trees of low vigor—a warning sign to would-be forestland buyers.

to face the reality of what you can actually invest. If you're fortunate enough to have a cool million dollars or more, then there are plenty of options for rural forestland. However, most rural properties that are on the market are being sold as future residential development sites; therefore, they have a much higher development value associated with them than land that is being sold solely for ongoing forest management. Further, land for sale within an hour's drive of most urban areas is more expensive than land in the boondocks. Just like buying nuts in bulk at the food co-op, buying land in bulk will net a lower per unit (acre) cost, and any real estate website will quickly reveal the high price variability of rural land.

Financing the purchase of rural land is very difficult. Few banks will lend on land that is not semi-developed (e.g., land that lacks a well, septic system, or foundation), so you may need to be prepared to make a cash investment or seek nontraditional financing. A range of farm credit agencies and organizations provide loans for rural land acquisition, but oftentimes these loans come at higher interest rates than conventional home mortgages and may require at least a 50 percent down payment. A general rule of thumb is that, over the long term, timber volumes and value on the west side of the Cascade Range appreciate at approximately 8 percent annually. This does not include appreciation of the land's value. This alone is a very reasonable investment while interest rates are low. However, taking into consideration the cost and interest of a loan, on top of stewardship costs, the investment may not make as much short-term revenue as other types of investments.

WHAT ARE YOUR OBJECTIVES?

Being clear on your objectives for owning forestland will help you or your real estate agent narrow the search. We've talked about your personal values when it comes to a forest, but what are your goals and objectives for owning one? Prospecting for forestland puts some of those goals to the test—in particular, if they're at all at odds with each other. So let's review.

Timber Production

If one of your primary objectives is timber production, you will want to find as productive a piece of ground as possible. This requires an understanding of soils and choosing land with a high Site Class or Site Index. This can mean loamy clay soils, valleys, lower hillslopes, and areas with higher rainfall and warmer temperatures. The most productive forest soils are on the west side of the Cascades—in particular, within the fog belt of the coast. As we describe in Chapter 10, you can generate soil maps online for information on a site's soil types and productivity.

When considering timber production, ask yourself how patient your capital can be before needing to generate a return on investment. Younger forests are typically much less expensive to purchase than older forests given the lack of immediately harvestable timber. A recently established plantation, for instance, likely represents the least expensive forestland available. However, it also requires a twenty-five- to thirty-year waiting period before seeing a return, as well as ownership and management costs along the way.

Relative to growing and selling trees, size does matter. You will need at least ten to twenty acres if you want to cut and sell trees and generate a dividend check every ten to fifteen years. As property size grows, so does your ability to log more frequently. For instance, with my family's two hundred acres of forestland, I anticipate commercially thinning some portion of our forest every five years.

Forest composition is also an important consideration. Unless each of the stands on the property is well stocked and growing vigorously, you may either incur short-term reforestation costs or forgo long-term revenue from unproductive acres. Sites with poor tree cover and a lot of brush are very difficult and expensive to transition back to forest.

Keep in mind, however, that there are financial assistance programs available to help forest owners offset the cost of restoring their forests. My family's Bucoda forest, for instance, has required a tremendous amount of restoration work (e.g., tree planting, invasive species removal, pre-commercial thinning). Basically, we bought a forest fixer-upper. The relatively poor condition of the timber allowed us to get a great deal on a large tract of land, and funding from both the federal Environmental Quality Incentives Program and Conservation Stewardship Program has covered more than 75 percent of the cost of doing the necessary thinning and replanting to get the forest tuned up and back into good growth. (We discuss this in more detail in Chapters

12 and 13.) This worked well for us, partly because we knew what we were getting into. We knew the site had fertile soils, and we knew how to access the available financial resources. You can do this too.

To Build or Not to Build

Most rural land on the market today is being sold as development property. The trend of moving to the country and building a home has become so popular that even surprisingly remote parcels, or ones that historically were devoted to timber production, are now being touted as future homesites. This is something to keep in mind if you do not intend to build a McMansion on your land. Most rural land has an inflated "development value" associated with it that dramatically increases the value of the land beyond that of the timber. If you're looking for land solely for producing timber, or solely for conservation purposes, and don't intend to build anything more than a tool shed on it, you will want to look for land that is not being marketed for residential development, or land that might already be encumbered with a conservation easement that prohibits development.

Conservation

Conservation and timber production are not mutually exclusive. However, if wildlife habitat and other conservation values are your primary objective, and you have absolutely no interest in generating revenue from your land, you may want to consider land that is thought of as degraded. Given the extraordinary regenerative capacity of this earth, sites

Aesthetic appeal may be an important quality when comparing one tract of forestland to another.

where the previous forest was removed and not replanted often have a very high diversity of shrubs, young trees, and other vegetation that provides rich habitat for birds, browsers, and bees. If you have the capacity to actively manage your land, these sites also provide plenty of stewardship opportunities in the way of removing invasive plants, planting additional trees, thinning to reduce competition, favoring the most wildlife-friendly

A Forest of Their Own

Abby Christensen and Jacob Covey were recently married and living in a condo outside Salt Lake City when they started looking for land so they could bring their love for the outdoors into their daily lives.

Initially, they considered ranch land in central Utah, but the filters they applied in their internet searches—anything over two acres and under $100,000—kept bringing them back to Washington's Olympic Peninsula. In autumn 2020, they drove west in a van they'd converted to a home on wheels to see the options in person. Ultimately, they made an offer on five acres of raw forestland near Port Angeles. Last logged in the 1980s, it nonetheless contained Douglas-fir, cedar, and alder trees up to sixty years old, along with younger trees. "There was so much life and material on the land that the accountant in me said, 'There can't be a better value than this,'" Jacob recalls. They sold their condo, bought the land free and clear, and moved onto it the following spring.

Over the next two years, they got to know their woods better, building trails through them, and discovering a forty-foot red alder that they've dubbed the climbing tree because of its perfect ladder-like arrangement of branches. "We were rock climbers—now we've transitioned to tree climbers," says Abby.

At first, because the road was too muddy to drive in the wet season, they spent winters living in town, where they plied their digital trades—he as a web developer, and she as an instructional designer. But now that they've improved the road and upgraded from a van to a 390-square-foot mobile home, complete with loft bed, kitchen, and airy living room, they intend to live on their property year-round, with the help of solar panels and satellite internet.

Abby and Jacob are still roughing it—showering at the gym, hauling in their water, and using a composting privy—but they get to drink their morning coffee overlooking the stream that runs through their woods. Their wooden gate, footbridge, and front steps are all made from trees they thinned from their forest and then hewed by chainsaw.

They took a sawmilling course together, and now Abby plans to enroll in a twelve-week intensive woodworking class, with the dream of launching a small business making outdoor furniture from their own western redcedars. Also on the agenda for the couple: starting a family in the woods.

The best part of the experience so far? "Getting to know a single place and seeing it through all the different seasons," says Jacob. "We're so lucky to have this beautiful spot," adds Abby. "We want to go slow, not mess anything up, and work with the forest."

—SZ

trees and shrubs, creating wildlife habitat structures, and on and on. This area could be a small parcel in your neighborhood or as large a tract as you want to manage.

Clarifying your conservation objectives will help you hone in on the right piece of forestland. If your objective is to offset your carbon footprint, for instance, you will either want land with good tree stocking or be prepared to invest time or money in restoring forest cover to degraded land. Similarly, if your objective is to restore old-growth forest structure to your land, you will also want some amount of trees to work with or be prepared to make that investment.

Conservation Easement

Whether your primary objective is conservation or timber production, you should consider the potential value of placing a conservation easement on your land after you've acquired it. We discuss conservation easements in Chapter 21, but I mention them here because, in some cases, a landowner can sell an easement, and this can be one method by which the initial investment in the land can be partially recouped. A conservation easement can also be donated, providing you with a significant income tax deduction, another strategy for recovering some of the purchase price. Some people are surprised to hear that many conservation easements allow timber harvesting. You can work with a local land trust to identify the best conservation easement options for your needs.

Recreation

If your primary objective is recreation, whether hiking, mountain biking, riding ATVs, hunting and fishing, bird watching, or just appreciating nature in general, you will want to look for land with special features. Active recreation is often more enjoyable on land with topographical variation (valleys, hills, etc.) or land that comes with views. Rivers, streams, or wetlands provide both wildlife observation and fishing or hunting values. A diversity of vegetation types ranging from forest cover to fields may also yield greater wildlife and game opportunities.

LOCATION, LOCATION, LOCATION

Based on my experience, the farther away your land is from where you live, the less likely you will be to visit and take care of it. Unless you really plan to visit your land only a few times a year, then I highly recommend you look for land that is less than an hour away from home. Of my three tracts of forestland, one is thirty minutes, another is forty-five minutes, and the third is sixty-five minutes away from where I live. The amount of time that I spend on each property is directly commensurate with their distance. The forest that is a little over an hour away only gets a visit once or twice per year. I visit the forest that is thirty minutes away at least once or twice per month.

I highly advise you to get a sense of the neighborhood and immediate neighbors. This will require a drive once you've identified a prospective property. There's no better way to get a sense of the vibe of an area than to directly see what the surrounding land and neighborhood look like. Neglected homes, profuse amounts of illegal dumping, abandoned vehicles, poorly managed or sickly looking forests, and the like may

Taking the time to walk through a new forest will reveal both its qualities and quandaries.

either deter you from visiting your forest as often as you would prefer or even make ownership and management difficult due to trespass, vandalism, or other buffoonery.

If timber production is one of your objectives, then access to mills is also an important consideration. The ideal (cost-effective) haul distance from your land to a mill should be less than one hour and no more than one and a half hours.

ACCESS AND ROADS

As you investigate forestland, confirm there is legal access to it. Access may be obvious if the parcel is adjacent to a public road and there is a forest road or driveway that leads directly into the property. However, if the property is accessible only through adjacent parcels, you will need to confirm the title to the property includes a legal road access easement. The easement may

or may not stipulate what the road maintenance agreements are between all users of the access road, and you will want to clarify these terms before purchasing the land.

Two of the forested tracts I purchased do not front on a public road, and the road access easement that came with each title restricted access to forest management activities only. This both limited my ability to develop either piece of land and dramatically reduced the purchase price of the properties because there was no development value associated with them. This worked in my family's favor as our objective was to manage these forests for timber and conservation anyway, and not to develop them. The reduction in value allowed us to buy more acres than we otherwise could have if the properties were developable.

An inspection of all roads is a must, as either road building or road maintenance can be very expensive. Ensure roads have good surfacing, are draining stormwater, and have new or properly functioning culverts.

REAL ESTATE AGENTS, CONSULTING FORESTERS, AND OTHER SPECIALISTS

Although I'm a professional forester and have a pretty good sense of what I'm looking for when prospecting for forestland, I still used a real estate agent for the last two properties I purchased. Real estate agents have access to a much broader range of property listings than are available on the internet. They also have the ability to customize their searches to a finer degree than is possible on most real estate websites. However, the greatest asset of a real estate agent is in their service of dealing with the bureaucracy of buying land. If you're like me and have a career, family, and a personal life, there's not much time left over to deeply acquaint oneself with the vagaries of title searches, drawing up and negotiating real estate purchase contracts, researching property access, filing all the paperwork with the county, and so on. Note that the sales price will usually include the seller's and buyer's agents' fees, as long as this is stipulated in the real estate contract.

I also highly recommend you retain the services of a professional consulting forester when prospecting for forestland. A forester can help you appraise timber value and forest ownership and management costs, which will be valuable as you negotiate the purchase price of the land. A forester can also evaluate the condition of the forest, estimate the value of long-term timber production, decipher state and local forest management regulations, and help you develop a forest management plan for the land.

You may also want to seek out other specialists and services, such as a financial advisor or a lender to identify affordability; a title company to process the sale; a county assessor; an attorney to interpret title documents, including access easements; surveyors if property boundaries are important; and hydrologists or geologists (timber companies often sell off twenty- to one-hundred-acre parcels that are not good for timber removal due to sensitive sites).

CURRENT USE TAXATION

The last morsel of wisdom I'll leave with you is about the current use taxation of the property you're intending to buy. Every parcel of land is assigned a valuation by the county assessor, which is based on its full market value, unless it is eligible to be assessed only at its value for forestry, farming, or open space. Most forestland that has been managed recently for timber production will be in the designated forestland (DFL) current use program. Land that has not been managed for timber production, or that can be converted to residential development, may be taxed at its residential value. Residential designation brings with it one of the highest annual property tax rates, whereas DFL enjoys the lowest annual property tax rate—typically only 10 percent of the residential rate!

If the land you are purchasing is already in the DFL current use program, then most counties will require you to submit an updated forest management plan that details how you will continue to manage your land primarily for timber production. See Chapter 10 for more about current use management plans, and be sure to check with the county assessor, because each county has a different policy on how soon an updated plan must be submitted.

If the land you are acquiring is taxed at any other rate than DFL, and if your primary intent is to manage for sustainable timber production, then it is advisable to apply to the county for a change in current use designation. There will be an application fee, an application process, and likely a waiting period before the land use designation can be changed, so it behooves you to engage the county early on to get this process rolling. One caveat to changing the land use designation is that either you or a future landowner may be responsible for paying back taxes at the highest rate if you choose to change the land use designation in the future.

THE ART OF COMPROMISE

As you get into the practice of forest management, you quickly begin to learn that you can't have everything. Regardless of how diverse a forest may be, it can't provide for 100 percent of your objectives everywhere all of the time. The most well-intentioned forest owner may have the desire to optimize carbon sequestration, wildlife habitat, biodiversity, fire resilience, sustainable timber production, and the ability of their forest to adapt to climate change. Those all sound like laudable goals, right? However, it may not be possible to optimize for all of those goals, as some of them are incompatible

with each other in either the short or long term, or both. For instance, optimizing for wildlife habitat and carbon sequestration in a young forest may not be compatible objectives because, arguably, the most effective method for sequestering carbon is to do nothing and let a forest naturally accrue biomass and carbon without intervention. In a young, regenerating forest, this can lead to stand conditions where there is so much competition that the stand remains homogeneous for decades and lacks the biodiversity and habitat structure necessary for wildlife.

There have to be trade-offs. So, the first principle of forest management is to learn to compromise. However, a lot of your goals may be compatible, or compatible to a lesser or greater degree, and if you prioritize them, you can develop *silvicultural systems* that balance these goals based on your priorities.

As this book progresses, we will take you through a process of evaluating the various natural resources in your forest, including flora and fauna, soils, hydrology, and climate, as well as the processes at work there, such as wildlife habitat, forest health, natural disturbance agents, and so on. With an understanding of these resources, and clarification of your values, you can better understand how closely your forest aligns with your values, and whether management may be necessary to adjust the composition and functioning of your forest. From this point, you can begin articulating goals for your forest and creating the framework for a forest management plan that will guide your actions going forward. We will begin with a qualitative evaluation of what we can see in the forest.

CHAPTER 5

What Lives Here? Making a Qualitative Assessment

BY KIRK HANSON

"Whenever I enter a forest, I first enter as a biologist, and ask myself what the right thing to do is for the biology of the forest."
—Rick Helman, senior forester, Northwest Natural Resource Group

A central feature of my job is to evaluate the condition of a particular forest and help owners match up the ecological characteristics of their forest with their objectives. I travel across the Pacific Northwest, visiting different forests and meeting with many forest owners who are all managing their land with a wide range of goals. In this chapter, I share with you the process that I use to conduct a qualitative forest assessment and how you can do your own evaluation.

When walking into a new forest, I find it incredibly important to have an open mind and just make qualitative observations. I think there is a tendency to jump straight into making management decisions, such as "Boy, this forest really needs to be thinned." But does it? Before you can get to the point of making any management decisions, you first have to evaluate what's going on in the forest, and this evaluation process is best started with objective observations.

THE OBSERVATION WALK

Upon first entering a forest, I like to relax, take the pressure off, and just look around—simply go for a walk and take notes on what I see. If I can divorce myself from my ego and open up to what's happening around

Use a compass to help you maintain a straight bearing through your forest while making a qualitative assessment.

me, I find this allows the natural process of revelation to take place, and deeper insights are gained into forest ecology. I'd like to say that my observation walks are systematic, orderly, and comprehensive. In reality, they're shaped by the moment, the needs of the project, the company I'm with, and other factors; they tend to be the observational equivalent of free association. Nevertheless, there is a common range of variables that, when combined, yield a comprehensive assessment of a forest's ecology. I list and

qualify these variables in this chapter, but I encourage you to come to your own conclusions during the observation walks you take.

TREE SPECIES, COMPOSITION, AND DISTRIBUTION

One of the first observations I make is of the general composition of trees including their age, species, and distribution. This provides clues to the origins of a particular forest—whether it naturally regenerated or is the outcome of deliberate planting. Here are some questions to ask as you observe the arrangement of trees in your forest:

1. **Does the forest appear to have trees of relatively the same age, or does it appear to be occupied by trees of multiple ages?** Trees that are all the same age are often the same height. A forest with trees of multiple ages will have trees of varying heights, including seedlings and saplings near ground level, low trees well beneath the canopy of the forest, trees that occupy mid-canopy positions, and dominant trees that create the upper canopy of the forest. Stands that are dominated by a single species and age of trees were likely either intentionally planted (e.g., Douglas-fir plantation) or naturally regenerated after a disturbance (e.g., dense red alder). Stands with multiple ages of trees likely naturally regenerated over a longer period of time and have gone through a process of self-thinning and continuing natural regeneration.

2. **Is the forest dominated by hard-woods or conifers—or a mix of both, and in what proportion to one another?** The presence and character of trees give important clues to the types of soils across a site (clay, rock, sand, loam, etc.) and their ability to hold moisture.

3. **Do you see a pattern where certain species are more common across the various soils, topography, and aspects of the site?** Tree species may be different on north-facing slopes versus south-facing slopes, on lower slopes, or in drainages versus on upper slopes or on ridges. All plants have a preferred habitat, as well as a range of tolerance. You will see trees thriving in their preferred habitats, and potentially struggling when they're in a location that's at the edge of their tolerance range.

4. **How many trees are there per acre—are there areas of high density (lots of trees close together), areas of low density (sparsely treed), or areas that lack trees altogether?** High densities of a pioneer species, such as alder or Douglas-fir, imply that a site was subject to a significant disturbance event such as land clearing, fire, disease, or some other disturbance agent. The density of trees has an influence on the growth of the forest. The canopy of a dense forest can suppress the growth of less dominant trees, frequently leading to their mortality. High densities can also cause trees to grow tall and skinny,

Recording observations in a notebook helps you to recall the nuances of a forest at a later date.

compromising their integrity during storm events. Gaps in the forest may be indicative of changes in soil type, hydrology, or the presence of root diseases.

5. **Is the forest composed of many small-diameter trees all packed together, or is the composition more open with fewer or bigger trees—or, again, maybe a mix?** Stands that are highly stocked with small-diameter trees likely naturally regenerated and are in a phase of self-thinning as individual trees compete with each other for sunlight and soil moisture. Sparsely stocked forests suggest a history of timber management, frequent fires, or drier soils.

6. **How structurally complex does the forest appear?** Look for signs of heterogeneity—for example, multiple ages and species of trees, numerous snags and downed logs, variable densities, and gaps in the canopy. Or you might notice the forest is highly simplified—dominated by one or two tree species, of a uniform density, with low shrub diversity in the understory and few snags or downed logs. The complexity of a forest, or lack thereof, can offer clues to the habitat potential for various wildlife species, and what it might need for forest restoration.

FOREST AGE

Before you attempt to determine the age of individual trees, you should step back and evaluate the age of the forest as a whole, although this can be challenging without much prior knowledge of it. Therefore, it's easier to lump forests into broad categories such as young, mid-aged, older, or mixed. Initially, that's all I really need to know in order to piece together more clues of the origin story of a particular forest. Younger forests tend to be more simplified in their species diversity and structural composition than older forests. Forests with multiple cohorts, or ages of trees, are more commonly older forests. I look to see if there are any trees naturally regenerating in the understory. Their species and distribution are indicative of the density of the canopy and the moisture regime of the soil. Dense forest canopies tend to support only shade-tolerant trees such as western hemlock, grand fir, western redcedar, Pacific yew, and bigleaf maple, whereas gaps in the forest canopy may support Douglas-fir, alder, or pine, depending on how wet or dry the site is.

Stumps or cut logs provide a simple way to determine the age of a tree or forest by counting the annual growth rings from the center out toward the bark. You can also purchase a simple tool called an *increment borer* that functions like a hollow drill bit to extract a cross-sectional core of a tree, revealing its annual growth rings and therefore its age. Tree cores and stumps also reveal patterns of growth and speak of the life history of a tree. Often annual growth rings are wide during the younger years of a tree, then gradually become tighter and tighter as the tree grows up and begins to compete for sunlight or soil moisture with other trees. A series of tighter growth rings amid otherwise wider ones may indicate a period of drought. Sometimes a long series of tight growth rings suddenly opens up into a period of wider growth rings, indicating either the forest was thinned or adjacent trees died, thereby increasing light and resources for the surviving tree and instigating a period of new growth.

CANOPY COMPOSITION

When I am walking through the forest, I spend a lot of time looking up into the canopy, where the crowns of the trees gather sunlight. The crown of a tree is the upper portion that is composed of branches and leaves or needles. I'm looking to see whether the trees are crowding each other or whether they are each in full sun. How do the crowns of trees interact with one another in the canopy of the forest? Do some trees have larger crowns than others or occupy more space in the canopy? Do some trees have very compressed, or very minimal crowns, and appear to be struggling in the understory of the canopy beneath more dominant trees? I'll either measure or, more likely, eyeball the live crown ratio of various trees in the forest, by determining the percentage of each tree's total height that has live green branches (see Chapter 10 for how to calculate the live crown ratio). The live crown of a tree is its growth engine, each leaf or needle a solar panel absorbing sunlight and producing carbohydrates that will form the tree's wood fiber. In nearly every case, the larger the live crown is, the larger the diameter of the tree, and the more dominant the tree is in the canopy. Vertically speaking, is the canopy composed of multiple layers of trees of different ages, species, and heights, which is more common in a naturally regen-

The extent of competition in a forest can be gleaned by observing the relationship between individual tree crowns in the canopy.

erated forest, or is the canopy largely composed of a single cohort of trees that occupy a single canopy layer, which is indicative of a manually established timber plantation?

STORM DAMAGE

In looking at the crowns of trees, I often notice evidence of past wind and ice storms. Some trees may have forked tops where the original leader was broken off during a storm and a side branch took over as the new leader. Other trees may have broken off at the last whorl of live branches, creating a platform beneath the canopy of the forest that often supports bird or squirrel nests. The presence of a large number of trees that are snapped off at their midsection or upturned with exposed root balls is likely evidence of a big windstorm, and the direction their tops face indicates the direction from which the wind came. Storms can also blow down entire sections of trees, or "punch a hole" in a forest by knocking down trees in a small patch.

TIMBER QUALITY

From the standpoint of ecological value, trees are just as good whether their trunks are straight or crooked. In fact, often the more "ugly" a tree is, whether it has a broken top or large, rotten hole where a branch broke off, the more valuable it is to wildlife. But at the mill, straightness is highly valued. So I will appraise the timber quality across a forest to ascertain its current or future potential to yield monetary value back to the landowner. The straight trees with minimal lower limbs and ample live crowns have a higher current and future timber value. I also look for signs of log "defect" within trees, or physical characteristics that may diminish the economic value of the tree. Common defects include spike knots, where a large branch connects to a tree at an acute angle, creating a large knot. Some trees may have a "dog leg" along its stem. This is a spot where the top broke out, and a side branch took over as the new leader for the tree, causing the base of the branch to twist up in the shape of an upside-down dog's leg. This, as well as other kinds of broken or forked tops, may diminish the length of merchantable logs the tree could someday yield. Trees with excessive sweep, or curved boles (trunks), can result from stretching for the sunlight or growing on

a steep and unstable slope, and this also diminishes their timber value.

MORTALITY AND FOREST HEALTH

My favorite forest structures are snags (standing dead trees) and downed logs. To some people, dead trees in a forest are an indicator of poor management or the unwanted presence of insect pests and fungal pathogens. However, large snags and downed logs are as architecturally grand as they are critical to the forage and shelter of myriad wildlife. Therefore, the impact of natural mortality agents must be weighed in balance with the objectives for a forest.

The pattern of tree mortality reveals many clues about the ecological processes going on in a forest. If mortality appears predominantly across a particular species, perhaps that species is not well suited for the site, such as western hemlock or western redcedar on soils composed of droughty glacial till. If dead trees occur in distinct clumps, they may indicate the presence of a pathogenic root fungus in the soil.

Looking back up to the crowns of the trees, do needles or leaves appear sparse and anemic rather than lush, full, and green? Again, this could indicate unsuitability to the soil or the presence of pathogens or other stressors. Other things to note in determining the health of the forest include the following:

- Sap or resin oozing (or pitch weeping) from the boles of trees, or an unusual discoloration of the bark
- Fungi that occur on living or dead trees that may lead you to wonder

about a disease on the site or a fungal pathogen that may be spreading from tree to tree

- Small holes or evident sawdust in or around the base of the tree that might indicate the presence of insects
- Trees that have an excessive number of cones or seeds, or produce cones or seeds consistently year after year—typically a sign of stress

UNDERSTORY VEGETATION

During spring, it's hard not to be dazzled by the brilliant new growth and showy flowers of understory plants. An old teacher of mine once opined, "Vegetation is an expression of the soil." As the trees give clues to the environmental conditions of a site, so can understory shrubs and groundcovers. A lack of diversity may suggest that a dense canopy is limiting sunlight to the forest floor, and I may look back up to the canopy of the forest to confirm that theory. Both the abundance and species of understory plants will change across the changing light conditions in a forest. Gaps in the canopy caused by disease or a micro-burst of wind, or areas of lower tree density, often support a much higher diversity and abundance of understory plants. Some plants, such as salmonberry and thimbleberry, are indicative of wet soils. Others, such as salal

As snags decay, they continue to provide crucial habitat for wildlife.

and Oregon grape denote dry soils, whereas plants such as sword ferns imply rich and productive soils.

By now I'm able to identify most native plants in the Pacific Northwest or, at a minimum, the ones that produce food! Berry- and nut-producing shrubs will improve forage options for wildlife, as well as snack options for hungry foresters. And some understory plants, such as bleeding heart and cleavers, have medicinal value. Others, such as salal and evergreen huckleberry, are valuable to the floral industry and may provide a non-timber forest product that forest owners can sell (see Resources for chapters 5 and 18).

OTHER NATIVE PLANT (AND NON-PLANT) SPECIES

The most mysterious denizens of a forest are fungi. Their ability to support the growth of forests through the exchange of nutrients beneath the forest floor is only rivaled by their simultaneous ability to kill and decompose certain trees. I keep an eye out for fruiting bodies popping out of the ground, on decaying logs and snags, and also from the trunks of trees that otherwise appear completely healthy. The ability to identify fungi helps me know what delicacies the forest owner may be able to add to their menu, which ones provide important medicines, and which ones will diminish the ability of the forest to produce merchantable timber. (See Resources.) Mosses and lichens can also be indicators of forest health; they are important contributors of nutrients to forests as rain washes minerals from their surfaces, or when they fall to the forest floor and decay.

NON-NATIVE PLANT SPECIES

As time passes, more and more non-native and highly invasive plants seem to be entering our region. They compose an international cast of interlopers that find homes within or immediately adjacent to our forests. The non-native plants that most people are familiar with include Himalayan blackberry, Scotch broom, ivy, holly, knotweed, and reed canarygrass, although there are dozens more. Many of these are aggressive, pioneering species, such as Himalayan blackberry and Scotch broom, quickly colonizing disturbed sites and outcompeting native plants. Others are extremely shade tolerant, such as ivy and holly, and will persist and slowly spread throughout the understory of the forest, gradually outcompeting existing native plants and often leading to a diminishment of plant diversity. We discuss invasive species and their implications in more detail in Chapter 8.

WILDLIFE AND HABITAT

As with my hunt for mysterious fungi, I also keep my eyes open for evidence of wildlife within the forest. I look for evidence of deer and elk: game trails, signs of browse on understory plants, or antler rubs on trees or saplings. I play "what made that scat?" and often hunch down to poke at animal poop to see what's in it. If large snags and downed logs are absent from the forest, with them go a wide range of cavity-dependent wildlife and the species that rely on the insects that occupy decaying trees. I listen. Do I hear birdcalls? How many different bird species can I distinguish? I may not be able to identify all of them, but at least I can get a clue as to the abundance of different species of birds, or the abundance of a particular species. In considering the composition of the forest in light of wildlife, I look at how complex the forest's canopy is and the diversity of tree species. I know that the more layers there are in a forest, the more bird species will occupy that forest, as different insects, the birds' prey, forage at different layers within the canopy.

TOPOGRAPHY

I'm mindful of the aspect of a site, especially if I'm on a slope. Both the species composition and topography can look quite different on a warmer, south-facing slope versus a cooler, north-facing slope on the other side of the hill. I also check my topo maps to confirm elevation. Elevation has a direct relationship with temperature and rainfall and can be a major determinant of what tree and plant species occupy a site. Is the topography flat, steep, or variable? Are there slopes greater than 40 percent, which can limit accessibility to logging equipment? Where does the forest occur on the topography: on a hilltop or ridge, midslope, down a ravine, at the base of a hill, on the valley floor? Topography and soil types directly influence moisture availability, a significant limiting factor in tree growth.

SOILS

Unless soils are exposed in some manner, such as a road cut, a stream, a riverbank, or some other form of disturbance, it may be hard to discern the composition of soils. Therefore, before I visit a forest, I always generate a soil map from the federal Natural Resources Conservation Service's website, as knowing the soils gives me the biggest clue as to what tree species will grow well on that site. (We discuss how to generate a soil map in Chapter 10.) However, without a soil map, my next best clue is the vegetation itself. As per my earlier discussion about

understory vegetation, I can get a good idea of what the general types of soils are, and their ability to hold moisture, by the plants that grow there. If the understory suddenly shifts from salal to sword fern, for instance, I know that I've just changed from a well-draining and drier soil to a richer and slightly wetter soil. Lastly, if I happen to have a shovel and I'm really curious about what's going on within the first few soil horizons, I'll dig a shallow hole. If I immediately hit rocks, I can assume the soil is well draining and may become droughty as the summer progresses. If instead I dig up dark soil, and can keep digging without hitting rocks, the soil may have the capacity to hold water much later into the season, and therefore be more productive for trees and other plants.

HYDROLOGY

My last observation of natural phenomenon is of the hydrologic nature of a site. Do I encounter streams, ponds, lakes, or other sources of perennial surface water? Are there wetlands throughout the forest, and do they appear to hold water throughout the year, or do they go dry during summer months? Both perennial and seasonal sources of surface water are important for supporting wildlife. I will also look at the condition of the forest adjacent to wet sites, referred to as riparian areas. Older mixed conifer and hardwood forests tend to provide more protective functions to streams and wetlands than younger forests. If streams and wetlands are exposed, I will begin thinking about how to restore forest cover to these sensitive sites.

Speaking of the importance of sensitive hydrologic sites, in the next chapter we'll take a closer look at the importance of streams and watershed hydrology.

FOREST ROADS, TRAILS, AND ACCESS

The final observation is of forest access routes. We discuss road analysis and management in Chapter 9, but here are some general observations to consider: Are the roads in good condition, and do they appear to drain stormwater properly? What are the roads surfaced with, and are there signs of erosion? Are ditches, cross drains, water bars, and other drainage systems clear and functioning? What are the conditions of culverts, bridges, and other stream crossings? Do any road crossings appear to impede streamflow? Are the roads clear for vehicular access? Are there areas of the forest that are inaccessible by road or trail, or areas farther than one thousand feet from a road that may require longer yarding distances when logging? Are there trails, either for walking or off-road vehicle use?

AT THE CONCLUSION OF YOUR QUALITATIVE forest assessment, you should have a notebook full of observations of the natural phenomena that make up your forest, and a much greater appreciation for the forest as a complex and dynamic ecosystem. As our book progresses, we will take you deeper into the process of evaluating the structure and biology of your forest, including how to measure aspects of your forest, quantify your observations, and finally, translate those observations to stewardship actions.

CHAPTER 6

A River Runs Through It: Streams and Watersheds

BY SETH ZUCKERMAN

The most important product of the forest would seem to be timber, but the value of wood harvested from Northwest forests pales in comparison to another stream of gifts that the forest showers upon us: clean water. There are other building materials and sources of fiber, but there's no other H_2O.

What do forests and water have to do with each other? The answer lies in the way precipitation filters through the tree canopy and forest soils to emerge clean, clear, and cool. In this chapter, we'll talk about how forests process the influx of snow and rain and transform it into free-flowing streams, how they shelter the watery habitat in creeks and rivers to keep them hospitable to fish and other aquatic creatures, and how you can tell whether your forest is doing a good job of protecting the streams that run through it.

WATER'S JOURNEY THROUGH A FOREST

Imagine what would happen if you sprayed a pile of dirt with a garden hose. The water droplets would splash onto the surface and begin to run off, coalescing into rivulets that cut channels into the dirt, washing some of it down to the edge of the pile. Essentially, that is what happens when rain falls on bare earth.

If the rain falls instead on a forest, each drop follows a more complicated path. For starters, if it lands on the tree's foliage, it might never even reach the ground. When you see fog rising from a forest, that's water that collected on the forest canopy, evaporated, and then condensed again into tiny droplets in the cool air.

Once enough water collects in the foliage that it begins to run off, not all of it drips straight to the ground. Some of it trickles down the branches and trunk, instead of striking the ground with brute force—a phenomenon that will be familiar to anyone who ever took shelter under a tree in a rainstorm.

When the rainwater reaches the forest floor, it encounters a layer of dead leaves, needles, and woody debris, known as duff, which acts like a sponge to soak up the incoming precipitation and release it into the soil over time. This process—of stretching out the time it takes for water to percolate through the forest and into the stream network—reduces the peak flows in the creeks that emerge from the forest, decreasing their erosive power and keeping them cleaner than if the impact of a cloudburst made its way to the streams immediately. The top of the duff layer, too, offers an opportunity for more evaporation before the water makes it to the soil below.

When it reaches the soil, the water continues to choose its own adventure. Absorbed into the soil, it may travel underground until it emerges at a seep, spring, or creekside . . . or it might be taken up in a plant's root system. If the rain reaches the soil surface faster than it can be absorbed, the excess will run off overland. Starting out as a thin layer called sheet flow, it collects in the folds of the terrain and runs downhill, eventually reaching a stream—a channel that has actually been cut into the landscape by the flow of water over the ages. Little streams merge together into creeks and even rivers, finally finding their way to salt water. Altogether, the land that drains into a single stream is known as a watershed.

You may be wondering, why review the hydrological cycle in a book about forests?

The way you manage your forest—and the way neighbors in the same watershed manage theirs—has a big impact on the health of the streams that run through it. Strip away too much of a watershed's forest cover in a few years, and peak stream-flows will increase, along with erosion and the streams' muddiness at high water. Degraded watersheds can affect not only values that the public has a stake in, such as water quality, salmon runs, and aquatic wildlife in general, but also private property downstream, through increased flooding and soil loss. Finally, because of all these potential impacts, states have adopted forest practice rules that stipulate some basic precautions that all forest owners must take to protect the streams in their care. As you steward your forest, you'll want to know those rules and follow them.

THE 6 RIPARIAN FUNCTIONS

Streams depend on their surrounding forest in at least six crucial ways.

Shade. Riparian (or streamside) forests cast shade on the creeks and rivers flowing through them, maintaining cool summer water temperatures for fish and amphibians. Besides keeping sunlight from directly striking the water, riparian forests also cool the air through evapotranspiration, like leafy swamp coolers.

Bank stabilization. Forests help stabilize streambanks by slowing the pulses of runoff, thanks to the processes described earlier in this chapter, spreading it out over time. In addition, forests hold the soil together with their roots, thus slowing the erosion of hillsides into streams. Streamside trees

Streamside trees provide shade and an input of nutrients that helps feed the aquatic food chain.

also calm the streamflow during high-water events, when floodwaters overtop the banks. Slower water has less erosive power, so the fringe of riparian vegetation keeps more soil in place.

Filtration. Forests filter the water flowing from the surrounding slopes into the creek. As water sheets off roads or patches of bare ground—such as the upturned mound of dirt where a tree recently blew over in a windstorm—it carries fine particles of clay and silt. If that runoff encounters a strip of forested ground before it reaches a stream, it will slow down and deposit those particles in the forest before they have a chance to enter the stream network and muddy the waters.

Nutrients. By dropping leaves, needles, and other debris into the stream, trees bolster the bottom of the aquatic food chain, providing food to the invertebrates that in turn are prey to the amphibians and fish inhabiting the stream. Trees even provide another intermittent source of food: insects that lose their purchase on an overhanging tree and land in the stream.

Woody debris. Forests serve as a source of logs and branches that fall into the stream or slide into it as the ground gives way. Natural streams aren't meant to be sterile conduits for water to get from point A to point B. Logs in streams create more varied habitat for fish, provide cover for them to hide from predators, and contribute to the formation of

What Good Are Logs in Streams, Anyway?

Trees that fall into streams create better fish habitat, such as this plunge pool downstream of a log.

Ironically, in the early days of stream restoration in the 1970s, the role of large wood was poorly understood and the ability of salmon to traverse logjams was grossly underestimated. As a result, a lot of effort was expended to remove logs from creeks before further research in the ensuing decade established how important large wood is to streams. If a chunk of streambank carries trees with it when it calves off and slides into the stream, those trees will help the stream "digest" that influx of sediment, trapping some of the dirt behind the trees to meter it out periodically in higher flows, and replenishing the stream's spawning gravels. The creek will be in far better condition than if the bank had given way and the associated dirt was deposited into a barren channel.

pools in streams where the water pours over them and digs out a depression below. They also provide places for juvenile fish to take shelter when rainstorms raise water levels and water speeds.

Streamflow regulation. Forested watersheds, particularly those covered in older trees, are good at absorbing precipitation as it falls and releasing it during the dry season. This has the beneficial effect (for humans and aquatic creatures alike) of reducing peak flows that can lead to flooding, and increasing summer water levels, when fish need it most.

How well a forest can perform these functions depends in part on how it has been managed. Each little disturbance—every road, every clear-cut, every culvert—has an effect on the whole. The first few disturbances may not have any visible impacts on the stream network, but when the amount of bare ground, or impermeable surface, or streams diverted by thoughtless roadbuilding reaches a certain threshold, then the effect of that last disturbance can be disproportionately significant. This phenomenon is known as cumulative impact, or cumulative effect, where the aggregate result of many small disturbances is greater than the sum of their parts. As an ecological forest steward, you will have the opportunity to take into account any cumulative effects you notice as you create a plan for your forest.

STREAM OBSERVATION

Armed with this understanding of forests and streams, you can investigate your forest and see how its riparian areas measure up. But what, exactly, constitutes a stream? For-

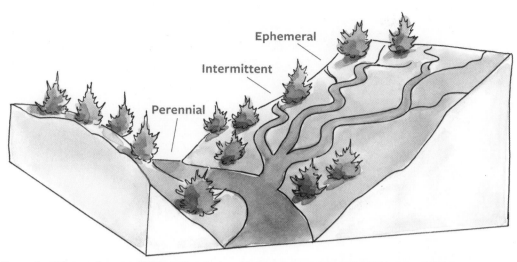

Figure 6-1. Ephemeral streams high on the hillside run only during rain or snowmelt, feeding intermittent streams that flow seasonally. Perennial streams flow year-round, often fed by underground aquifers.

esters divide streams into three main categories: perennial, intermittent or seasonal, and ephemeral (see Figure 6-1).

- You'll find flowing water in **perennial streams** all year-round. This category needs the greatest protection, since it can accommodate the widest spectrum of aquatic life.
- **Intermittent or seasonal streams** run for months at a time during the rainy season, once the ground becomes saturated enough to feed them.
- **Ephemeral streams** run only during rainstorms or immediately thereafter, or when the snow is melting.

It's worth remembering, though, that even when streams dry up on the surface, they are often flowing belowground through pores between the gravel and soil particles, in a process known as hyporheic flow (which can also help moderate stream temperatures in the summertime, as water seeps through the cool earth). But how far up the channel does an ephemeral stream actually extend? Foresters and hydrologists recognize the beginning of a stream at the point where it has defined banks and can move sediment with the force of its flow. Above that point, it may be considered a swale, but doesn't enjoy the bragging rights or legal protections of full stream status.

If the underbrush isn't too thick and the streams are not too deep, try to walk the length of the streams that traverse your forest. Depending on their size and the season, this may require mud boots or even waders! Be sure to choose your clothing and the time of year accordingly.

As you walk the streams, look up into the canopy and imagine the high path of the sun on a summer's day. Would the forest canopy block the sun? If you are conducting this survey in the winter, the alder, bigleaf maples, willows, and cottonwoods—four common Northwest riparian trees—will be leafless, so you will have to imagine them after they leaf out. As you consider the species growing in the riparian zone, bear in mind that red alder trees start dying back at about age sixty. If older alder are the dominant species, look for conifer saplings in the understory to see if any are ready to fill the growing space as the alder give way. If not, you might consider creating some small openings and planting conifers, which have a life span measured in centuries.

Take note, as well, of the streambanks. Do you see a lot of bare soil that suggests the banks are actively eroding, or are they well vegetated? The occasional bare spot is just part of normal geomorphic processes by which precipitation whittles away at the region's mountains. But a large slide can impact the quality of habitat in the stream. Depending on the cause, you may be able to treat the influx of dirt to the stream by planting willow wattles or seeding the bare dirt, or you may be able to alleviate the root causes if they are linked to, say, faulty road design or maintenance. As for vegetation, keep a sharp lookout for invasive species in the riparian area, because that can be an especially destructive place to find them. Not only do some impair the functioning of the riparian area by displacing more valuable native vegetation, but they can easily propagate far afield if seeds or sprigs that can take root are washed downstream.

Next, look down at your feet, at the substrate (the material at the bottom of the streambed), which keeps score on the health of the stream. The beds of small streams should ideally be covered in clean gravel or rock, since the spaces between the gravel are essential to many aquatic species. Salmon and trout lay their eggs in nests (known as redds) that they dig in the streambed, and they depend on the flow of oxygenated water through the pores between chunks of gravel to keep their developing offspring alive. The aquatic insects that fish feed on, such as mayfly and dragonfly larvae, also inhabit those spaces between the gravel. In fact, a good indicator of whether the stream is sufficiently free of mud and silt is to turn over a few rocks in the stream near the edge of the water. Look for little invertebrates scurrying for a place to hide, which will indicate that the stream is clean and clear enough for them. The technical term for how much the silt and sand in a stream bottom has cemented the gravel together is *embeddedness*. If a streambed's gravel is more than 25 to 50 percent embedded, that's a sign you might want to focus some of your stewardship activities on reducing the influx of sediment into your streams.

Finally, look for the size, type, and amount of woody debris in your streams. As trees fall over, some will land in the stream and turn what would otherwise be a raw bar for kingfishers and raccoons into a place where juvenile coho, cutthroat, or steelhead trout can spend the summer fattening up on stream bugs before braving the ocean. There is no one standard for how much wood should be in a stream the way there is for the number of standing dead trees per acre (see Chapter 17). But you do want some, and you want to think about the flow of new wood to replace what is already there as it

Old, undisturbed forest next to streams keeps them flowing clear and clean.

decays or gets washed downstream. Tree trunks with stout roots still attached are particularly valuable in streams, with the more rot-resistant species such as cedar and Douglas-fir being especially prized. Letting trees grow old and tall next to the creek ensures that, eventually, some will fall over and contribute to this crucial element of riparian habitat.

As you walk up the streams, take note, too, of how past management has affected the stream. Before the importance of riparian areas was well understood and enshrined in state forest practice rules, it was common to log right down to the edge of the creek, and even to use streams as routes to transport logs. Even after the end of the splash-dam era, dry streambeds were used by tractors to skid logs to landings, since they were often the most level and convenient routes available. You can sometimes find evidence of these obsolete uses; consider whether affected areas need active restoration to recover fully.

For future management, it will be important to distinguish intermittent from perennial streams. Therefore, it's a good idea to walk your streams at the driest part of the summer and map the extent of the flowing water. That said, it's also important to check on them during the wettest part of the year, when bare soil upstream will muddy the waters. If you have any stream confluences in your forest, the wet season is a prime time to check out which stream forks stay clear for longer, since those are likely to be the healthier subdrainages with the least watershed disturbance. For that matter, it's worth walking them in the shoulder seasons as well, just because a streamside walk through the forest in spring or fall makes for a pleasant outing. In fact, aside from the middle of a flash flood, there isn't a bad time to explore the streams in your forest. It's by spending time with them that you will develop your eye for the processes at work and how you might shape them.

CHAPTER 7

Forest Health

BY KIRK HANSON

The perspective that ecological forestry brings to insect and disease management in Northwest forests is a bit different from what is taught in many conventional silviculture classes. As practitioners of ecological forestry, we should first seek to understand what is happening at a biological level before making any management decisions. Most insects and fungal pathogens in forests are naturally occurring organisms and are part of the complex range of natural disturbance regimes that affect forest structure and composition. My euphemism for most of these organisms is that they are "agents of stand diversification." They create gaps in the forest, recruit snags and downed logs, and lead to greater structural and species diversity, to name but a few outcomes.

In my experience, in forests where ecological objectives are prioritized, rarely do insects or pathogens occur to such a degree as to be deemed detrimental. There are exceptions, of course, such as sudden oak death in Southwest Oregon and the pine beetle epidemic that has swept across most of the Rocky Mountains. I often find the best strategies for limiting the impact of insects or pathogens are to manage for tree species diversity and increased tree vigor. Nature abhors a homogenous plantation, whether it is an even-aged Douglas-fir stand west of the Cascades or a pine plantation east of the Cascades, and will find every opportunity to diversify it. If we follow this natural trend by thinning to promote tree diversity and vigor, as well as planting tree species appropriate for the site, we typically observe a dramatic decrease in the presence or impact of insects and diseases. Diversity is the key to healthy communities. What a relevant message for these times we live in.

OPPOSITE: *Fruiting body of red ring rot* (Porodaedalea pini), *a heart rot fungus that causes stem decay*

FIRST, A WORD ABOUT FOREST HEALTH

I find the term *forest health* is often used casually to express how a forest appears to an observer ("This forest doesn't look healthy") or describe a goal for a forest ("I want my forest to be healthy"). I still use the term at times out of laziness or a desire to simplify a conversation. My problem with the term is that it is commonly used to frame the role of natural disturbance agents—such as pathogens, insects, windstorms, fire, and drought—as negative influences on a forest's ability to produce timber. As such, forest health is put into an entirely human-centered and economic context that does not recognize the role of natural distur-

bance on the development and ecological functions of a forest. From a purely ecological perspective, dead, diseased, insect-ridden, wounded, old, and slow-growing trees of all species and ages can be part of a healthy forest ecosystem.

The practice of ecological forestry recognizes the role of natural disturbance agents and events and seeks to approximate their effects on a forest through active management in order to achieve similar outcomes in a more controlled fashion. This reduces the potential for natural disturbance events to become catastrophic or unduly impact other desired outcomes such as timber harvesting or carbon sequestration.

Table 7-1: Causes of Tree Damage and Mortality

BIOTIC			ABIOTIC		
Insects	Pathogens	Wildlife	Human origin	Weather	Other
Bark beetles	Root disease fungi	Bears	Herbicides	Drought	Fire
Wood borers	Dwarf mistletoes	Ungulates	Air pollution	Wind	Poor soil
Defoliators	Canker-causing fungi	Rodents	Displaced soil, construction	Frost	Nutrient imbalances
Terminal and shoot borers	Stem decay fungi	Sapsuckers	Soil compaction	Flooding	Landslides
Root feeders	Other brooming agents		Poor planting technique	Winter desiccation	Avalanches
Sucking insects and mites	Foliar pathogens		Off-site seed source	Temperature extremes	
				Lightning	
				Snow, ice	

Source: Ellen Michaels Goheen and Elizbeth A. Willhite, *Field Guide to the Common Diseases and Insect Pests of Oregon and Washington Conifers* (R6-FHP-RO-2021-01, USDA Forest Service, Pacific Northwest Region, 2006).

I argue that *forest resilience* is a more appropriate term. Rather than striving for a vague or poorly informed state of forest health, ecological foresters should instead strive to improve the resilience of forests and foster their ability to rapidly recover after disturbance. Management strategies that improve a forest's resilience to insect and disease damage, drought, and other stressors, such as the effects of climate change, are therefore the subject of ecological forestry. Relative to the goals and objectives for a particular forest, a forest can be managed to both improve resilience and mimic or incorporate a certain degree of ongoing natural disturbance while providing desirable ecosystem services and valuable forest products.

Naturally occurring disturbance events that affect a forest can be divided into either biotic or abiotic agents (see Table 7-1). Biotic agents include insects, pathogenic organisms such as fungi, parasitic plants such as dwarf mistletoe, and animals. Abiotic damage agents include wildfire; weather-related events such as wind or ice storms, frost, and saturated or droughty soils; and human-caused impacts such as herbicides, soil compaction, or air pollution. Biotic agents such as pests and disease are described in greater detail later in this chapter, as they are factors that can be more readily identified and addressed through management. Natural abiotic agents, however, are often beyond a forest manager's control and must be adapted to. We will discuss how to manage for their impacts in later chapters. First, let's talk about assessing your trees and the health of your forest.

ASSESSING TREE AND FOREST HEALTH

When assessing the health of a forest, I like to keep in mind a quote from Kevin Zobrist, an extension forester with Washington State University:

> When considering tree health, it is important to remember that tree health and forest health are not the same thing. Tree health refers to the health of an individual tree, whereas forest health refers to the health of an entire forest system, including trees, plants, soil, wildlife, and water. A certain amount of insect activity, disease, mortality, and decay is normal and healthy within a forest system, and damaged, deformed, dying, and dead trees provide critical habitat for wildlife.

THEREFORE, AN OBJECTIVE ASSESSMENT OF forest health involves determining the extent to which trees appear to be ailing and how this affects the goals and objectives for a forest.

Quite often, more than one factor contributes to tree mortality or damage, and some factors commonly occur together, such as drought stress and bark beetles, mechanical damage and root diseases, trees inappropriate for the site and foliar diseases (described below), and rodents and fungi that attack the interior of a tree.

Evaluating the health of trees within a forest can largely be accomplished with qualitative observations that include symptoms of the host tree, signs of the damage or mortality agent, patterns of both signs and

Table 7-2: Diagnosing Tree and Forest Health

SYMPTOMS	SIGNS
Expression of the host	**Expression of the agent**
• Sparse foliage	• Fruiting body on a needle
• Resin flow	• Insect galleries
• Swellings	• Fungal mycelia
• Crown dieback	• Conk on a bole
• Yellow foliage	• Chewed or webbed needles or leaves
• Pitch tubes	
• Branch dieback	
PATTERNS	**CONTEXT**
Within and among trees	**The setting of the observed damage**
• Portion of the tree	• Geographic location
• Age of affected needles	• Stand history
• Mortality progresses slowly over time in the stand	• Setting
• Windward or exposed side	• Topographic location
• Tree species	• Weather history
• Mortality has occurred within a short time period	• Forest characteristics

From: Goheen and Willhite. *Field Guide to the Common Diseases and Insect Pests of Oregon and Washington Conifers.* (R6-FHP-RO-2021-01, USDA Forest Service, Pacific Northwest Region. 2006.)

symptoms within and among trees, and the overall environment of the site (see Table 7-2). Look for these common clues that may indicate the presence of insect activity or diseases.

Symptoms:
- Discrete groups of standing dead trees, typically of the same species
- Discrete areas of downed trees, also typically of the same species

- Thinning or diminishing live crowns
- Tops of trees dying back
- Pitch weeping from the lower portion of a tree's trunk or discoloration of the trunk
- Discolored or deformed foliage
- Wood-boring dust or shavings emerging from the bark, or around the base of a tree
- Pitch tubes or pitch streaming from multiple points on bark

Signs:
- Large numbers of insects on stems, leaves or needles, sticky leaves or needles, or the presence of insect webbing, cocoons, or nests on leaves or in branches
- Distinctive foliage chewing patterns
- Fungal fruiting bodies emerging from leaves or bark
- Tunneling patterns under bark
- Heavy and consistent cone or seed production

With a list of any of these observations, you can match your findings with the various common diseases and insect pests in Northwest forests.

FOREST DISEASES

Management of diseases must be consistent with the goals and objectives of the forest owner. Unless fungal pathogens are demonstrably and excessively impacting the management objectives of a forest, consider accepting them as a natural part of the ecosystem and observing how they function as agents of stand diversification. Containment and reduction of fungal diseases can require cutting all of the infected trees, along with trees that appear healthy but are in close proximity to known infected trees, which often results in a large patch cut. This approach may affect the character of the forest in ways that are not compatible with the goals and values of many small woodland owners. Therefore, less intrusive management strategies should be considered.

The most common diseases that affect forests in the Pacific Northwest can generally be placed into one of five categories: root diseases, stem decay, foliar diseases, canker diseases, and dwarf mistletoes.

Root diseases are typically confined to the roots and lower bole of a tree and spread via root-to-root contact between trees. They can be difficult to detect as trees tend to die slowly, especially when older. Mortality may occur among groups of trees in a discrete area or individual trees scattered through a stand. Many root diseases are considered diseases of the site, as they can persist between generations of trees on roots, stumps, or decaying wood of dead trees. Laminated root rot (*Coniferiporia sulphurascens*), for instance, is a common root disease, pathogenic on Douglas-fir and other commercially important conifers in the Northwest, though hardwoods, including red alder and bigleaf maple, are immune.

Although hundreds of species of fungi feed on dead trees and downed logs, there are about fifteen species of fungi known as heart rots that can infect live trees and lead to the decay of the wood within the tree. Heart rot fungi do not typically infect intact trees; they require an opening, such as a wound caused by fire, storm damage, injured roots, or pruned branches, to gain entrance

Heart rot fungi, such as Indian paint fungus (Phaeolus schweinitzii)*, often produce fruiting bodies on the trunk of a tree that can aid in their identification.*

to a tree. These fungi often go unnoticed but can produce fruiting bodies called conks on the stem of the infected tree. Red ring rot (*Porodaedalea pini*) is a common stem decay in the Northwest, affecting numerous species of trees, including Douglas-fir, pines, and true firs. Other common heart rot fungi include Indian paint fungus (*Echinodontium tinctorium*), which is most severe on true firs and hemlocks, and velvet-top fungus (*Phaeolus schweinitzii*), which infects Douglas-fir, spruce, fir, hemlock, pine, and larch. Western gall rust (*Endocronartium harknessii*) is another common fungal pathogen found on both the east and west sides of the Cascades, primarily infecting lodgepole and ponderosa pine.

Foliar diseases damage leaves and needles and reduce the photosynthetic capacity of a tree. Although many foliar diseases affect hardwoods, the diseases that affect conifers have the most impact on forest management given the focus on conifer timber production in the Northwest. Foliar diseases can affect tree vigor by causing foliage loss, and they tend to be more common in areas where there is either high humidity or poor air circulation, or where trees are not suitable for the site. Swiss needle cast (*Nothophaeocryptopus gaeumannii*) is an example of a widespread foliar disease that affects Douglas-fir and occurs predominantly in wet coastal areas.

Hundreds of species of fungi cause canker diseases that result in dead branches, dieback of tips, top mortality, girdling of stems, swelling of trunks or stems, and whole tree mortality. Disease occurrence is frequently tied to the introduction of trees that are not suitable for the site, drought, sunscald, and periods of severe weather or particular climatic conditions, such as high humidity or low air circulation, that favor infection or disease development. White pine blister rust (*Cronartium ribicola*), caused by a non-native pathogen, is an example of a canker disease that has had severe impacts on five-needle pine species, such as western white pine, both in the Northwest and across the country.

There are about a dozen species of dwarf mistletoes in Oregon and Washington, solely affecting conifers, and each one typically infects only one or a narrow range of tree species. Mistletoes are parasitic plants that depend almost entirely on their hosts for food and spread seeds in a localized manner from one tree crown to another. Mistletoe infection causes branch deformities that manifest in brooms (dense clusters of abnormally shaped branches or twigs) and can reduce tree growth, kill the top of a tree, and even lead to mortality.

FOREST INSECTS

I have to admit that I have very little direct experience with insects that adversely affect forests in the Pacific Northwest as, for the past twenty-five years of my career, I've seldom had to take management actions specifically intended to target forest insects in western Washington. This alone may be a meaningful testimony to the limited impact insects have on forests in western Washington where I do most of my work. However, insects have had, and continue to have, significant impacts on forests east of the Cascades, and we do not yet know what effects climate change will have on insect populations across our region.

Forest ecosystems host an extraordinary number of insect species, all of which perform important ecological functions such as aiding in the decomposition process of organic matter, pollinating, controlling other insect populations, and providing food for birds and animals. The term *pest*, with its negative connotation, is used to single out insects that can have a harmful effect on forest management. Once again we must keep in mind that we are typically viewing the function of insects from a very human-focused perspective, and relative to the goals and objectives for a forest. Therefore, an insect can become a pest when its impacts are in conflict with our goals and objectives. Otherwise, insects that lead to low or moderate levels of damage or mortality in trees, just like naturally occurring forest diseases, are contributing to the structural diversity, complexity, and habitat values of a forest ecosystem.

Trees and forests that are stressed or have experienced a disturbance event are the most vulnerable to insect outbreaks. Consider the mountain pine beetle (*Dendroctonus ponderosae*) outbreak that ravaged hundreds of thousands of hectares of forests across British Columbia beginning in the late 1990s. For decades the timber industry clear-cut the original, diverse old-growth forests and replaced them with highly stocked, homogeneous plantations of lodgepole pine, its primary host. When trees are stressed, they emit volatiles that are detectable by bark and wood-boring beetles. Combining thousands of hectares of homogeneous and highly stressed trees with a booming population of bark beetles has proven to be a recipe for catastrophic tree mortality.

The most common insects that affect forests in the Pacific Northwest can generally

Bark beetles, such as the mountain pine beetle, are identified by the galleries they create immediately beneath the bark of a tree.

be placed into one of four categories: bark beetles, wood borers, chewing and defoliators, and sucking defoliators. Bark beetles spend most of their lives between the bark and the sapwood of living trees and can kill a tree. Wood borers attack only dead or dying trees. As per their name, chewing and defoliating insects primarily feed on the foliage of trees, and sucking defoliators, such as adelgids and aphids, may also feed on twig bark. Bark beetles are ubiquitous and omnipresent in most forests. However, defoliating insects tend to follow a boom-and-bust cycle, and their effects can be

limited to isolated areas. Therefore, a defoliating insect that doesn't seem important here and now could become a headache for someone in the future, causing dieback of tree crowns and loss of growth. Some good examples are western hemlock looper, western black-headed budworm, balsam woolly adelgid, western spruce budworm, Douglas-fir tussock moth, and white pine weevil.

Insects are further categorized as either primary or secondary agents depending on their ability to kill trees in the absence of other factors. Primary agents can directly kill the trees they attack, acting either alone or in concert with other insects, diseases, or other abiotic factors. Secondary agents typically attack a tree after it's been weakened by another insect, disease, or other factor but will rarely kill a tree on their own.

HOW TO MANAGE FOREST DISEASES AND PESTS

Listed here are a series of general ecosystem-based strategies for managing forest insects and diseases.

Tolerance. Be clear about your objectives and the actual impact of diseases or insects on your forest. If your objectives are focused on habitat or biodiversity, then these agents may serve as an ally by creating habitat structures (e.g., snags), thinning canopy trees, creating gaps where other plant species can thrive, and providing a food source for birds, animals, amphibians, and other forms of wildlife.

Thinning. Overstocked stands are more susceptible to forest diseases and insects as competition between trees increases stress and decreases their vigor. All plants have defensive systems and a certain ability to withstand disease or insect damage. Thinning reduces competition, increases the availability of light and water, and therefore increases the vitality of trees. Vigorously growing trees not only are less appealing to insects but also have improved ability to resist and recover from their attacks. In particular, resinous conifers will often pitch out wood-boring insects that attack them. Thinning can reduce the spread of mistletoes but may increase the spread of certain fungal diseases that enter trees through wounds to the stem or roots.

Diversifying. Given that most common fungal pathogens and insects tend to be species-specific, increasing species diversity is a key strategy for limiting the severity of their impacts in a forest. If a particular tree species is affected, the disease or insect may not be able to travel as far, or as quickly, in a forest that also contains tree species that are not susceptible to these agents.

Planting. Similar to diversifying, planting nonsusceptible tree species into a site infected by a particular disease can help transition the site away from disease impacts. For instance, it's an effective strategy to plant areas affected by laminated root rot with either western redcedar, pines, or hardwoods.

Minimizing tree damage. Some fungal pathogens enter trees through wounds on the trunk or roots. Although many wounds occur naturally and cannot be avoided, such

The Douglas-fir beetle (Dendroctonus pseudotsugae) *is one of the most destructive insect pests to affect Douglas-fir in the Pacific Northwest.*

as during storm events when one tree falls and scrapes bark off its standing neighbors, other wounds result from human influence. Damage to trees can occur during logging, either when skidders roll over tree roots that are close to the surface of the ground or logs scrape against trees while being transported. Using appropriate equipment and well-trained operators is key to reducing logging-related damage. Pruning cuts can also serve as vectors for disease entering a tree, and some tree species, such as hemlock, spruce, and true firs, are more prone to infection this way.

Minimizing dead wood accumulation. Since bark and wood-boring insects are attracted to dead or dying trees (their ecological function is to begin the decom-position process), avoiding sudden large pulses of freshly dead wood into your forest can help reduce the occurrences of these insects. Outbreaks may occur in recently cut downed logs, and wood-boring insects, in particular Douglas-fir beetle and Ips pine engravers, can move into living trees.

For more information on identifying forest diseases and insects, as well as specific control strategies, see Resources. In the next chapter, we will turn our attention to the presence of non-native plants in Northwest forests. Unlike insects and diseases, non-native plants need to be viewed a bit more critically, and timely intervention is often warranted to prevent these plants from gaining too much ground in your forest.

CHAPTER 8

Where'd That Come From? Invasive Species

BY KIRK HANSON

Among the community of native plants that occupy my family's forests are several interlopers that have traveled great distances to be here. They include a cast of characters who are thuggish, persistent, thorny, stinky, and rude. They have formed a cabal that is seemingly intent on attracting new members every year, displacing the native population, and claiming this land as their own.

Plants in their native range have a sophisticated system of checks and balances. When they get displaced, things can get out of whack. So, when some of these plants got shipped oceans away from their native range, they were able to establish freely, without the limits that have evolved to keep them in check.

However, despite their indisputable negative impacts and these obvious anthropomorphic allusions, it is important to recognize that these plants still provide eco-logical benefits: wildlife forage and shelter, soil stabilization and fertility, erosion control, shade, and more. It takes some effort to view these plants objectively, given the strained relationship I've had with many of them over the years, but I've found it necessary to regularly reconsider my relationship with them as I observe their behavior, both in my own woodlands and wherever they occur across the region.

A CORNUCOPIA OF TERMS FOR THESE PESKY PLANTS

You may have heard the terms *noxious weeds*, *non-native plants*, and *invasive plants* used interchangeably in the past. The truth is the terms overlap but are not the same.

Non-native plant is a general term referring to species that have been introduced from other regions or continents. *Invasive plant* is a more general term usually applied to non-native plants whose introduction causes, or is likely to cause, economic or environmental harm or harm to human health. A plant can be non-native but not invasive. *Noxious weed* is a legal term used by state and local agencies. Both Oregon and Washington maintain noxious weed lists, and although their systems for classifying them differ, they both adhere to a similar definition of noxious weeds: noxious weeds are invasive, non-native plants that threaten agricultural crops, local ecosystems, or fish and wildlife habitats. Note that not all invasive plants are listed as noxious weeds. To be considered a noxious weed, a plant must be nominated by a member of the public, then voted on by a series of boards. In short, not all non-native plants are invasive, and not all invasive plants are noxious weeds; but all noxious weeds must be non-native and considered invasive.

IDENTIFYING NON-NATIVE PLANTS

If you're not familiar with the non-native plants in your area, you can visit the website of the Noxious Weed Control Board for your state or county or invite a natural resource professional from a local, state, or federal agency to visit your land to help you identify them. It's important to identify the locations and extent of non-native plants in your forest so that you know where the problem areas are.

Himalayan blackberry (*Rubus armeniacus*) is one of the most ubiquitous uninvited guests on Northwest forestland. It flourishes in full sun and always seems to discover recently disturbed sites where soils have been exposed. Confusingly, the thicket-forming plant is not from the Himalayan mountains, but in fact from the Lesser Caucasus region, which includes Armenia and northern Iran, hence its Latin name. It was introduced into the United States in the 1870s as a food crop and, I have to admit, does feed a lot of people . . . and wildlife.

Another common invasive plant in the Northwest is Scotch broom (*Cytisus scoparius*). Native to northern Africa and parts of Europe, Scotch broom was brought to the west coast of the United States as an ornamental and later planted widely for erosion control. I occasionally see Scotch broom for sale at plant nurseries, which baffles me, given how invasive it is. With a seed viability of up to eighty years, this plant is often the first to pop up following a disturbance, and once it gets established, it is difficult to contain. That said, its showy yellow flowers are lovely, and ecologically speaking, it fixes nitrogen in the soil, is a great pollinator plant, builds soil through rapid organic matter accumulation, and shades the ground, thus minimizing soil transpiration.

Then there are the trio from England: English ivy (*Hedera helix*), common holly (*Ilex aquifolium*), and cherry laurel (*Prunus laurocerasus*). Introduced to the United States as ornamentals in the late 1700s and early to mid-1800s, these enthusiastic colonizers immediately wandered out of gardens and are now settling into the understory of many forests across the Northwest. These particular plants are so shade tolerant that they can persist beneath even the densest of forest canopies.

There are other non-native plants in my family's woods: Robert geranium (*Geranium robertianum*), tansy ragwort (*Jaco-*

It fixes nitrogen, makes beautiful flowers, and takes over: It's the highly invasive Scotch broom (Cytisus scoparius).

baea vulgaris), various thistles (*Cirsium* spp.), and reed canarygrass (*Phalaris arundinacea*). With these plants, and others, my relationship ranges from casual observation, to annual pulling, to a maddening series of ongoing attempts at control—many unsuccessful.

Once you have identified and listed the non-native plants on your land, you should seek to understand the basic ecology of each plant. What is its preferred habitat—does it like dry, wet, shady, or sunny sites? How does it spread—do birds disperse it, or

does it climb or creep? How aggressive is it—is it outcompeting other native plants or just puttering along on the forest floor? What ecological functions is it performing? With this knowledge, you will have a better understanding of both the natural limitations to the ability of these plants to spread and when, how, or even whether to apply effective control measures.

If I were to distill my years of accumulated knowledge into a single truism, it would be this: if you want to be successful at controlling non-native invasive plants on your land you must be persistent, use a demonstrably proven control strategy, be diligent in your follow-up, and be prepared to pay—either in the form of your own labor or the cost of a contractor.

MANAGEMENT OPTIONS

Dealing with non-native plants is likely one of the greatest headaches of forest management a landowner will face. That's why the old adage "An ounce of prevention is worth a pound of cure" should become your mantra every time you are conducting some sort of management activity in your forest. Regularly monitor your forest for signs of non-native plants colonizing new areas, and be prepared to respond rapidly to any new occurrences. Below are some ecologically focused strategies for dealing with non-native plants. Ultimately you may need an integrated pest management strategy that combines several strategies for an effective outcome.

Prevention

The first strategy for addressing non-native plants is to prevent them from arriving in the first place, or not inviting more to join the party. Many non-native and invasive plants catch a ride on equipment entering a forest, tangled up in the roots and soil of transplants, or even inadvertently spread through a seed mix or hay mulch. Here are some tips for preventing the spread of unwanted plants in your forest:

- Ask your logging contractors (or other contractors who come to your forest) what steps they're taking to clean their equipment to avoid tracking in seeds. Require all equipment to be washed before it enters the forest.
- Know the origin of all plants or transplants that are brought to the site. Purchase seed mixes and straw or hay that are certified weed-free.
- Routinely check any recently disturbed sites, such as log landings or new roads, as exposed soils are very attractive to non-native plants.
- When manually removing non-native plants, safely dispose of them. Flowering or reproductive parts should be put in the garbage. If retaining plant material on-site, cuttings, root balls, and rhizomatous plant parts should be allowed to dry out without touching the ground. (Avoid large piles, as these can pose a fire hazard.) Check your county's policies before disposing of non-natives in yard waste.

Shade

The shade of a forest's canopy is the best strategy for controlling all but the most shade-tolerant plants. Scotch broom, Himalayan blackberry, tansy ragwort, thistles, and many other non-native plants prefer full sunlight. Once trees close the canopy over them and exert the suppressive effect of shade, these weeds begin to struggle, and their populations decline. This is one of the strongest arguments for maintaining a continuous forest cover and avoiding clearcutting your forest. Following the thinning of your forest, some non-native plants may creep in from the surrounding area and find refuge beneath the temporarily open canopy, or on skid trails and log landings. You may choose to proactively remove these, or wait for the forest's canopy to close and once again shade these plants out.

Tolerance

The key question that should be asked of existing non-native plants is whether they are indeed impacting your ability to grow trees or achieve other objectives, and to what degree. Some tender non-native plants, like Robert geranium, may linger in the understory and have a negligible effect on other surrounding native vegetation. Conversely, dense patches of Himalayan blackberry may inhibit the ability of native trees, shrubs, and groundcovers to thrive on a site. Pick your battles, then prioritize them based on your forest management objectives. Plants that have the least impact may be tolerated for a period of time, while plants that have a significant impact should be targeted for control. You may choose to tolerate some non-native plants in certain locations (e.g., the "sacred" Himalayan blackberry pie patch) but otherwise remove them wherever else they occur. One hundred percent eradication may not be necessary (or possible), compared to limiting the impact or spread of plants until other natural control mechanisms, such as shade, come into effect. If you don't know where to begin with a target species, you can start on the edges of the infestation (least weeds) and work your way toward the densest portion (e.g., monoculture).

Manual

Most invasive plants can be controlled using manual methods, such as a machete, loppers, or a shovel. If you're persistent and patient, manual removal over the course of a few years is usually effective in limiting the impact of small to medium-sized populations in your forest. Given how labor intensive manual control can be, you may want to consider the judicious use of this technique, such as only cutting back competing vegetation from around tree seedlings versus attempting to completely eradicate a particular non-native plant. Depending on the plant you're dealing with (e.g., blackberry or holly), combining manual cutting with a secondary method (e.g., sheet mulching or herbicide) can prove to be effective.

Mechanical

Mechanical control implies the use of heavier equipment or handheld power tools such as a brush cutter or chainsaw. Heavy equipment is usually used to masticate vegetation across larger sites and can include a brush hog, which is like a large deck mower that is typically pulled behind a tractor, or a flail mower, which is a rotating series of heavy metal teeth that is typically mounted on a mini-excavator or articulating arm on a tractor. Use of these types of equipment is best applied to larger patches of non-native plants. Avoid mowing when unwanted plants are in flower or seeding as this will just spread the infestation, and always clean your equipment before and after use. Mowing or grinding up plants just one time is rarely effective in eradicating them. Repeated mowing, annually or semi-annually, may eventually exhaust the carbohydrate reserves in a plant's roots, thereby impeding its ability to regrow. However, mechanical treatments are typically most effective when followed up by either an herbicide application or repeated manual treatments.

Herbicide

Herbicides should be a last resort when it's known that either manual or mechanical treatments alone won't be effective or are too cost prohibitive. Before using an herbicide, carefully consult your state and local laws. Not all herbicides should be used in all places! Care should be taken in ecologically sensitive areas, such as streams and wetlands. If you choose to apply an herbicide, closely read the label. A herbicide label provides important information about a chemical, its appropriate use, and the precautions needed to avoid off-target impacts. Legally, you must follow label instructions.

An abundance of information can be found online to aid in identifying and controlling invasive plants (see Resources for suggested websites). I urge you to add invasive plants to your regular forest monitoring program so you know when they appear, if they're increasing in abundance, and whether they're negatively impacting any part of your forest.

In the next chapter, we'll start taking a look at the infrastructure of your forest, namely roads and the various components associated with them, such as stream crossings and drainage systems.

CHAPTER 9

Roads in a Wood

BY SETH ZUCKERMAN

Roads in a forest are a mixed blessing. On the one hand, they make it possible to access land more easily—to truck in seedlings for planting, transport crews to the forest to care for those trees, extinguish unwanted fire, and ship logs to market. But as earth scientist Danny Hagans says, "There is nothing in Nature that mimics a road." A road sturdy enough to haul timber makes a qualitatively different impact on the forest than even the largest elk. Without proper care, those roads can muddy the streams that flow through the forest, sacrifice valuable topsoil, and become undrivable. In this chapter, I'll describe how you can evaluate the roads in your forest, what road features to pay attention to, how to decide which roads to keep, and what kind of maintenance is required.

ANATOMY AND PHYSIOLOGY OF FOREST ROADS

Until I lived in a rural area where I had to maintain the access to the house I was renting, I took roads for granted and didn't think much about how they came to crisscross the landscape. But then, walking the driveway during winter storms, carrying a shovel or hoe to keep it in good condition, I came to understand their anatomy and physiology.

Forest roads aren't constructed in the way that a house or table is built—rather, they are sculpted from the land so that a vehicle can travel reliably across uneven terrain without sinking up to its axles in mud. In some places, that sculpture is a process of subtraction, carving a flat bench in a hillside that slopes off to one side of the direction of travel. That subtraction might be balanced with addition, in which the material scraped off the uphill portion of the road is piled and compacted on the downhill side to widen the level bench—called the running surface—on which the vehicle will drive. If the road is to be used in the wet season, it will need a layer of gravel that sheds water and keeps the roadbed firm enough to support the weight of the vehicles traveling along it.

The large rock on the right is a base layer, covered with finer rock to make a smooth driving surface.

A road sculptor must also consider how to cross streams of all sizes. While a shallow streambed across flat terrain may be crossed on what is known as an "armored ford" of cobbles, most streams require more elaborate crossings. The assignment: allow the flow of the stream to pass under the road while traffic passes above. For the largest of streams or those whose channel is most deeply incised into the hillside, a bridge is required. But most forest roads are built more modestly, with streams channeled into culverts.

That describes the anatomy of a road. Its physiology comes into play when it is subjected to rainfall or snowmelt, since flowing water is the biggest challenge that roads face on a regular basis. A healthy road sheds water quickly. If roads are built carelessly, they become watercourses themselves, collecting and concentrating water that flows along the direction of travel. That water carries with it surprising erosive power, turning a smooth, easily driven road into a bumpy, gullied mess after just a few downpours. Tire tracks become ruts that cut down into the roadbed the more water flows along them. The art in road design and maintenance is to direct the water off the road before it builds up the volume and power to do any damage. Water can wind up on a road even in less obvious ways. When a road-builder cuts into a hillside to create a level driving surface, that cutbank exposes layers of the soil through which water is percolating. That water then emerges onto the road and needs to be drained from it.

ROAD ASSESSMENT

Not all roads are created equal, and not all should be built to the same standard (see sidebar below). Explore the road network in your forest with a critical eye. As you traverse the forest roads, you can make a map—using smartphone apps such as Google Maps or Avenza Maps—to keep track of trouble spots that need repair or areas that you want to revisit in the rain to see how they are draining. (See the next chapter for more on maps.)

Part of your mission is to fix or maintain what you can address quickly with the tools at hand, and create a list of the sites that need more extensive work. But another part requires a more strategic perspective: deciding whether each road should remain as part of your long-term stewardship of the forest or whether it ought to be put to bed—decommissioned so that it can safely

Types of Roads and How They Function

The different types of roads that traverse a forest each serve a specific function and should be built to the standards that suit their uses and the vehicles that will travel them, from log trucks to ATVs. As you inventory your roads, think about where each one fits along this continuum.

The king of roads is the **surfaced, all-weather road**, meant to be drivable through all seasons (as long as it is free of snow). These roads are topped with a layer of compacted gravel, which is impermeable to water and provides better traction than bare soil. The gravel makes the road firmer, keeping vehicles from sinking into wet ground. On especially muddy terrain, that gravel may be underlain with a sheet of filter fabric, which keeps the gravel itself from sinking into the clay below.

Next is a **seasonal road**. This is a permanent part of the transportation network, but it doesn't have a gravel surface, so it can be used only when the soil has dried out enough to support the vehicle's weight. Gravel isn't cheap, so this is a good choice if you can confine the road's use to the dry season. Because it is a permanent feature of the landscape, its stream crossings need to be robust to the highest expected flows, and its road surface needs to disperse water effectively so that it doesn't wash out.

Temporary roads are built to access parts of the forest for a specific management need but are at least partially decommissioned after the project is over. This makes it possible to remove stream crossings so they don't need to be monitored and maintained, and to build drainage structures across the road (to direct water off the road) that are beefier than what's practical for roads that are in regular use.

Equipment trails or skid trails are built with the least disturbance to the ground, often just by removing trees and driving along the route with heavy equipment. As long as they didn't interrupt natural streams, these are likely to disappear into the landscape as they become grown over.

Landings are flat areas constructed as a place to stockpile logs before loading them onto trucks for shipment. Depending on whether they will be used in wet weather, they may or may not be rocked. Although not technically roads, they can have a similar impact on forest drainage.

Measure the Slope of a Road

If you know the height of your eye above the ground, you can use your smartphone and a measuring tape to estimate the road's slope. Use an angle measurement app on your smartphone to hold it level, and sight along it to a point farther up the road that is even with your eye. Measure or pace out the distance to that point, and divide your eye height by that distance. That decimal fraction, converted to a percentage, is the approximate road grade.

be abandoned. The more roads you have, the easier it is to access each acre of forest, but that access comes with two price tags: the cost and effort to maintain the road, and the area you remove from production. Half a mile of sixteen-foot-wide road occupies an acre of ground.

The location of the road on the landscape matters too. The easiest roads to maintain in general are roads that follow the ridges, since streams don't cross them. The hardest are those that snake along the middle of a hillside, where they have to contend with both sloping terrain and frequent stream crossings. In between are roads in the valley bottom, which sometimes present the paradoxical challenge of being so flat that they are hard to drain, and can compromise water quality if they are situated too close to a stream. But if they are set back far enough from the bank and their stream crossings are well built, they can be a valuable part of your road network.

You will notice a lot more if you walk the road than if you drive it, so if you have the time and your forest parcel is small enough, try walking the entire road network. In addition to a notebook and smartphone, bring a shovel along so that you can correct small problems on the spot. For larger road networks, you may need a motorized vehicle (ideally an ATV, to give you a broad view of the landscape). If possible, take a partner along so that one person's attention can stray from the task of keeping the vehicle on the road. Bring a chainsaw if you can, since drivability is a matter of vegetation as well as road construction. Trees and shrubs grow quickly, and the exposed mineral soil of roads makes a great seedbed for pioneering species such as red alder and Douglas-fir. If a road has been unused for years, it may take some tree cutting to open it up again. Fortunately, there is no easier firewood to gather than from trees that have grown up in a road! If you're on foot, bring a folding orchard saw and either a machete or loppers to clear brambles, brush, saplings, and branches.

Besides the obvious issues that affect drivability, such as boulders and slides in the road or encroaching trees and branches, pay close attention to the road's durability, which is mainly a matter of its ability to handle flowing water. If you're inspecting the road in the dry season, you will need to do some sleuthing, looking for evidence of running water on the roadbed, much like an astronomer scrutinizing the Martian surface. As you inspect, triage the problem: issues you can fix on the spot, issues you can fix yourself later, and issues that can be addressed only with heavy equipment.

OUTSLOPE VS. INSLOPE

First, pay attention to the way the roadbed is pitched across the direction of travel. The simplest roads to drain are outsloped— canted slightly so that rain landing on the road will run off to the downhill side and diffuse onto the hillside. On outsloped roads, check to see that road grading hasn't left a berm that interrupts the sheeting of water across the road or, if there is a berm, it is interrupted often enough that runoff doesn't build up to the point of eroding the road. Simple as it is, outsloping is a viable solution only for roads whose grade is up to 8 percent—that is, which rise 8 feet for every 100 feet of driving distance.

Steeper roads are usually insloped— tilted slightly to the inside of the hill. In climates prone to ice and snow, this design choice also stems from safety consider- ations, so a vehicle that loses traction will slide into the roadbank instead of off the edge. In general, these roads are prone to more headaches than the other varieties. Insloping concentrates runoff in an inboard ditch, which needs to be drained across the road through culverts spaced periodically so that it doesn't carve a deep channel into the hill. Unlike culverts for stream cross- ings, ditch relief culverts discharge water right onto the hillside and should have rocks at their outlet to diffuse the energy of the gushing water and minimize the poten- tial for erosion. The last relief culvert before a stream crossing is especially important, because it keeps muddy road drainage out of the stream.

If a road segment was insloped when it could have been outsloped, you might con- sider switching to an outslope next time you

Figure 9-1. Road drainage geometries: outsloped (top), insloped (middle), crowned (bottom)

commission heavy equipment work in your forest—it will pay off in less maintenance later.

If the road is on flat ground or carries a lot of traffic, it may sensibly be crowned— highest in the center and draining to both sides. On a slope, the downhill side of a crowned road drains as if it were outsloped, while the uphill side drains into an inboard ditch, which requires all of the maintenance and drainage structures of an insloped road (see Figure 9-1).

DRAINAGE

Gullies in a roadbed are a sign that too much water has concentrated on the road surface, gathering enough power to erode it. If you find a gully, walk up the road to where you first start to see that it has created its own channel, and then examine the ways the roadbed has been shaped to direct water off the road. Chances are that the road builders' method for draining the road has fallen into disrepair, and you might be able to set it right.

The simplest of drainage structures are known as water bars, consisting of a shallow trench—one to three boots' length wide and about ankle-deep—that guides the water across the road to its downhill side (see Figure 9-2). These can fill in with silt so that the water overtops them, and often a few quick passes with a shovel are enough to make sure they catch the water running down the

Figure 9-2. Water bars are effective at draining water from a road, but they are easily breached by vehicular traffic and therefore require diligent maintenance.

Figure 9-3. A rolling dip is broader than a water bar, so it stands up better to the passage of vehicles and can be driven over more easily. You'll need heavy equipment to build one, though.

road and steer it out of harm's way. The outlet of the water bar can also fill in with silt and debris, damming up the flow and preventing the water bar from working properly—something else you can easily fix. Or you might find that the hump on the downhill side of the water bar has been breached by tire tracks from vehicles that crossed it.

In that case, rebuild the berm with dirt and gravel dug from the trench. But don't waste time being mad at the drivers who broke the water bar—just keep them off the road in the winter. This type of drainage isn't well suited to roads that are open for traffic.

For roads in regular use, engineers recommend a rolling dip, which is similar in its function to a water bar but wider and more gently sloping (see Figure 9-3). The idea is the same: to catch water running down the road and shunt it across to the downslope side. But because it is broader and shallower, it isn't damaged when it's driven across. Rolling dips can be maintained with hand tools but require heavy equipment to build and are suited only to road grades up to 12 or 15 percent.

One tricky situation arises where the road has been carved lower than the level of the surrounding terrain on both sides. For the entire length of this feature, known as a through-cut, it's hard to disperse runoff from the road. Usually, these through-cuts are short, so if you make sure the road has been well drained just above it, and create drainage immediately below it, the road won't erode. If it is longer than one or two hundred feet, however, you might need to maintain a ditch at the side of the road that will collect the runoff, and then drain it at the lower end of the through-cut.

STREAM CROSSINGS

Finally, your mission as you inspect the road network is to assess the state of the stream crossings. As a first cut, you want to make sure that the culverts are in working order— that their inlets aren't blocked by dirt or debris, that they haven't gotten filled in with gravel, and that their outlets are not carving gullies into the earth. If the stream is flowing, it'll be easy to see whether the culvert is passing water. But if it's dry, you'll want to become a culvert detective. Peer up the culvert outlet to see if there's light at the other end. Look on the roadbed for signs that the flow has exceeded the culvert's capacity and

overtopped the road. If the culvert is open and you still see signs that the culvert overflowed, that might suggest it is undersized. A previous owner trying to construct a road on the cheap might have installed a culvert that was too small (and thus less expensive). Another indication, on steel culverts, is to look for the rust line where gravel moving through the pipe has worn away the galvanized coating. If that rust line extends more than 20 percent up the diameter of the culvert, chances are that it is undersized for the stream. Bear in mind that peak flows are predicted to increase with climate change, so if a culvert seems only marginally big enough, consider it for a possible upgrade.

The biggest reason culverts fail isn't too much water—it's that they get plugged with debris. On streams big enough to transport sticks and logs at high flows, something as simple as a fencepost driven into the streambed upstream of the culvert can turn the debris so that instead of lodging sideways it gets flushed through the culvert. Other options include trash racks of various designs, which all need to be cleaned out periodically so they themselves don't obstruct the stream on its implacable journey toward the ocean.

Even the best of culverts can clog, so the prudent roadbuilder makes sure that the water has a good second option if it can't fit through the pipe. The best practice is to create a "critical dip" in the road just downhill of the culvert, meant to guide any overflow back into the stream channel (see Figure 9-4). Escaped water can erode the fill from the stream crossing into the creek or—even worse—find a rogue path downhill that destabilizes the slope and triggers a

Figure 9-4. A critical dip (at left, arrows) is insurance against the chance that a culvert will plug or be too small for the stream flow, causing water to overtop the road. If that happens, the extra water is meant to flow across the critical dip (the lowest spot) and back into the stream it came from, thus preventing further damage to the road, the hillside, or an adjoining watercourse.

landslide. If you don't see one of these dips, add it to your wish list for the next time you have road work done.

Ideally, roads are as invisible as possible to the stream that crosses it, but in practice, roadbuilding carries trade-offs of cost and impact. The greater the biological value of the stream, the more significant are those impacts. So if the road crosses a stream used by salmon or trout, the fish should be able to migrate up and down the stream as though the road wasn't there, which means maintaining the natural gradient of the stream and its natural streambed. For bigger streams, a bridge or pipe arch (a half

culvert supported on either side with concrete footings) is best; but in small streams, an adequately sized culvert can work fine. Crucially, the culvert outlet should be at the level of the stream, not suspended above it in what is known as a shotgun culvert. Not only do high culverts prevent fish from accessing the upper watershed, but they are also prone to causing erosion as the water shoots out of the culvert and plunges to the streambed below.

When thinking about fish passage, remember that it isn't just about adults migrating upstream to spawn—juvenile fish move up and down the stream network during the year and need to be able to swim up tributaries in search of food and cooler water. A jump that would be easy for an adult to negotiate is insurmountable for a fingerling.

Road design and placement are especially critical if a road roughly follows the course of a stream. In the best-case scenario, the road stays on one side of the stream and is separated from it by a generous strip of forest. Roads that are built right next to a stream should be considered for retirement, and typically will require special permission to use for timber harvest.

ROAD CONSTRUCTION AND PERFORMANCE CONSIDERATIONS

Every state has its own standards for forest road construction, and rules about stream crossings and how closely a road can follow a watercourse. Some forest stewardship activities, such as timber harvest, may trigger a requirement to upgrade your road to modern standards. In addition, each state offers programs that can help landowners remove barriers to fish passage on roads that were built before their impacts were fully understood.

If all this sounds like a lot to keep track of, it's because roads are the Achilles' heel of forest management. We need access to the land for vehicles and heavy equipment, and to create that access, we have to create a vulnerability that can cause more lasting damage than any kind of vegetation management. A sloppy clear-cut will grow back in decades, but a road washout can carry away millennia of topsoil in an instant. Don't let this paralyze you! Instead, take it as a reason to keep a sharp eye on your roads.

As you are driving your forest roads, you can keep an eye on their performance by glancing in the rearview mirror, says Peter Marshall, the training officer for a local volunteer fire company in Northern California. "If you see a cloud of dust behind you," he says, "slow down!" Fast driving in dry weather mobilizes the finer particles of the dirt road into the air, leaving a bumpy road surface, made up of larger rocks, but nothing between them. "If you see ruts on your road in wet weather," Marshall adds, "it means the road needs more rock."

Windshield rules of thumb aside, there is no substitute for inspecting your road in the middle of a rainstorm. So put on your best rain slicker and gum boots, and see how the drainage on your roads comes to life in wet weather. Muddy water flowing through your inboard ditches is a good clue that there is work to be done. Standing water on the road surface is a sign of poor drainage, and will lead to potholes if the road is driven on when wet. Don't forget your shovel!

CHAPTER 10

Forest Inventory and Management Planning

BY KIRK HANSON

One of the things I enjoy most about visiting a new forest is what happens before the visit. I relish collecting information on a place that is new to me and preparing to venture into the unknown. I seek to both inform myself about what I can expect and remain open to the element of surprise. If my site visit is aimed at developing a forest management plan, which I discuss at the end of this chapter, then I will come armed with maps, tools, and a methodology for observing, measuring, and documenting what I find—a process referred to as a forest inventory.

There is a science to designing a forest inventory system that results in a high statistical accuracy of the data collected. You should consider taking a formal forest inventory, or timber cruise, if you're managing your forest as a business, for tax or estate planning purposes, prior to conducting a commercial timber harvest, prior to the sale of the land, or if you have an abundance of time and want to geek out in your woods. In that case, I direct you to the bevy of forest inventory resources on Northwest Natural Resource Group's website (nnrg.org). For the rest of us, the methodology outlined in this chapter falls under the category of "good enough" and will yield a quicker and less costly forest assessment.

A forest inventory builds on the qualitative assessment, described in Chapter 5, by adding a quantitative element to the process, identifying resource concerns or potential problem areas in the forest, and formulating management options that will help achieve the desired future condition. Beyond simply observing forest phenomena, we are now evaluating how much the forest is already meeting our objectives, or how much we need to tinker with it to make sure it's on track to meet those objectives. A

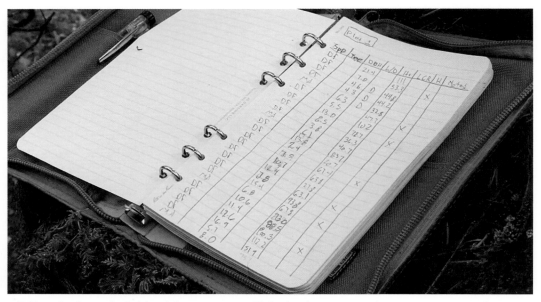

A field notebook organized with a plot measurement table is a handy way to record tree measurements in the woods.

forest inventory aims to answer the following questions:

- Are there forest health issues that affect my ability to meet my goals and objectives?
- Are there limiting factors that reduce the ability of wildlife to prosper in my forest?
- Is my forest capable of producing a sustained yield of forest products?
- Is my forest resilient to climate change?
- What will happen to my forest if I do nothing?
- How do soils, aspect, elevation, topography, hydrology, and climate affect my forest?

In this chapter, I describe a series of steps that compose a forest inventory. Completing these steps will provide you with the information you need to develop a forest management plan. For a forest owner with twenty to forty acres, this process could take the better part of a day or longer, depending on the tools you have, and another day to both prepare for the inventory and process the data you collected. It may behoove you to work with a professional forester at first, to get acquainted with the tools and techniques of conducting an inventory, before proceeding on your own.

PREPARING TO CONDUCT A FOREST INVENTORY

Although I have access to professional cartographers and hundreds of dollars' worth of forest inventory equipment and tools, I can't assume that you do. This section covers tools and strategies that are accessible to the layperson and come at little to no cost, as well as some key professional forestry tools for you gearheads.

Resource Maps

The first step in preparing for a forest inventory is to collect a series of resource maps. Even without a sophisticated geographic information systems (GIS) department, you can create or find a wide array of maps that provide very useful information about the natural resources on your land. These maps will articulate the topography of the land; identify the potential for streams to support fish or whether streams are perennial or seasonal; express patterns of vegetation and forest cover; describe the soil's composition, productivity, and its ability to retain moisture; and reveal the history of land use. Table 10-1 lists the types of maps and map data that are available on the web.

Tools to Bring

You will need several tools to conduct a forest inventory, and you can decide how crazy you want to get with buying gadgets. As with anything these days, you can spend as much as you want. I advise temperance. If you're running your forest as a business or have a larger ownership, then you may want to invest in a set of professional forest inventory tools, which I describe below. Otherwise, you may already have everything you need at home . . . or in your pocket.

Here are the tools and supplies that I carry in my forester's vest and use on a routine basis: smartphone with external Bluetooth GPS receiver (improves the accuracy of a phone's GPS), compass, laser rangefinder, manual clinometer, increment borer, diameter tape, basal area angle gauge, plastic flagging, weatherproof notebook, first-aid kit, water bottle, pens and pencils, snacks, gloves, and an emergency whistle.

Excluding the smartphone, which you likely already have, the remainder of the tools add up to less than $1,500—a fairly reasonable start-up expense that will definitely increase the efficiency and accuracy of collecting forest inventory data. However, you can get by with just the following if necessary: smartphone, 100-foot fiberglass

Drawing Boundaries, Roads, and Trails with Google Earth

Google Earth uses recent imagery to produce an aerial view of the land, and also has an archive of historical imagery. It's an all-around great tool for generating aerial photos and resource maps and can help you record useful monitoring information.

One of Google Earth's most useful features is its suite of mapping tools that, among many other functions, allow you to draw polygons to identify property and forest boundaries, as well as lines to identify roads and trails. The mapping tools also calculate area and distance. Google Earth does not include parcel data, so you will need to estimate the location of parcel boundaries using another map as reference. Using the line tool, you can also either trace visible roads and trails or estimate their locations to the best of your knowledge.

measuring tape or a carpenter's laser, and brightly colored plastic flagging or rags. If you were going to buy just two or three more tools to complement this basic, low-end toolkit, I suggest an increment borer in order to determine the exact age of your

Table 10-1: Resource Maps

TYPE OF MAP	ONLINE SOURCES	INFORMATION PROVIDED	NOTES
Aerial photo (recent or historical)	Google Earth, county assessor, WA DNR, ODF	Current and historical land use, vegetative cover	WA DNR and ODF only provide current aerial photos on their websites.
Soil types	Google Earth, NRCS Web Soil Survey	Soil types and descriptions based on NRCS soils data	To generate a soil type map in Google Earth, you must first download an extension from the NRCS's website.
Site class	WA DNR	Site productivity ranked I–V, with Class I being the most productive	These maps provide a very simple ranking of soil productivity.
Site index	NRCS Web Soil Survey	Site productivity based on average tree height over 50 or 100 year timeframes	These maps provide a more accurate estimate of soil productivity and can be used to determine the volume of tree growth over time.
Steep and unstable slopes	WA DNR, ODF	Presence of potentially unstable slopes	Forest practices may require special permission on steep or potentially unstable slopes.
Hydrology (streams and wetlands)	Google Earth, NRCS Web Soil Survey, county assessor, WA DNR, ODF	Rivers, streams, lakes, wetlands, and fish use	WA DNR and ODF hydrology maps also identify if a stream is fish bearing. These maps are frequently erroneous and should be ground-truthed.
Topography	Google Earth, NRCS Web Soil Survey, county assessor, WA DNR, ODF	Contours of mountains, hills, ridges, valleys, lakes, and rivers	To generate topo maps in Google Earth, you must first download an extension from the USGS website.
Hillshade/ terrain	County assessor, WA DNR, ODF	Highly detailed imagery of minute topography	These maps can be very useful for identifying old road grades and landscape features that are not visible either in aerial photos or on conventional topographic maps.

Note: NRCS = Natural Resources Conservation Service; ODF = Oregon Department of Forestry; WA DNR = Washington Department of Natural Resources; USGS = US Geological Survey.

An increment borer is used to extract a "core" from a tree so its annual growth rings can be counted to determine its age, without killing the tree.

trees and observe growth rates, a basal area angle gauge, and a 100-foot logger's tape, often referred to as a Spencer's tape or diameter tape, which measures distance on one side and tree diameter on the other.

Before venturing out to conduct a forest inventory, make sure your smartphone is charged up and ready. And by ready, I mean equipped with some useful tools for conducting a forest inventory. Numerous free apps enable you to download aerial photos, topographic maps, soil data, geo-referenced PDF maps, and other resources that will aid you in navigating across a property and collecting information. Some common apps include Avenza Maps, Gaia GPS, Guru Maps, and onX. When researching apps to use for a forest inventory, confirm they can perform the following minimum functions:

- Record a track as you walk around the land.
- Drop a pin or create a placemark and add notes and photos to the placemark.
- Download the data in various file types—at minimum, either .kml or .kmz, as these are compatible with Google Earth and can be imported to other GIS software.

COLLECTING INFORMATION IN THE FOREST

Equipped with your tools, resource maps, and a rudimentary understanding of the

Table 10-2: Tree Spacing and Recommended Inventory Plot Size

TREE SPACING (FT.)	TREES PER ACRE	RECOMMENDED PLOT SIZE	PLOT RADIUS (FT.)
>7×7	800+	1/100th acre	11.8
7–10	400–800	1/50th acre	16.7
10–17	150–400	1/20th acre	26.3
17–25	75–150	1/10th acre	37.2
<25	<75	1/5th acre	52.7

land, you should devise a route that will allow you to visit all parts of the land. During the inventory, you will delineate your forest into distinct *forest management units*, collect sufficient information to characterize and quantify these units, and begin to hypothesize management options for moving your forest along the path toward its desired future condition. A forest management unit is a discrete area of forest that will be managed in a manner that is different from another area of the forest. Based on aerial photos, you may have already identified different stand types on your land. Each distinct stand may be its own forest management unit, or may be divided into more than one unit. I usually distinguish forest management units using the following criteria. However, there are no rules as to what defines a management unit, and this determination is up to you.

- Is there a distinct age difference between stands?
- Is there a distinct change in tree species between stands?

- Is there a geographic feature that separates one stand from another, such as a stream or road?
- Do you intend to use a different management strategy in one stand versus another?

Along with visiting the different stand types, you will want to visit these other prominent features:

- Streams and wetlands
- Steep slopes
- Forest edges
- Property boundaries
- Roads, trails, and stream crossings
- Areas of natural disturbance (disease, windthrow, fire, landslide, etc.)

Forest Inventory Plots

Forest inventory plots are used to collect a data sample of a forest. The simplest way to use inventory plots is to walk a route that will take you through every distinct part of the forest, stopping to make observations and collect measurements within a "plot" whenever you observe a discernible change in the composition of the forest. Inventory plots comprise a circular area of a specific size, and the size of the plot is determined by the density of the trees. Where there is a high density of trees, plots can be smaller. Where trees are sparse, plots must be larger. The plot should be sized to include at least seven to nine dominant trees. The two most common plot sizes I use are 1/20th acre and 1/10th acre, or 26.3 feet and 37.2 feet in radius, respectively. See Table 10-2 for common plot radii.

The more plots you install, the better you'll get to know your forest, the more accurate your data sample will be, and the better your resulting forest management unit map will be, as you will use these plots to help differentiate one management unit from another. Wherever you choose to establish a plot, hang a ribbon on a branch of a tree or shrub, or scratch out a small patch of bare soil that's easily visible. This will be the center of your plot. All further measurements will occur within a specific radius of that plot center.

PLOT MEASUREMENTS

For the purposes of a forest management plan, I recommend you collect data from at least one plot in each distinct stand in your forest. This will not result in a statistically valid representation of your forest but will still provide meaningful metrics you can use to make basic forest management decisions. As you observe a discernible change in the composition of the forest, stop to take photos and record the following information within a plot:

- Age
- Tree species (Spp)
- Tree height (Ht)
- Tree diameter at breast height (DBH)
- Tree live crown ratio (LCR)
- Tree height-to-diameter ratio (HDR)

A chart can be helpful. Solely recording the species, diameter, and height of each tree in a plot will provide enough information to allow you to develop rough estimates of the volumes of wood, biomass, and carbon in your forest.

Although in this book I advocate for a quick-and-dirty, and therefore non-statistically valid, approach to forest inventory, it's still important to collect the data in a systematic and disciplined fashion. To that end, here are a couple of recommendations:

- Always start counting or measuring trees with the tree closest to north, and work your way clockwise around the plot.
- Staple a small piece of paper, hang a ribbon, or make a chalk mark on each tree as you take its measurements to ensure you don't either double count or miss a tree.

Now let's discuss gathering information and taking measurements from your forest plots.

Placemark and photos. The first step once the plot center is established is to create a placemark in your mapping app and label it (e.g., Plot 1). Most mapping apps also allow you to take and attach more than one photo to a placemark. If yours does,

PLOT #	TREE #	AGE	SPP	HT	DBH	LCR	HDR

Figure 10-1. A sample plot measurement table. Use multiple rows for each plot, with each tree getting its own rows. In even-aged stands, measure the age for just one tree per plot; in uneven-aged stands, measure multiple trees.

then take a series of photos in each of the compass directions, starting with north and proceeding clockwise, as well as photos of the canopy immediately above the plot center and the understory vegetation within the plot.

Age. The two most reliable ways to determine the age of an older tree (i.e., one that is twenty years or older) are to count the rings on a stump (which implies the tree is dead) or to take a tree core and count the rings (which implies you have an increment borer). If a tree is a younger conifer (i.e., less than twenty years), you can count the whorls of main branches. If you're not willing to spend a couple hundred bucks on an increment borer and you don't want to cut the tree down, then you're left with estimating tree ages, or the age of the stand in which they're growing, unless you happen to know the history of the forest. Historical photos found on Google Earth, your county assessor's website, or through other sources can also help you hone in on the year a stand was cut or planted. Without these clues, it's fine to generalize the age of a stand using three or more categories depending on your needs—for example, young, mid-aged, and older. A quick (though not always accurate) way to estimate stand age is to use average tree diameters such that trees up to eight inches in diameter are usually young, trees eight to fifteen inches in diameter are usu-

ally mid-aged, and trees greater than fifteen inches in diameter are usually older.

Species. Of course, you will need to be versed in common Northwest tree species before getting too far along in your journey as a forest steward (see Resources for suggested identification guides). It's useful to note which species are most dominant, either in the canopy or in overall abundance, as they will give you important clues as to the soils, hydrology, and microclimate of a site.

Trees per acre. Determining the trees per acre (TPA) provides a useful metric for understanding the influence of stand density on tree growth. Younger trees can grow at a higher density than older trees. Shade-tolerant trees can also grow at a

The History of Timber Harvests on Your Land

Both the Washington Department of Natural Resources and the Oregon Department of Forestry retain records of timber harvests on private lands in free online databases. These resources are called, respectively, the Forest Practices Application and Review System (FPARS) and the Forest Activity Electronic Reporting and Notification System (FERNS).

A smartphone with a clinometer app can be used to measure tree height.

higher density than less shade-tolerant trees. Therefore, determining the degree of competition within a stand is based on the species, density, and age of the trees.

Calculating TPA can be as simple as counting all of the trees within a plot and multiplying by the size of the plot. For instance, if 9 trees are counted within a 1/20th-acre plot, they represent 180 TPA (9 × 20 = 180). You can introduce more nuance to measuring tree density and composition depending on how complex the forest is and what your objectives are. Here are some options to consider:

- Segregate dead trees (snags) from live trees, but record all additional measurements of dead trees (e.g., height, diameter, species).

- Don't include seedlings or saplings in your tree count. Instead, tally them separately and by species.
- Count only the dominant and codominant trees to get a sense of competition within the canopy of the forest.
- Count only trees with a diameter of six inches or more to determine the merchantable timber volume of the stand.
- In uneven-aged stands, segregate trees by canopy layer. For instance, count the number of dominant trees, the number of mid-canopy trees, and then the number of understory trees, and tally these numbers separately.
- Segregate the trees by species, and record the number of trees by individual species.

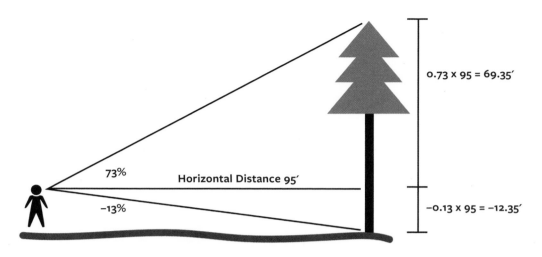

0.73 × 95 = 69.35′

73%

Horizontal Distance 95′

−13%

−0.13 × 95 = −12.35′

Formula for Total Tree Height
(Upper Slope–Lower Slope) x Horizontal Distance: (0.73-(-0.13)) x 95 = 81.7 feet

Figure 10-2. How to measure tree height.

Tree height. You will need to know the height of a tree (see Figure 10-2) if you want to determine the volume of wood or carbon in it, and to calculate either the tree's live crown ratio or height-to-diameter ratio, both of which are discussed below.

Measuring tree height requires some tools and a bit of math. You can avoid the math and speed things up considerably by purchasing a laser rangefinder that is programmed to calculate height from distance and angle to the top and bottom of the tree. The low-cost method involves a smartphone with a clinometer app and a nylon measuring tape or carpenter's laser, and goes like this:

1. Find your distance from the tree. Attach the nylon measuring tape to the tree with a nail, then walk far enough away to where you can see

the top of the tree. Alternatively, you can use an inexpensive carpenter's laser to shoot the distance to the tree. Record your distance from the tree.

2. Set the clinometer on your phone app to read percent (%) slope.

3. Measure and record the upper slope, which is the angle from horizontal (at eye level) to the top of the tree's crown.

4. Measure and record the lower slope, which is the angle from horizontal (at eye level) to the base of the tree.

5. Calculate for tree height using this formula: (Upper slope – Lower slope) × Distance = Height.

For example, I am standing 95 feet from a tree. The angle of the upper slope between the top of the tree and the horizontal is 73 percent. The angle of the lower slope between the horizontal and the base of the tree is –13 percent. Therefore, the calculation for height goes like this: (0.73 – (–0.13)) × 95 = 81.7 feet. (Remember that subtracting a negative number is like adding its positive version.)

Tree diameter. Diameter is reckoned based on the circumference of the tree, at 4.5 feet above ground level, known in forester's terminology as the diameter at breast height (DBH). If you are on a slope, stand on the uphill side of the tree to measure the trunk. Once you know the circumference, you can calculate the diameter based on this formula:

$C/\pi = D$, or circumference ÷ 3.14 = DBH

If you anticipate measuring a lot of trees, then I highly recommend you invest in a logger's tape which is calibrated on one side in diameter equivalents of circumference.

Live crown ratio. The live crown ratio (LCR) of a tree is an indicator of the tree's growth and vigor. Typically, smaller or sparser crowns lead to slower growth and less vigorous trees.

After you've calculated the height of a tree using the method described earlier, measure the height from the base of the tree to the lowest live branches at the base of the tree's crown (these branches should have fairly continuous live branches above them, and for this purpose you can ignore small, superficial branches found lower on the bole). Subtract this number from the tree's total height to determine the height of the remaining live crown, then divide the height of the live crown by the total tree height to find the LCR (see Figure 10-3). The formula looks like this:

Height of live crown ÷ Total tree height = LCR

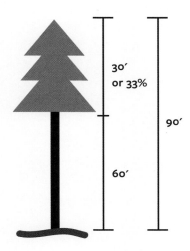

Formula for Live Crown Ratio
(90–60)/90 = 30/90 = 33%

Figure 10-3. A live crown ratio of 40 percent or less indicates that trees are so densely packed that they are competing too hard with their neighbors for light.

For example, I've measured a tree's total height at 90 feet. I've then measured the height from the base of the tree to its bottommost living branches at 60 feet. I subtract this number from the tree's total height (90 – 60 = 30). The tree's live crown is 30 feet tall. To find the LCR, I divide the height of the live crown by the tree's total height:

30 ÷ 90 = 0.33, or 33 percent live crown

All of this being said, the LCR is the one variable that I estimate the most often. Sometimes I default to simply noting either greater or less than 40 percent, as this threshold, as discussed later, is important to understanding the future growth potential of a tree.

Height-to-diameter ratio. The height-to-diameter ratio (HDR) of a tree indicates how prone a tree is to breaking during storms, tipping over, or bending severely

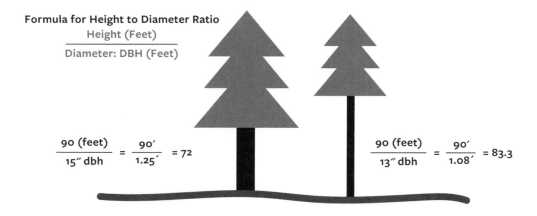

Figure 10-4. A height-to-diameter ratio of 80 or more (as seen in the right-hand tree) suggests that the tree is especially vulnerable to wind damage.

enough to affect growth and timber quality. Tall, skinny trees with a high HDR can be unstable, and entire stands of trees with high HDRs are very vulnerable to wind and ice storms. HDRs of 80 or higher indicate very skinny and therefore very vulnerable trees. To calculate the HDR, refer to Figure 10-4 and use this formula:

Total tree height (ft.) ÷ Diameter (ft.) = HDR

Here's an example: I measure a tree's total height to be 90 feet tall. The tree's diameter is 13 inches. Converted to feet, the diameter is 1.08 feet. The calculation is then

90 ÷ 1.08 = 83. A tree with an HDR of 83 is at increased risk of storm damage.

Basal area. Basal area refers to the cross-sectional surface area of a tree, or stand of trees, measured at breast height, or 4.5 feet off the ground, and is used to describe stand density (see Figure 10-5). The basal area of a stand of trees is expressed in square feet per acre. Knowing the basal area of a stand can help determine if a site is fully occupied by trees and therefore optimizing the growth of a site, or if a stand is either understocked or overstocked.

Calculating Timber Volume

Here's a formula for very rough estimate of timber volume using basal area:

Basal area (in ft² per acre) × Average height (in feet) × 1.5 = MBF per acre

Note: The standard unit by which timber is measured and sold is one thousand board feet, often abbreviated as MBF.

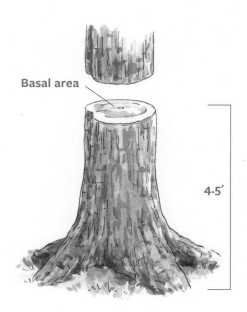

Basal area

4.5′

Figure 10-5. Basal area is the cross-sectional surface area of a tree measured at breastheight, or 4.5 feet from the ground.

The easiest way to measure basal area is to use a basal area angle gauge. The angle gauge is held a fixed distance from the eye when the forester is standing over the center of a plot, and as the forester turns in a circle, all trees within the plot whose diameter is larger than the angle gauge are counted. Each angle gauge is set at a certain *basal area factor* (BAF), and each tree that is counted represents that many square feet of basal area per acre. The BAF is multiplied by the number of trees counted in the plot to give basal area per acre.

For example, using the BAF 20 on an angle gauge, a forester counts ten trees in the plot. Therefore, this plot represents two hundred square feet per acre of basal area.

The advantage of this kind of sampling is that you don't have to measure the distance to the tree from the plot center: a tree is only counted if it appears wider than the angle gauge. To interpret the basal area of your stand for its particular age and species, refer to Oregon State University Extension's publication, Competition and Density in Woodland Stands, listed in Resources.

QUALITATIVE NOTES

A forest inventory and a qualitative assessment, as described in Chapter 5, can be done simultaneously. Even if you did a prior qualitative assessment, I suggest you also record similar qualitative observations at each inventory plot. Observations will run the gamut from forest composition to forest health; wildlife features such as snags, downed logs, and forage; forest roads, stream crossings, erosion; and more. Revisit the main themes presented in Chapter 5, and add to this list to suit your objectives.

MAKING MANAGEMENT OBSERVATIONS

The final bit of note-taking in the forest involves speculating about management options. Even before your management savvy has been enriched through experience and professional consultation, you can make some basic observations that begin to shape a pathway forward for the forest:

- Are there many small-diameter trees with small live crowns that appear to be competing with each other? If so, thinning to reduce competition may be warranted.

It is useful to collect information even in newly planted areas or in areas where no trees exist.

- Are there groups of dead trees that may indicate disease or unsuitability for the site, offering an opportunity to plant something else?
- Are there large areas dominated by invasive plants that could be restored to native trees and shrubs?
- Are trees large enough, and high quality enough, that commercial thinning may be viable? An average diameter of at least ten inches DBH is usually a good cutoff to consider commercial thinning.
- Are roads and drainage systems well maintained, or is maintenance necessary to prevent stormwater erosion?
- Is there a lot of fine dead wood accumulation, both standing and downed, that may need to be mitigated to reduce the risk of fire?
- Is there a deficit of snags and downed logs that may limit habitat options for wildlife?

- Are there known strong winds on one side of the forest that warrant retaining a higher density of trees on the forest's edge in order to protect interior trees?
- Are riparian areas dominated by hardwoods and would therefore benefit from planting additional conifers?

PULLING TOGETHER WHAT YOU'VE LEARNED

If you complete a forest inventory along these lines for your forest, you will end up with a notebook filled with measurements and observations, and a smartphone full of placemarks and photos. This is the raw material that will compose the guts of your forest management plan and inform the management decisions you make.

While your memory is still fresh from the inventory, download placemarks and photos to your computer and import them into whatever mapping program you are using.

Make sure the placemarks appear within the property boundary you drew earlier. If you're using Google Earth, when you click on a placemark, the photos and notes you took should automatically open.

If you've already drawn the locations of streams, wetlands, roads, and trails on your map, revise them as necessary based on your field data. Using the mapping tools in your mapping program, draw polygons around the forest management units that you observed during the forest inventory. This is a good time to review the plots you installed and compare forest composition between the plots. If your forest is small and homogeneous in species and age, then you may have only one forest management unit. If your forest is larger or more complex, you may have several management units. If similar stand types occur in different places

around a property that you intend to manage the same way, then identify them on the map as the same forest management unit. Label all of the units using a common code, such as FMU 1, FMU 2, and FMU 3 (or more descriptive names such as Lower East Side, Bowery, etc.).

Summarize the forest inventory data you've collected and calculate averages for each forest management unit (e.g., average TPA, average DBH, average height, average LCR, and average HDR). NNRG's website offers several Excel-based forest inventory programs that you can download and enter this data into. These programs handily calculate a variety of summary data, including trees per acre, HDR, wood volume, carbon volume, and more.

Now that you have a custom forest management unit map and detailed notes on

Remember to consider the health and vigor of the understory when you are crafting your management plan.

An Example of a Forest Inventory

On my family's Bucoda land, we have a fifteen-acre plantation of twenty-seven-year-old Douglas-fir. A couple years ago, I took a walk through this stand and, based on a cursory review, determined that it should be thinned in order to reduce competition between the trees. Although my professional judgment led me to this conclusion based solely on observations, I wanted to reinforce my opinion using forest inventory and other resource data. When I prepared the forest management plan for this land several years ago, I obtained a site class map from the WA DNR's website, which identified the soils as Class II, or the second most productive soils in Washington State. This told me that trees on this site would grow faster and have the ability to achieve a merchantable size much sooner than trees growing on lower-productivity soils. What I needed to determine was whether the stand should be pre-commercially thinned (at a cost to me), or if I could commercially thin it and use the revenue to pay for the thinning. With my kids' help, I installed seven forest inventory plots and collected all of the forest inventory data I described in this chapter. Averaging the data across the plots yielded the following results:

Sample Forest Inventory Table							
AGE	SPP	TPA	BASAL AREA	HT	DBH	LCR	HDR
27	DF	331	147	62'	8.8	<40%	85

From my qualitative assessment of the stand, I could see that the live crowns of the Douglas-fir were receding quickly given the dense canopy of the stand. As the live crowns receded, the growth of the stand was beginning to taper off, and there was a clear distinction between dominant trees (larger crowns and larger diameters) and suppressed trees (smaller crowns and smaller diameters). The diminishing live crown ratio across the dominant and codominant trees (less than 40 percent) was the singular metric that led me to conclude this stand should be thinned. The remaining metrics just reinforced this opinion.

I assumed this stand was originally planted at a conventional reforestation density of 350 TPA, so the fact that there was still an average of 331 TPA told me that there was either a high survival rate over the intervening years or additional trees seeded in. This high density was causing the competition in the canopy and the reduction in live crowns. As the trees competed for sunlight, they were putting most of their energy into height growth at the cost of diameter growth. This was contributing to an average HDR of 85, which indicated a stand that was becoming increasingly vulnerable to storm damage.

Lastly, with the use of an increment borer, I cored trees in each plot to look at the annual growth. Over the preceding eight years, annual diameter growth had begun to taper off significantly—another clue that the stand was in a highly competitive growth phase. Since diameters across the stand averaged ten inches, I concluded that the stand was just barely of a merchantable age and size to be commercially thinned. What helped convince me of the merchantability was the fact that a fair number of dominant and co-dominant trees had storm damage in their tops and would yield larger diameter (and therefore more valuable) logs when they were cut. There were also a sufficient number of suppressed and intermediate trees in the eight- to ten-inch DBH range that would yield saleable chip-and-saw logs.

Using the timber volume formula, I determined that the stand averaged 13.6 MBF/acre ($147 \times 62 \times 1.5 = 13{,}671$ MBF). I estimated a commercial thinning would yield approximately 5.5 MBF per acre of merchantable logs by thinning from below and removing approximately 40 percent of the trees (13.6 MBF $\times 0.40 = 5.5$ MBF). This would reduce the stand's density to an average of 180 to 220 TPA. The cut trees would yield 40 percent pulp logs (too small and low quality to make sawlogs) and 60 percent sawlogs, making for an economically viable logging project. I have since obtained a permit for the timber harvest and am now debating whether to hire a logger or attempt to thin the forest myself.

your forest, you're ready to begin organizing this information into a forest management plan.

A COMPREHENSIVE MANAGEMENT PLAN

Think of a forest management plan as a living document for a forest. It should describe the natural resources that combine to create a forest ecosystem, articulate a vision, and evolve as the circumstances of a forest change. One of the greatest values of a management plan is the process of creating one.

I still have a copy of the management plan I wrote in 1998 for the first tract of forestland I acquired. I had enrolled in the Coached Forest Stewardship Planning Course hosted by Washington State University Extension Forestry, a nine-week course that guides small woodland owners through every step of writing a management plan for their land while introducing them to all of the information, resources, and technical and financial assistance available to them. The program brought in specialists who talked about how soils affect tree growth, ways to improve wildlife habitat, managing for timber quality and production, forest management regulations, non-timber forest products, and many other topics I found fascinating. At the end of the course, an extension forester came out and walked my land with me and helped interpret what was going on in my forest. He also provided tips on how I could better manage my woods to meet my goals and objectives. He then reviewed my draft plan and gave feedback.

It's entertaining to read the nearly thirty-year-old plan now that I've been a professional forester for over twenty-five years. I was incredibly naïve in predicting how my forest would develop over time, and ignorant of proper management practices to effectively steward it. Regardless, the plan serves as a useful snapshot in time, and thanks to the coaching of the extension forester and the course he hosted, it does serve as a proper catalog of the resources my land and forest started with.

Most forests will benefit from our stewardship, and a forest management plan is the best way to arrive thoughtfully at the course our stewardship should follow. Putting together a plan requires a concerted effort to collect and understand data from your forest, make informed observations, familiarize yourself with the climate and other natural and anthropogenic influences on your forest, and get very clear on what your goals and objectives are and whether they're appropriately matched to the forest. If a family or group of people are involved in your forest, then the planning process provides an opportunity to galvanize everyone around a shared vision and logic for its management.

Here are some other reasons why a comprehensive forest management plan is a valuable investment:

- It provides a vehicle for efficiently organizing a wide range of information about your forest that otherwise may remain scattered.
- It may qualify you for a reduction in annual property taxes through your county's current use programs.
- It may qualify you for financial assistance through federal, state, and local government conservation funding programs.
- It may qualify you for a variety of forest certification programs offered by government and private agencies.

There are enough resources out there to assist you with writing your own plan that I won't go into much detail about them here. Instead, I provide suggestions on how to choose a type of plan that best suits your needs and how to find the templates and guidelines to compile the plan yourself.

Writing a Basic Plan for Current Use Designation

Oregon's and Washington's timberland and designated forestland classifications reduce taxable land values for owners whose lands are primarily used for growing and harvesting timber. These designations allow the land to be assessed for its forest use rather than the land's highest value use (e.g., residential development). A *timber management plan* is required when applying for either of these land use designations, and it must describe timber harvesting and associated activities. This type of plan tends to be the simplest to put together, and after reading this book, you should be able to write the plan yourself.

Most, if not all, county assessors have an outline on their website for a minimalist timber management plan that specifies what information is needed to qualify for current use designation. The county may require you to submit a management plan prior to closing on the purchase of your land or within a short time after purchasing your land. Here's some of the basic information that must be included:

- A description of the ownership goals for the land and an outline of the intended management practices
- A brief description of the timber (major species, size, age, and condition), including an inventory of the forest types and stands, tree densities, and health conditions

Professional foresters can help you collect forest inventory data and write a forest management plan.

- A description of reforestation plans if the land has been recently logged, or if the land has no trees growing on it, a description of the plans to restock within three years of designation
- A description of whether the land is in compliance with minimum state stocking requirements, including the number of trees per acre
- A map or aerial photo showing the property lines, access roads, topography, water, or other physical features of the property

Writing a Comprehensive Forest Management Plan

For those of you who want to embark on the journey of writing a more comprehensive plan, you can turn to an abundance of resources. State forestry agencies have templates that help landowners qualify for stewardship certification programs and state conservation funding. State university forestry extension services have their outlines. The Natural Resources Conservation Service has an outline of the minimum required content for a *conservation activity plan* that qualifies you for federal funding through the Environmental Quality Incentives Program. The national American Tree Farm System has a template and guidelines for forest owners to develop a plan that will qualify them for third-party certification.

Several years ago, local, state, and federal natural resource agencies in both Oregon and Washington worked together to create templates for forest management plans that would satisfy the requirements of each entity. These two templates are referred to as the *Washington State Integrated Forest Management Plan Guidelines and Template* and the *Oregon Forest Management Plan Guidelines and Template.*

Getting Assistance

Writing a comprehensive forest management plan is not in everyone's wheelhouse. It takes time, a minimum level of experience, a lot of research, and at least some basic forestry skills. Plans that I write for small woodland owners frequently take me at least thirty-two to thirty-six hours to complete, including the site visit. Keep in mind that I'm a professional forester who has fancy tools, a GIS cartographer on staff, a well-honed methodology, and over twenty-five years of experience sticking my thumb in the air and saying, "That's about right." So how long will it take you? Twice as long? Three times? Finding the time, and discipline, to translate all of your notes,

research, and ideas into the format of a management plan can be surprisingly elusive. I want to encourage every do-it-yourself person out there to write their own plan, but take some time to think about it and decide if it's something you truly can and want to take on independently.

NOW THAT WE'VE SUMMARIZED A VARIETY OF strategies for evaluating your forest and land, we are going to pivot to the economic side of ecological forestry. No conversation about ecological forestry is complete unless we talk about how we're going to pay for the ownership and management costs of a forest. However, one of the benefits of living in the Northwest is that many of our forests grow on highly productive soils, and opportunities to manage for both sustained revenue and improved ecosystem services abound, as we'll begin to discuss in the next chapter.

CHAPTER 11

The Economic Benefits of Ecological Forestry

BY SETH ZUCKERMAN

So far in this book, we have barely mentioned the reason many people buy and hold forests: to grow their wealth and generate income. That isn't because we discount the importance of revenue, but because revenue is just one of several objectives for practitioners of ecological forestry. When managing the forest as a whole system, revenue comes second behind the health, integrity, and resilience of the forest, since the capacities of the forest are what make it possible for the forest to yield a stream of forest products, and thus income.

At the same time, we wouldn't want to avoid the topic of income entirely. Forest stewardship entails actual costs—whether for property taxes, road maintenance, or forest improvements such as tree planting, seedling release and protection, and pre-commercial thinning. Unless an outside source of funds is subsidizing your forest, it's worth pondering how much of its own way your forest can pay. If we ignore revenue entirely, in the words of Northern California poet Jerry Martien,

It will turn out money was just another
kind of love we thought we could live without

Thinking about money doesn't turn forestry into a get-rich-quick scheme. Just as ecological forestry takes a long-term perspective on the forest's life cycle, it has a patient outlook on the forest's ability to provide harvestable logs and other saleable products—which turns out to be a good match to the stately pace of forest growth. It's a happy coincidence that some of the by-products of forest restoration—the timber from trees you thin from the forest—can be sold for cash money.

In this chapter, we will explore how that approach can translate into a stream of income from forestland—a get-rich-slow

A load of logs leaves the landing after a thinning operation in Ashford, Washington.

proposition, if you will. We'll focus on timber, which is the highest-priced product that most forests provide, while in later chapters, we will touch on other products and services that can be sold from forestland, from wild mushrooms to carbon offsets, and from floral greens to conservation easements. This chapter will sound somewhat mercenary compared to most of the rest of the book, but don't take it to mean that we are exclusively about the Benjamins.

If the only kind of timber harvest you've seen is clear-cutting, it might have shaped your preconceptions of what logging means and how it leaves the land. So if you are recoiling from the idea of logging because that's what logging evokes in your mind's eye, we ask that you suspend judgment and consider that there are other ways to cut timber that might be aesthetically and ecologically friendlier. In fact, chances are that you have driven past forests that have been harvested in other ways—such as

thinning—that didn't have the same stark visual impact, and they didn't even register as forests that had been logged.

THE RHYTHMS OF FOREST GROWTH

Before we describe how income from timber harvest can fit into a plan for ecological forest management, it's important to understand some basic patterns of forest growth. For example, consider a moderately good site where the previous cohort of trees had been clear-cut or flattened in a windstorm. A new stand of trees emerges, whether human-planted or from seeds that blew in from nearby woods. As seedlings and even as saplings, the stand has no timber volume because the trunks of the trees are too small. But at some point, perhaps in their early to mid-twenties, a few trees begin to grow into a merchantable size—that is, they are big enough that a logger could cut them down and manufacture a log that a mill would purchase. (The actual ages when the stand shifts from one phase to another will vary, but the sequence is true across most forest types.) The minimum size of a saleable log depends on the kind of product that the tree will ultimately be made into—and the mill's requirements—but for lumber, it means a tree that is at least five or six inches in diameter, inside the bark, at a height of eighteen feet off the ground (sixteen feet for the log, plus an allowance for the height of the stump and a little extra for the mill to be able to square off the ends of the log). As the forest grows, more trees reach a merchantable size, and about the same time, they enter the fastest growth phase of their lives. The trees have spread their canopy across the site, their needles are capturing nearly all the available sunlight for photosynthesis, and they are tapped into a network of subterranean fungi that help them scavenge the soil for water and minerals. On a decently fertile and productive site, a twenty-five-year-old tree could put on two or three feet of height per year, and lay down a quarter of an inch of wood or more all the way around the trunk. The volume of wood in the stand shoots up like a gangly teenager.

Around age thirty or forty, the forest's growth eases up. The additional wood grown each year, which foresters call the annual increment, begins to decrease as the trees physiologically mature, and, if unmanaged, begin to crowd one another. But it is still higher than the *average* growth up

to that point in the tree's life, the *cumulative* average production of wood per acre. That average continues to rise, albeit more slowly, until the annual increment slips below the cumulative average—a transition that occurs around sixty to one hundred years in Douglas-fir on the west side of the Cascades. If your sole interest lies in maximizing the timber production of that piece of ground, that age—known as the culmination of mean annual increment—would be the time to cut the stand and start over (see Figure 11-1). As we describe in Chapter 14, that's not the only option.

If you clear-cut the forest earlier than that, you would forgo some of the land's productive potential. That's the course chosen by the industrial forest owners described

Culmination of Mean Annual Increment

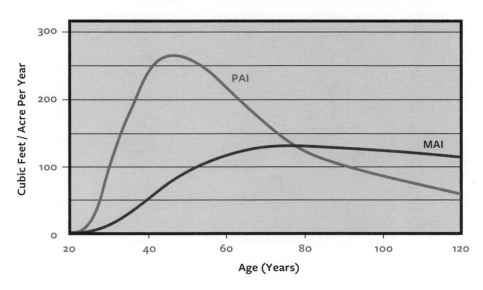

Figure 11-1. A representative pattern of timber growth in a stand of trees that all took root about the same time. The PAI (periodic annual increment) is the additional growth in any given year, while the MAI (mean annual increment) is the annual growth averaged from the establishment of the stand up to that point in time. Where they cross marks the maximum of the stand's average growth, also known as its culmination. Actual ages and volumes vary by site and species.

Short-rotation industrial forestry near Port Ludlow on the Olympic Peninsula

in Chapter 3 who practice short rotations. They reap a smaller harvest than if they raised older forests, but they realize those harvests sooner, which suits their cash flow needs.

SHORT- VS. LONG-ROTATION FORESTRY

When you think about the biophysics of forest development, it makes sense why frequent clear-cutting would reduce productivity. It takes ten years or so for the forest to reoccupy the site and rebuild its photosynthetic apparatus. Until the branches of the young trees, planted some ten or twelve feet apart, reach one another and form a continuous forest canopy covering the ground and capturing almost all the available sunlight, some of the site's wood production potential is wasted when the sunbeams land on the ground between the trees. In a short-rotation regimen, the forest spends more time in the part of its cycle that squanders sunlight as the new trees build their leafy canopies. Northwest Natural Resource Group (NNRG) foresters used a US Forest Service model to compare the results of short- and long-rotation forestry and found that two forty-year rotations back-to-back produce about 25 percent less timber than a single eighty-year rotation. That 25 percent drop is the penalty in timber production that a landowner incurs when they cut the trees so young.

Raising older trees doesn't mean you need to keep your saw holstered until the stand is eighty years old. To understand why, compare two stands in your mind's eye: young trees that are clustered closely together and an older stand where the trees are larger but spaced farther apart. A few decades previously, the older stand was thronged with younger, more densely packed saplings. What happened to all the missing trees? If the stand was unmanaged, they were probably crowded out. Their neighbors overtopped them and left them in such dark shade that they couldn't survive. They died and fell over; in a managed stand, they might have been cut and removed. Either way, as the forest ages, you expect to find larger trees but fewer of them per acre (as we'll see in greater detail in Chapter 13). That creates an opportunity for land stewards looking to mimic natural processes: thin the forest to harvest some of the trees that would die anyway.

In a neighborhood near where King County Department of Natural Resources and Parks was selectively logging a tract of parkland, the agency put it this way on a sign announcing their project: "Making room for larger trees." Who can argue with that? From an economic standpoint, repeated thinning can provide more frequent cash income, preserve a wider spectrum of options for future landowners (perhaps the children and grandchildren of the present owners), and ultimately increase the total timber yield from a piece of ground. In the rest of this chapter, we'll see how.

THINNING FOR GROWTH

The precise way you harvest your forest will depend on its natural gifts and your objectives. For starters, consider a tract of forestland that originated as an industrial plantation and whose owners want it to eventually develop mature and even old-growth forest characteristics. At NNRG, we help a lot of forest owners with forests like these, whether they are land trusts that have acquired the land for restoration and habitat, small family forest owners who have bought the land for recreation, or a rising generation of owners who want to set their family land on a new path.

We find that forests on the west side of the Cascades are ready for their first commercial thinning sometime in their thirties. At this point, we usually recommend a thinning that removes most of the weaker and slower-growing trees, those with poor timber form or meager crowns, and those that are too close to the trees we want to retain for at least the following decade or two. The net effect is to give the vigorous trees more room and improve the quality of the stand; this is accomplished by removing about half of the trees in the stand if it hadn't previously been pre-commercially thinned or 30 to 40 percent if it had. Along the way, the harvest produces about four thousand board feet of logs per acre—roughly a truckload—of which a substantial amount might be of such low quality that it can be sold only for pulp. Depending on logging costs, proximity to the mill, and log prices, the harvest might produce a small profit (in the early 2020s, a few hundred dollars per acre) or barely break even. Either way, the harvest benefits the forest, as it spreads the resources of the site—water, sunlight, and soil nutrients—among fewer trees so that the remaining stand can grow faster than if it hadn't been thinned, and it is more resilient to a warming climate.

Ten or fifteen years later, depending on growing conditions and log markets, it would be time to return for another thinning. By this time, most of the trees will already have grown to sawlog size. In an industrial model, this is when the forest would be clear-cut. But seen through the eyes of an ecological forester, the forest is just entering its prime growing years. At this point, you might remove a third of the trees (in later chapters, we'll address how you choose which ones), and each acre would yield about one and a half to two and a half truckloads of logs for market. This time around, the trees yield some higher-grade sawlogs, which are more valuable to a mill because they can be used to produce a wider variety of lumber sizes, and so fetch a higher price per board foot. Because the loggers are dealing with fewer, larger stems, their work is more efficient and they charge a smaller percentage of the gross log price that the mill pays. Between the higher volume removed, the higher price per thousand board feet, and the lower logging cost, this is likely the first harvest that will deliver significant profit to the landowner after all expenses are accounted for. Net income of

How Much Can I Plan to Cut?

To harvest your forest indefinitely, you must remove no more timber than your forest grows—a concept referred to as sustained yield or annual allowable cut (AAC). Usually measured as a rolling average, given that timber harvest may not occur every year, the AAC is based on your site productivity, as well as the age and composition of your forest. You can find your site productivity, expressed in cubic feet of timber per acre per year, in the Natural Resources Conservation Service (NRCS) soil survey for your county or via the NRCS Web Soil Survey. This productivity rate is based on a well-stocked fifty-year-old stand of Douglas-fir. If your forest is younger, composed of other species, or not well stocked, you will need to adjust this growth rate subjectively. Further, you will want to deduct areas of your forest where you never expect to harvest timber, such as riparian zones, steep slopes, and areas of high conservation value.

Here's an example: A thirty-acre parcel of land has a forty-year-old Douglas-fir-dominated stand, of which twenty-five acres are accessible for timber production (the remaining five acres are in wetlands and stream buffers). Based on the NRCS data, the property can produce 150 cubic feet of timber per acre per year once it reaches age fifty. At five board feet to the cubic foot, that amounts to 18,750 board feet per year (150 × 5 × 25). Given that you probably want to rebuild your forest and make allowance for unexpected eventualities, we'd consider the AAC to be at most 90 percent of annual growth, or about 17 MBF per year, suggesting that you could harvest about 170 MBF or about 40 truckloads each decade.

This harvest amounted to about one-third of the timber on a parcel near Silverdale, Washington.

a couple of thousand dollars per acre is easily achievable, even more if forest or market conditions are favorable.

From that point onward, you can likely return to the forest every fifteen years or so for another thinning, each time harvesting fewer but larger and higher-value trees. If your objective is to continue the forest's development toward old-growth conditions, you can continue doing this nearly indefinitely. Even in the second entry, you can thin some parts more than others, to break up the forest canopy and create more diverse habitat. You (or your successors) might start to create some small openings, mimicking the conditions that would be created if a windstorm or root rot fungus took out a clump of trees. Or nature might do that for you every decade or two, giving you the opportunity to salvage the logs—meaning, haul them to market after the trees

have already died—if you choose to do so and there are enough to interest a logger in coming to haul them away.

REGENERATION HARVESTS

Depending on your objectives and your financial needs, you could also choose to carry out what is called a regeneration harvest—logging that sets the stage to establish a new cohort of trees across the entire stand. Clear-cutting is probably the best-known style of regeneration harvest, but you might want to consider a variable retention harvest, which leaves in place 10 to 30 percent of the trees to provide a biological legacy and more complex habitat as the next cohort of trees grows up. By thinning the forest up until that point, you have kept your options open: You can harvest nothing, carry out a thinning to harvest a portion, or harvest the stand

Measuring Timber

When you are estimating the amount of timber on your land, the appropriate unit depends on the product you will sell. For small trees that will be used for pulp and paper production, the appropriate measure is the cubic foot. Regardless of the shape and size of the log, it will all get ground into chips and sold by the ton.

For sawlogs, a better measure is the number of board feet that can theoretically be milled from a log that size. (A board foot is the standard measure of lumber and sawlog volume, and is equivalent to a one-by-twelve-inch board, one foot long.) The estimate of board feet in a log is based on its length and the diameter of its smaller end, with an allowance for the amount of the log that would be turned into sawdust as it is milled. Some loss occurs on the edges as well, in the process of transforming a tapering cylindrical log into a bunch of rectangular slabs (boards). As a result, a ten-cubic-foot log will usually be estimated to yield just fifty or sixty board feet, even though ten cubic feet of lumber would amount to 120 board feet since the entire volume of the boards would contribute to the cubic volume. See Figures 11-2 and 11-3.

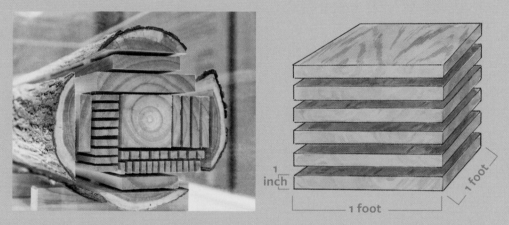

LEFT: *Figure 11.2. Although small trees might yield only 2x4s and chips that can be made into oriented strand board, if you wait another couple of decades, they can be milled into quite a range of lumber dimensions.*
RIGHT: *Figure 11-3. This stack of six one-by-twelve-inch boards, each a foot long, amounts to six board feet, or half a cubic foot.*

and start over when you decide to. On the other hand, if you had harvested all of the trees when they first reached maturity, you would have limited options: just keep the trees alive until the new stand reaches merchantability again.

These choices might look very different depending on the size of your forest. If you own only a small patch of forest, a regeneration harvest would set the entire forest back to the seedling stage, and it might not meet your other objectives. On the other hand, if you are managing scores or hundreds of acres, you might see fewer drawbacks in regenerating one patch of forest while leaving the bulk of it to keep maturing.

The forests described here are just examples. How you manage your forest will also depend on its composition. In the ponderosa pine region, your thinning might be dictated by a desire to remove more fire-vulnerable species and reduce the fuel ladder so the stand is more resilient to fire. A maturing sixty-year-old stand of alder that is well on

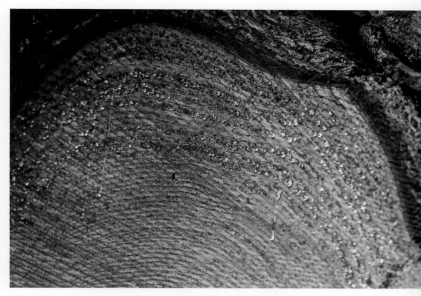

The width of a tree's annual rings tells the story of its prosperity and vigor from year to year.

its way to decay might be ripe to be replaced with a young cohort of cedar and fir. In ecological forestry, the economic opportunities grow out of the biological imperatives of the site, blended with your objectives.

A FOREST SAVINGS ACCOUNT

From a financial standpoint, think of the forest as a savings account or an endowment. When you don't need to make a withdrawal, you can let the principal sit and earn interest—the additional timber volume that the forest puts on. Periodically, it will pay a dividend, when it comes time every fifteen or twenty years to thin it. And if necessary, you can withdraw the principal entirely by harvesting the forest and replanting.

From our experience, most small forest landowners don't want to get to that place of liquidating the principal. But since it

takes a substantial investment to acquire forest land, it's good to know that those assets are not permanently tied up in forestland. Rather, they can be turned into cash through harvest, or by selling the property if you need to, which allows you to recoup both the value of the land and the value of the timber you have raised.

COVERING THE COSTS OF FOREST OWNERSHIP

We've focused here on the income side of the equation, but any business plan for forest ownership needs to take the costs into account as well. Land taxes are an obvious and inescapable expense. (As mentioned in Chapter 4, you may be able to reduce property taxes by enrolling in a current use program with your county assessor.) Roads need maintenance so they don't fall into disrepair and cause erosion problems (see Chapter 9). And young trees need care to ensure they don't get engulfed by shrubs, or crowd together so densely that they choke off one another's growth. Fortunately, numerous local, state, and federal programs can pay a good portion of the cost of developing a management plan, preparing ground for new trees, purchasing and planting seedlings, and protecting them from voracious deer. Program rules vary between Washington and Oregon, so it pays to check with local agencies to see what is available in your area. Some programs will cover about half the cost of a management plan and two-thirds or more of the cost of reforestation and the care of young seedlings. You can think of it as payment for the public goods that a forest provides—such as clean water, oxygen, and habitat—even if it grows on private land. Without that cost share, landowners might underinvest in young forests, since they won't be able to harvest those trees for decades.

Harvestable or not, from the standpoint of financial return, those trees are becoming more valuable even before they are ripe for the saw. A forest five years away from harvest will be more valuable than one that is twenty years away. So even though forestland may not provide the spectacular profits (or risks!) of a meme stock, it can provide a steady and respectable return. In Part III, we'll turn from understanding to action, and show you what forest stewardship looks like in practice.

OPPOSITE: *In a forest on Washington's Kitsap Peninsula*

- Planting trees
- **Protecting seedlings**
- **Foraging**
- **Building trails**
- **Harvesting timber**
- **Fire and forests**
- **Welcoming wildlife**

PART III

Stewardship in Action

CHAPTER 12

Stand Establishment: Planting, Seedling Protection, and Seedling Release

BY KIRK HANSON

I love planting trees . . . almost as much as I love cutting them down. The latter is a thrill—a test of skill, mettle, and art. The former is an exercise in gratitude and an opportunity to give back to a world that gives so much to us. There's something deeply humbling about the experience of planting a tree that will not only outlive me but also may grow for hundreds of years. When my kids help me plant trees, I always tell them, "That tree may live for centuries; you can take five minutes to plant it well."

One winter I bought some western white pine seedlings to plant on my family's land near Bucoda, in honor of our Midwest silvicultural heritage. As my dad, who was ninety-five at the time, stooped over to tie a ribbon on a stake that marked the location of one of the seedlings, I was reminded of a Greek proverb: "A society grows great when old men plant trees beneath the shade of which they will not sit." I would amend that quote to read "old humans," as my mother is a force of nature unto herself and has surely planted enough trees in her lifetime to offset the carbon footprint of our entire family. Planting trees offers more than just a feel-good moment, however, and can be part of bigger ecological and financial investment. To do it well requires a plan with many considerations, and in this chapter I discuss how to develop and implement a successful

OPPOSITE: *A brave beginning*

planting plan and maintain your seedlings once they're in the ground.

A NATURAL CAPITAL INVESTMENT

During the winter of 2019–2020, my family planted approximately eighteen acres of brushy land back into trees on our land near Bucoda. Along with restoring a mixed-species forest habitat to the site, this planting is intended to be a long-term investment for our family. I estimate that in twenty-five to thirty years, each acre we planted will have grown approximately 15,000 board feet, or 15 MBF, of wood volume. (Recall from the previous chapter that MBF is the standard unit by which timber is measured and sold.) At a conservative estimate of $600 per MBF, that represents a gross value of around $162,000 across the eighteen acres. Although we're not intending to clear-cut the trees when they reach a merchantable age, we could, if necessary, to meet any financial needs we have at the time—similar to selling stock or cashing in an annuity. Assuming a (clear-cut) logging and hauling cost of approximately 50 percent, this yields about $81,000 of net value to my family. The cost of the investment was approximately $8,865, as shown in Table 12-1. Therefore, given a final net income of $81,000, this translates to an annualized return on investment (ROI) of 7.65 percent. Not bad in the world of investing, and this doesn't account for either the value of the land or any of the other ancillary benefits my family, and society, receives from this forest. How many other kinds of investments can you walk through, breathe deep of, find solace in, and occasionally nibble on?

Table 12-1: Return on Investment for Planting 18 Acres	
Cost of investment (tree planting and property taxes)	$40,615
Less: EQIP* cost share	$31,750
Net cost	$8,865
Gross value at 30 years	$162,000
Less logging costs of 50%	$81,000
Return on investment	$81,000
30-year annualized ROI	7.65%
*Environmental Quality Incentives Program	

THE STAGES OF A PLANTING PROJECT

There are innumerable reasons to plant trees and other native shrub and plant species: sequestering carbon, restoring forests on non-forested sites, improving wildlife habitat, and investing in long-term timber production. As you delve more deeply into the art and science of ecological forestry, reasons may become more nuanced, such as replanting a patch cut in order to replicate the process of natural regeneration in a root rot pocket, underplanting a forest with shade-tolerant trees after a selective thinning, increasing the population and diversity of drought-tolerant trees to improve climate resilience, or restoring forage for birds or pollinator insect species.

Whatever the situation, most planting projects can be divided into the following stages:

- Identifying goals and objectives
- Developing a planting plan
- Developing a budget
- Applying for cost-share funding (optional)
- Ordering seedlings
- Preparing the site
- Planting
- Maintaining seedlings after planting

Through the remainder of this chapter, I describe each of these stages in detail.

Identifying Your Planting Goals and Objectives

The goals of a planting project will directly inform the species selected for planting. For instance, the species you plant for long-term timber production, such as ponderosa pine or Douglas-fir, may be different than what you'd plant for wildlife habitat, such as Oregon oak or bigleaf maple. If your objective is to optimize long-term carbon sequestration, you may opt for a combination of fast-growing and longer-lived conifers, such as Douglas-fir and western redcedar. If you want to restore biodiversity to your site, you may select trees that are underrepresented in your forest, such as Pacific yew, incense cedar, or tanoak. You also need to be mindful that what you want to plant may not be suitable for the soils or microclimate of your site.

The primary goal of my family's 2019 planting project was to establish a plan-

tation for long-term timber production. Therefore, we planted Douglas-fir, western redcedar, and western hemlock, as each of these species has significant commercial value. However, as good ecological foresters, my family also wants to restore biodiversity and enhance wildlife habitat. Cedar and hemlock occur only in low numbers on our land, so planting them helps restore an underrepresented species. Red alder and bigleaf maple were already present on the site, and these and other hardwoods, as well as grand fir, are naturally regenerating at a high rate all across our land, so I didn't feel the need to plant more of them.

DEVELOPING A PLANTING PLAN

After defining your goals and objectives, it's time to develop a planting plan. You will want to start planning at least twelve months in advance of planting. Contractors, seedling nurseries, materials suppliers, and financial assistance programs all require a significant lead time, and you don't want to get stuck hastily planning your planting project only to find that seedlings are all sold out, the cost of hiring a contractor is beyond your means, or you missed the application deadline for a funding program.

There are several other factors to consider when developing a planting plan. These include species composition, aspect and slope, soil type, and tree density. Let's look at each of these in more detail.

Species Composition

You should always consider planting more than one species of tree or shrub. When planting multiple species, however, you need to understand how various species interact. Growth rates, shade tolerance, and density preferences, in particular, inform how well plants of different species will get along together. The gardening practice of companion planting comes to mind, as trees and shrubs, just like vegetables, often prefer to grow in companionship with different species or, conversely, may not tolerate the presence of a particular species.

The soils, rainfall, and microclimate of your site, and what currently exists on the site, inform the palette of plants that will thrive there. If you're starting with a blank slate, such as a field or recently cleared area, then your choices will primarily be informed by your goals and suitability to the site. However, if you're planting where there are already trees and shrubs, then you may choose to prioritize underrepresented species, species that perform a specific function (timber production, wildlife forage, etc.), or species that are shade tolerant.

Aspect and Slope

The aspect and slope of a planting site impact soil moisture and the exposure of tree seedlings. Southerly and westerly aspects, as well as areas higher on a slope's profile, tend to be drier and should be planted with more drought-tolerant species. In western Washington, that includes trees such as Douglas-fir, pines, oak, madrone, and maple. Conversely, north- or east-facing slopes, areas down in draws (gullies) and near seasonal stream valleys, and the base of slopes tend to be wetter and may be more suitable for shade-tolerant and moisture-loving species such as cedar, hemlock, spruce, grand fir (or other true

firs, depending on the forest's elevation), cottonwood, and alder. However, in drier climates, such as southwest Oregon or the Klamath Basin, you might choose to plant Douglas-fir on northeast-facing slopes, as the cooler and moister microclimate supports their growth.

Soil Type

As the saying goes in the tree-planting industry, "Right tree in the right location." Forest owners should know their soil type before planting, as not every species is suited to every type of soil. For instance, heavy clay and loamy soils tend to stay wetter than gravelly soils, and therefore are more suitable to trees and shrubs that are more moisture dependent. As discussed in Chapter 10, you can generate a soil map for your land online using the Natural Resources Conservation Service's Web Soil Survey. Once you've identified the various soil types, you can then read about the characteristics of your soils in your county soil survey. The descriptions of the soils often also include a list of native trees and other plants that naturally occur on them.

Tree Density

Tree density—how many trees there are per acre—affects how trees compete for sunlight, water, and soil nutrients. It also relates to how much wood volume will be available for future cutting. And when it comes to newly planted trees, density also translates to how much work you need to put into seedling care.

When you look at a recently planted timber plantation west of the Cascades, for instance, the standard reforestation

Table 12-2: Planting Densities Based on Shade Tolerance and Species

SHADE TOLERANCE	SPECIES	MINIMUM REFORESTATION SPACING (FT.) DENSITY	TREES PER ACRE
Very shade tolerant	Subalpine fir Pacific silver fir Western redcedar	9 × 9	538
Shade tolerant	Western hemlock Sitka spruce Engelmann spruce Grand fir Bigleaf maple	10 × 10	436
Moderately shade tolerant	Douglas-fir (west of Cascades) Madrone	11 × 11	360
Moderately intolerant (moderate soil moisture)	Douglas-fir (inland) Ponderosa pine Western white pine	12 × 12	302
Intolerant	Red alder Western larch Lodgepole pine Black cottonwood Oregon oak	13 × 13	258
Intolerant (low soil moisture)	Douglas-fir (inland) Ponderosa pine Juniper	14 × 14	222
Intolerant (low precipitation)	Douglas-fir (inland)	15 × 15	194

Source: US Department of Agriculture, *Forest Stand Density Guide* (Spokane, WA: Natural Resources Conservation Service, November 1982).

density is typically 350–450 trees per acre (TPA). I know some forest owners who plant at a higher density (600 TPA) in order to ensure the trees fully colonize the site. This is often done on sites where there is an expectation of high mortality, either

Table 12-3: Spacing and Trees per Acre	
SPACING (FT.)	TREES PER ACRE
4 × 4	2,700
6 × 6	1,200
8 × 8	680
10 × 10	436
11 × 11	350
12 × 12	300
13 × 13	250
15 × 15	200
17 × 17	150
20 × 20	100
25 × 25	75
30 × 30	50
50 × 50	25

ones. Table 12-2 provides the optimal ranges for replanting an area with trees based on their relative shade tolerance in order to fully colonize a site and optimize its photosynthetic potential. If you're interested in a species of tree that is not listed in the table, you can find information on its biology and management at both the Forest Service and state extension services websites (see Resources).

Some states have minimum stocking requirements. For example, Washington and Oregon state laws require replanting after logging, and also require a minimum number of surviving seedlings per acre that can range from 150 to 200 TPA (see Table 12-3).

Developing a Budget

One of the biggest constraints on your planting ambitions may be the cost of the project. To give you an idea of both the elements of a planting project and their relative costs, in Table 12-4 I provide the detailed budget of the 2019 planting project at my family's forest. Obviously the more work you do yourself, the less out-of-pocket costs you incur. Fortunately, local, state, and federal financial assistance programs are available to help offset the costs of planting trees and caring for them.

I chose to hire a professional tree-planting crew to install the 5,200 tree seedlings on our eighteen-acre planting project. As much as I enjoy planting trees, I can plant about one hundred trees per day before the novelty wears off. The professional crew, composed of eight tree planters, planted all 5,200 seedlings and installed tree cages on the cedar in two days.

due to droughty soils or intense brush competition. The idea behind this is that it's cheaper to overplant at the beginning than to come back and replant if there has been a high rate of mortality. However, if there is a high survival rate, then pre-commercial thinning may be necessary to reduce competition before the trees can be commercially thinned.

One of the simplest guides to the density for tree planting is the species' shade tolerance. Shade-tolerant trees can grow at a higher density than less shade-tolerant

All non-industrial forest landowners, including family forests, conservation groups, tribes, and small companies, qualify for cost-sharing financial assis-tance through the Environmental Quality Incentives Program (EQIP) managed by the USDA's Natural Resources Conservation Service. Oregon and Washington

Table 12-4: 2019 Planting Budget for Hanson 18-acre Reforestation

ITEM	DESCRIPTION	UNITS	COST PER UNIT	TOTAL COST	EQIP REIMBURSEMENT
Site preparation	Flail mower cutting of heavy brush	18	$1,160	$20,880	$16,000
Tree protectors	4" × 24"	2,600	$0.35	$910	
Tree seedlings	Douglas-fir, western redcedar, western hemlock	5,200	$0.56	$2,912	
Bamboo stakes	3' 3/8" (8–10 mm) bamboo stakes	7,500	$0.10	$750	
Orange ribbon	50 rolls	50	$1.25	$63	$12,300*
Cedar planting	With cages and 2 stakes	2,400	$0.97	$2,328	
Douglas-fir and western hemlock planting	No cages, one stake	2,800	$0.50	$1,400	
Planting bonus				$272	
Seedling release 1	Seedling release	18	$150	$2,700	$1,150
Seedling release 2	Seedling release	18	$150	$2,700	$1,150
Seedling release 3	Seedling release	18	$150	$2,700	$1,150
				$37,615	$31,750

*$12,300 reimbursement was for the entire reforestation process

have different rules and deadlines; find the relevant state's sites with an internet search. Cost-share funding pays a portion of the expenses of a conservation practice by reimbursing the landowner for an agreed amount. Other funding programs are available to forest owners and managers through state natural resources agencies, local conservation districts, and other sources (see Resources).

ORDERING SEEDLINGS

When it comes to ordering seedlings, two main considerations are stock types and seed zones. A seedling's stock type refers to its size, age, and suitability for planting into specific sites. The three most common conifer seedling stock types in the Pacific Northwest are 1+1, P+0, and P+1. Hardwood seedlings are sold as "bare root" and come in different stem thicknesses and seedling heights. Here's how the Washington Department of Natural Resources describes them:

> **1+1 seedstock** designates a seedling grown for one year in a seedbed, harvested, root pruned to five inches, and transplanted back into a nursery bed for an additional year. The transplanting process results in a thicker stem and a more fibrous root system, which allows the seedling to survive on an infertile site, compete with other vegetation, and give it a better chance of surviving browse damage.
>
> **P+0** (a.k.a. plugs) seedstock is a seedling grown in a greenhouse in containers that are narrow and deep. For some species, this stock type reduces the time between request and outplanting. [It may

also be necessary because of low germination and early growth.]

> **P+1** (a.k.a. plugs plus 1) seedstock is grown in a greenhouse for a year, then the seedling is extracted from the container, root pruned at five inches, and transplanted in a nursery bed for an additional year. As with the 1+1, the root pruning and transplanting generates a thicker stem and more mass in the root system. Cedar, hemlock, larch, and some species of pine and true firs are propagated as Plug+1.

Seed zone refers to where the seeds originated. Forest owners typically source seedlings from the same seed zone (region and elevation) as their forest. Increasingly, however, forest managers and owners are sourcing seedlings from areas where the current climate approximates the climate projected for the location of their own forest. The Seedlot Selection Tool (SST) is a web-based mapping application that matches seedlots (where seedlings are grown) with planting sites based on climatic information.

Every year seedling availability is limited. Seedlings usually need to be ordered by September if you want to plant the following winter. If you wait until December or January to order seedlings, it will be extremely difficult to find them, as nurseries are typically sold out by then.

There are two primary ways to order seedlings:

- Ordering directly from a reforestation nursery
- Working with a planting contractor who purchases seedlings on behalf of their clients

For my family's 2019 planting project, I ordered the seedlings myself in September from the Webster Forest Nursery in Olympia, Washington, along with planting supplies (e.g., tree cages, bamboo stakes, orange flagging) from a forestry supply company. I picked up the bags of seedlings just prior to planting in early January (although tree planters can pick them up also) and had them on-site, along with the planting materials, when the crew arrived.

PREPARING THE SITE

The most important step in the tree-planting process is preparing the site. Without proper site preparation, seedlings can face a grueling first year as they compete with encroaching vegetation for both sun-

light and soil moisture. How you prepare a site for tree planting depends on the existing vegetation. This section addresses some of the most common planting scenarios.

Replanting after Logging: Light to Moderate Brush

On sites where the prior tree canopy was relatively dense, the understory shrub layer is often fairly sparse. These sites tend to be the easiest to plant into and therefore the least expensive. Depending on the abundance and species of shrubs present on the site, only minimal site preparation may be necessary. For instance, sites that are dominated by sparse sword fern or other low-growing shrubs may not require any site preparation, and tree seedlings can be

A mini-excavator equipped with a flail mower can be used to prepare an area for tree planting by masticating brush and other competing vegetation.

planted directly into the ground. If there is an abundance of low-growing shrubs, then a three-foot-diameter circle should be scarified (cut to bare soil) of all vegetation at each planting site.

Replanting after Logging: Heavy Brush

On sites where the prior tree canopy was less dense, the understory shrub layer may be considerably more diverse, lush, and composed of multiple layers of shrub species. These sites are much more difficult to prepare for planting and therefore time consuming and expensive. A forest manager has two basic options: hand preparation or full mastication.

Prepping a site by hand involves cutting all vegetation within a planting spot. Along with scarifying a three-foot-diameter circle, all overhanging vegetation within a 45-degree cone of light should be cut back around the planting site. This can be done with a machete, chainsaw, or heavy-duty mechanical brush cutter.

Full mastication involves the use of machinery to grind shrubs and small trees into mulch. The most common is a flail mower mounted on an excavator or tractor. Rather than preparing individual planting sites, these machines are used to masticate the majority of the shrub layer. Although more expensive than hand crews, mastication results in ideal conditions for the planting crew and may result in lower planting costs.

Replanting Fields and Pastures

Agricultural sites dominated by grass are the most difficult sites to reforest. As rhizomatous species, grasses are extremely difficult to kill, compete aggressively for soil moisture in the same soil horizon as the roots of tree seedlings, and can grow tall and shade tree seedlings and provide cover for mice and voles who often girdle the seedlings. As if that wasn't enough, grasses also produce an allelopathic (suppressive) chemical that inhibits the growth of nearly anything in its presence. Yes, grasses engage in chemical warfare under the soil.

Although I typically avoid herbicides, this is one scenario where a limited and targeted use of herbicides can make the difference between a successful planting and abject failure. During mid- to late summer, I recommend mowing all of the grass throughout the

A mechanical brush cutter with a string-line attachment can be used to scarify an individual tree planting site.

planting area, then using one of the following strategies:

Herbicide. In late summer, after the grass has had a few weeks to regrow, spray either individual planting sites, planting strips, or the entire area with an herbicide that is specifically formulated to kill grass.

Non-herbicide. In late summer, after the grass has had a few weeks to regrow, scarify the planting site to bare soil using either hand tools (e.g., shovels, hoedads) or a mechanical brush cutter.

Mechanical. In late summer, after the grass has had a few weeks to regrow, an excavator or tractor equipped with an auger can be used to dig individual planting holes. This serves the dual purpose of incorporating together organic matter and the upper soil horizons at the same time the planting hole is dug. This technique is typically used only when bare-root hardwood trees are being planted.

Replanting Neglected Sites with Heavy Brush

There are many sites that have been logged in the past and not replanted, or have been left fallow (idle) following a prior use of the land, and have consequently become colonized by a dense brush layer. These sites must be prepared for planting using the same techniques as sites with heavy brush that were recently logged.

Replanting Sites Dominated by Invasive Species

Preparing sites that are dominated by invasive species will utilize a combination of the steps described previously, with some additional nuance. Similar to grasses, the success of replanting may be significantly increased with a targeted use of herbicides. Here are some suggestions.

Mowing. Most invasive species should ideally be mowed early in the growing season, left to regrow throughout the year, then mowed again in mid- to late summer. Knotweeds are an exception to this; they should be sprayed and never mowed, as even small pieces of the plant can root and regrow.

Herbicide. In late summer, after the invasive species has had a few weeks to regrow, spray either individual planting sites or the entire area with an herbicide that is specifically formulated to kill that particular species.

Non-herbicide. In late summer, after the invasive species has had a few weeks to regrow again, scarify the planting site to bare soil using either hand tools (e.g., shovels, hoedads) or a mechanical brush cutter.

PLANTING

There are, of course, right ways and wrong ways to plant a tree or shrub. The most basic advice, which my dad gave me as a kid, is that the green part of the seedling should always point up. Beyond that, it's all about nuance. Here are some quick tips to planting both conifer seedlings and bare-root hardwoods; see Resources for more detail.

Plant all seedlings within a week of obtaining them from the nursery. If seedlings can't be planted that quickly, they should remain in as cool of a location as possible, and roots should remain moist. It's a good idea to dunk the roots in a bucket of water before planting them.

When planting seedlings, take a small amount out of the bag they were packed in,

Next to each seedling, place a three- to five-foot bamboo stake with bright orange plastic ribbon tied to the top. Staking seedlings in this way can aid in locating them in future years. Bamboo stakes will last three to five years in the ground, at which point your seedlings will either achieve a free-to-grow height above the brush or at least be large enough that you can see them readily.

When planting adjacent to existing trees, plant outside the drip line of the crown of the existing tree (unless you are intentionally underplanting).

MAINTAINING SEEDLINGS

Once you or your planting crew have safely ensconced every seedling in a nice, brush-free spot, the work isn't over. It's important to ensure your seedlings are getting adequate sunlight, water, and nutrients to thrive, and are protected from browse damage. Caging, mulching, and seedling release are three ways to protect seedlings during their early, vulnerable years.

Caging

If either deer or elk frequent your land, you will want to cage all cedar and hardwood seedlings. Cedar is often referred to as "deer candy" and will suffer severe browse damage that either stunts its growth or outright kills the seedling. I've found that Douglas-fir can tolerate browse, and will eventually shoot up a leader above browse height within a few years, and therefore typically don't require caging. Pines, hemlock, spruce, and grand fir are all generally unpalatable species to deer and elk, so do not require caging.

Planting trees is a great activity for all generations.

and plant them before returning for more seedlings. This will help ensure roots do not dry out.

Plant when raining or when rain is in the immediate forecast. Do not plant when temperatures are below freezing, as the roots of the seedlings may be damaged.

Periodically check cages, adjusting, straightening, and cleaning them out as the leader of the seedling grows. Expect to maintain cages for three to four years, until the seedling is tall enough to get above the hungry mouth of a deer. In my experience, deer rarely browse the leader of a tree once it's about five feet tall. Ungulates tend to keep their noses lower to the ground, or may browse the side branches of a seedling, which doesn't particularly affect its growth. Deer often rub their antlers on the stems of older cedar seedlings, which damages the thin bark of the young tree. If this happens, once the seedling reaches about five feet tall, slide the tree cage back down to protect the middle of the tree until it gets a little bigger and the bark firms up.

Mulching

Placing mulch around tree seedlings is a rare activity in industrial reforestation projects due to the cost of materials and labor. However, for the small woodland owner, mulching may be a more accessible option, and certainly will improve the drought resistance of your seedlings, particularly if you have gravelly or otherwise well-draining soils. You can use a wide range of materials for mulch. I've seen folks use bark, branches from pruning, newspapers, and even old mail. The operative principle here is that anything is better than nothing. In my experience the dream team of mulch is a couple layers of cardboard with wood chips placed on top. The cardboard functions as a weed barrier, especially if it's applied during the late spring after the main flush of growth has passed. The wood chips not only serve as a sponge but also provide a medium for mushrooms to get established, which improves soil health and nutrient availability to seedlings. I recommend placing a doughnut of chips within at least a two-foot radius of the

Tree protectors, used to prevent deer browse, need to be lifted annually to protect the growing tip (leader) of the tree.

seedling, being sure that the chips don't come in direct contact with the stem of the seedling, as this can cause it to rot.

Seedling Release

The most vulnerable window of time for your newly planted tree and shrub seedlings is the first three to four years after planting. During this time, surrounding vegetation will grow back vigorously, often outcompeting your planted seedlings in height growth, and will therefore threaten to overwhelm them. Vegetation in immediate proximity to your seedlings—grass, in particular—will also compete for soil moisture. Dry planting sites are especially important to keep clear, as competing vegetation will gleefully suck moisture from the soil around seedlings. Therefore, it's critical to have a plan in place to deal with competing vegetation during the first growing season following planting. This practice is often referred to as *seedling release*, as you are effectively "releasing" your planted seedlings from the surrounding vegetation in order to optimize their growth.

A young tree is typically considered free to grow when its leader is at least three feet above the surrounding vegetation. It could take three to five years for the seedlings to reach free-to-grow height, depending on the species and the site productivity. Until then, expect to invest in some serious labor every spring. In my experience, it takes an average of a minute per seedling to clear competing vegetation around it. Therefore, for the 5,200 trees my family planted across eighteen acres in 2019, it would have taken us approximately ninety hours per year to conduct the seedling release. Given the scale of

the project, we opted to hire this process out to a contracted crew.

Seedling release strategies generally fall into two categories—manual release and herbicide release—and the two activities are often combined.

Manual release. Manually releasing tree seedlings from competing vegetation involves using either hand tools, such as a machete, or mechanical tools, such as a chainsaw or brush cutter, to cut back plants that are encroaching on the seedlings. Seedling release is typically conducted from late May to early July, and should occur after the primary flush of spring growth has ended.

All vegetation within a two-foot radius of a planted seedling should be cut back. Additionally, if taller shrubs are overhanging the planting site, they should be cut back to create a 45-degree cone of light to the seedling.

Herbicide release. Herbicides can be used in lieu of, or in combination with, manual seedling release. As you might expect, the use of herbicides entails directly spraying competing vegetation in order to kill or stunt its growth. Given the high cost of hiring a contractor to annually conduct a manual seedling release, I am left to wonder if it would have been both less expensive and more effective to have sprayed the competing vegetation the first year after planting. I have been reluctant to use herbicides on my land, but spending $3,000 a year for three to four years on manual seedling release is a big expense to swallow.

Herbicides can be used at various times of year depending on the plant species being treated and the timing of the project.

A follow-up herbicide application may be made the first spring after planting when shrubs are just beginning to grow but have not yet developed much height. During a spring herbicide application, care must be taken to avoid spraying the tree seedlings. An expensive but very effective technique is to manually cut back competing vegetation in late spring or early summer, then spray the vegetation in late summer.

Stand Release

Stand release is similar to seedling release but is used when trees are five to fifteen years of age. Shrubs, naturally regenerating trees, sprouting hardwoods, and other types of competing vegetation are cut back to ensure the sapling has plenty of room to grow. Stand release can be used to restore young plantations that received little or no post-planting maintenance where seedlings are being overwhelmed by brush or other trees. Some elements of pre-commercial thinning (discussed in the next chapter) may come into play here as well in order to reduce competition between planted or naturally regenerated tree seedlings and to adjust species composition.

With your new forest well established and growing vigorously, it's time to turn your attention to its next phase of growth as a young stand. In the following chapter, we'll pick up where we left off after releasing the seedlings from competing vegetation and look at how the trees start competing with one another, and when to thin them to maintain their optimal growth.

CHAPTER 13

Young Stand Thinning

BY KIRK HANSON

To acquire as much productive ground as possible, my family has consistently purchased land stocked with young forests, since they are less expensive by the acre than older forests. This approach has resulted in an intriguing hodgepodge of forest types and management conundrums, such as conifer seedlings struggling against native shrubs and invasive blackberry, dense thickets of naturally regenerated hardwoods, and young, homogeneous Douglas-fir plantations that are just beginning to achieve a merchantable age and size.

In every scenario, some form of stand release or thinning has been necessary to reduce competition, either between densely packed trees or from encroaching brush, to ensure that the trees we want have room to grow. As I work with older forests for other clients, some of whose forests were thinned at any early age and some of whose were not, I am constantly reminded that thinning is an essential tool for nearly all ages and types of forests.

Learning how to thin to an optimal density and species composition is a fascinating study, and requires an understanding of the ecological characteristics of individual tree species, the soils on which they grow, and the objectives for a particular forest.

THE ARGUMENT FOR THINNING

Most forests today have too many trees. This might seem like an appalling statement to the conservation-minded, so bear with me. Over the past 150 years, more than 95 percent of the original old-growth forests across the Pacific Northwest have been converted to other uses, primarily even-aged, homogeneous, Douglas-fir-dominated, industrially managed plantations stocked with trees at a very high

OPPOSITE: *A young, overstocked stand in the competitive exclusion phase of growth*

density. I recently saw this tagline in an email from an individual who works in the forest products industry:

> It's OK to print this email. Paper is a biodegradable, renewable, sustainable product made from trees. Growing and harvesting trees provides jobs for millions of Americans. Working forests are good for the environment and provide clean air and water, wildlife habitat and carbon storage. Thanks to improved forest management, we have more trees in America today than we had 100 years ago.

Aside from the advocacy of wanton wastefulness, the claim that we have more trees in the United States today than we did one hundred years ago is incredibly misleading. Converting a modestly stocked old-growth forest to a highly stocked plantation may net you more trees per acre, but what is lost in wildlife habitat, carbon storage, and other ecological values goes unaccounted for when you simply count the number of trees.

For most landowners I work with, the desired future condition for their forest is an older one that provides similar structure and functions as an old-growth forest. Therefore, I posit that the single most effective tool to achieve this objective is thinning, and, in fact, thinning multiple times over a span of decades. Why? Consider the following. When I hike in old-growth forests across the Northwest, regardless of whether they're on the coast, in the Olympic Mountains, or along the Cascade Range, I often notice the density of the very large, dominant trees. There may be innumerable understory seedlings and saplings beneath these dominant trees,

but when most people visualize old-growth forests, they think of the big trees, and these trees nearly always occur at densities ranging from twenty-five to, at most, one hundred trees per acre. Therefore, it can be argued that the carrying capacity of most soils in the Northwest for very large old-growth trees is significantly less than one hundred trees per acre. The term *carrying capacity* refers to the ability of a site to support a population of a particular species. If a given acre of forestland can support only twenty-five to one hundred very old trees under historical climate conditions, then it's also conceivable that it will support even fewer under the hotter and drier climate predicted for our region.

Now, if we're starting with a young, recently established plantation, or a naturally regenerated stand of trees, then we're likely dealing with a forest that has more than three hundred to four hundred trees per acre, or three to fifteen times the long-term carrying capacity of the site. Therefore, if we want to restore the functions and characteristics of older forest types, we need to dramatically reduce the number of trees per acre. We have two fundamental pathways to get from here to there:

1. We let nature run its course. Leave the forest to self-thin as it passes through the competitive exclusion phase and gradually succeeds to an older forest composed of fewer dominant trees.
2. We actively thin the trees in order to accelerate the process while also benefiting from what the forest can offer.

Many conservation-minded folks ask me, "Why can't you just lock the gates and let nature run its course?" My response is: you certainly can. I think it's a legitimate option in some locations but very hard to justify in most others. There are consequences to doing nothing, the outcomes of which may be in conflict with some of your objectives. Specifically, overstocked stands lack resilience.

Let me give you some reasons why: Trees that grow in competition with one another achieve a high height-to-diameter ratio (see Chapter 10) that makes them very susceptible to breakage or blowdown during wind and ice storms. High densities often result in highly stressed trees as they compete for increasingly limited resources. Highly stressed trees are more vulnerable to insects and diseases. If the limiting resource is water, then highly stocked stands are also much more prone to drought-induced mortality. Overstocked stands tend to accumulate large amounts of small-diameter dead and dying trees that place them at higher risk from fire. They also provide very simplified habitat and have limited value to wildlife. Lastly, overstocked stands result in very slow-growing trees, which delays the ability of the forest to produce merchantable timber and may result in overall lower-value timber.

Consider the following four points:

- Most of our forests are in a disturbed condition relative to their historical norm.
- Most of our forests are overstocked relative to the long-term carrying capacity of the site.
- The future climate regime will be different from the past and may support even fewer trees per acre.
- Doing nothing may incur increasing risks for most forests.

If we can agree on those points, then it stands to reason that one of our best strategies for improving the condition of our forests is thinning—the judicious cutting and, in some cases, removal of various trees. How we go about doing this carefully is one of the key aspects of ecological forestry.

WHEN TO THIN

The first step in determining whether to thin a stand is to evaluate the species composition, density, size of live crowns, and average diameters of the trees. As I alluded to in the previous chapter, the optimal density of a particular tree species at any given stage in its development is, in part, dependent on its shade tolerance. In short, shade-tolerant trees can maintain optimal growth at much higher densities than shade-intolerant trees. For instance, you will notice that shade-tolerant trees maintain live branches much lower to the ground in dense forests than shade-intolerant trees, which tend to self-prune beneath a dense canopy.

Using Live Crown Ratio as a Guide

A good indication of when to thin is expressed in the average live crown ratio of dominant and codominant trees in a stand. As I discussed in Chapters 5 and 10, the live crown is the growth engine of the tree. As live crowns gradually diminish due to competition in the canopy, so does the growing capacity of those trees. In general, in order to optimize the growth of a stand of trees, we want to keep at least 40 percent of the dominant and codominant tree's total height covered in live branches—in other words, with an average live crown ratio of at least 40 percent. When a tree's live crown decreases below 40 percent of the total tree height, the tree will grow more slowly and likely become suppressed in the canopy as

more vigorous and dominant trees overtake it. Therefore, if the average live crown ratio of the dominant and codominant trees is less than 40 percent, the stand should be thinned by removing trees with the smallest live crowns, giving more room to the trees with larger crowns. Once that is done, the dead branches on the remaining trees won't come back to life, but the trees will continue to grow upward, adding

Table 13-1: Optimal Densities for Young Stands

SHADE TOLERANCE	SPECIES	SPACING	OPTIMAL DENSITY (FOR TREES 2"–9" DBH)
Very shade tolerant	Subalpine fir Pacific silver fir Western redcedar	9'–11'	360–538 TPA
Shade tolerant	Western hemlock Sitka spruce Engelmann spruce Grand fir	10'–12'	302–436 TPA
Moderately shade tolerant	Douglas-fir (west of Cascades)	11'–13'	258–360 TPA
Moderately intolerant	Douglas-fir (inland, site index >100) Ponderosa pine (site index >100) Western white pine	12'–14'	222–302 TPA
Intolerant	Red alder Western larch Lodgepole pine Black cottonwood	13'–15'	194–258 TPA
Intolerant (low soil moisture)	Douglas-fir (inland, site index 80–100) Ponderosa pine (site index 80–100)	14'–16'	170–222 TPA
Intolerant (low precipitation)	Douglas-fir (inland, site index <80)	15'–17'	151–194 TPA

Source: US Department of Agriculture, *Forest Stand Density Guide.*

more live branches, while the lowest live branches will stay alive, since they are no longer being shaded as much by the surrounding trees. A tree may also sprout *epicormic* branches along its stem, or very abbreviated branches that emerge from latent buds in the bark, which also aid with photosynthesis.

The principle of thinning using the live crown ratio as a guide can also be applied in mixed species stands that are composed of both shade-tolerant and shade-intolerant trees, as well as in multi-aged stands. In mixed species and age stands, the live crowns of shade-intolerant trees will recede faster than shade-tolerant trees, and these stands will gradually become dominated by shade-tolerant species unless action is taken. As the live crowns of shade-intolerant trees diminish in a mixed species stand, a forester is presented with a two basic options, the choice of which will be determined by the objectives for the forest: (1) proactively remove the shade-intolerant trees before they succumb to suppression mortality and, in so doing, shift the stand toward dominance by shade-tolerant trees, or (2) thin shade-tolerant trees in order to release shade-intolerant trees.

Using Tree Diameter as a Guide

The average diameter of trees throughout a stand can also be an indicator of the effects of density and when to thin. There is a direct relationship between the size of a tree's live crown (growth engine) and a tree's diameter. The larger the live crown, the larger the diameter. Therefore, a mid-aged or older stand composed of small-diameter trees likely has small live crowns and should be thinned to improve growth. Measurements will need to be taken to determine both the average diameter of trees and whether average diameters vary in different parts of the stand. Areas of the stand with smaller diameters (higher densities) should be prioritized for thinning.

Table 13-1 provides a useful guide for determining the optimal density young stands should be thinned to when tree diameters range from two to nine inches at breast height.

MANAGING A FOREST THROUGH MULTIPLE THINNINGS

Given the productive nature of the soils and climate across most of the Pacific Northwest, many forests can be thinned every ten to twenty years in order to minimize competition and adjust species composition. Forests in the drier parts of the San Juan Islands in northwest Washington and east of the Cascades, where growth rates are considerably slower, may be able to be thinned only once every twenty-five years or more. Using a variety of thinning techniques (described throughout the rest of this chapter), the density of trees within a stand is gradually reduced over multiple thinnings. During initial thinnings, the majority of the suppressed and damaged trees are selected for removal in order to retain and release the most vigorous, dominant, and highest-quality trees of each species that are suitable for the site. Some dominant trees may also be selected for removal where they will release vigorous understory trees, thereby increasing the vertical heterogeneity of the forest canopy.

Looking Sharp: Chainsaws

If you're looking after a forest, you will need that most basic of modern woods tools: a chainsaw. Whether you're thinning Douglas-fir that are too crowded, dismantling a maple that has fallen across your access road, or turning alder logs into firewood, a chainsaw will enable you to accomplish more in minutes than you could in hours of hand-sawing.

For smaller jobs, a battery-powered chainsaw is a good option, particularly if you're new to the experience. The lower noise and vibration level, and the ability to start cutting with just a squeeze of a trigger (instead of the pull-start of a two-stroke gas engine), makes it my personal choice for light-duty sawing. A model with a 16-inch bar and an extra battery will set you up to work for an hour or two at a time, allowing you to thin trees up to twelve inches in diameter, trim off their branches, and cut them into stove-length rounds or into longer chunks for use as poles or in a wildlife habitat pile (see Chapter 17).

Make sure to equip yourself with all the appropriate safety gear: eye and ear protection, hard hat, gloves, and chaps. (Helmets that integrate a face screen and ear muffs are a convenient choice.) You'll need to maintain your saw and sharpen its chain—see the vast library of online videos for how to best care for your saw. When your chain starts throwing smaller chips, it's getting dull, creating a work environment that isn't just ineffective, but also dangerous. Your kit should include a chain file, extra chain(s), and a bar tool to adjust the tension in your chain or replace it. A felling lever is helpful when cutting smaller-diameter trees in dense stands, as it allows you to twist a tree out of the canopy if it gets hung up.

If you want to tackle larger trees, you'll need to learn how to assess the hazards that come with guiding multi-ton objects safely to the ground. Use a saw that's the appropriate size, with a bar slightly longer than the width of the largest tree you're cutting. A saw that's too large will quickly tire you out. You'll also need at least two felling wedges and a felling ax, and possibly a felling lever to tip the trees where you want them to fall.

—SZ

During later thinnings, trees are thinned to variable densities, and small gaps (e.g., 0.25 to 1.0 acres) may be introduced to increase horizontal heterogeneity within a stand and create opportunities for less shade-tolerant trees and plants to prosper. Reforestation largely comes from naturally regenerating seedlings, and natural regeneration is stimulated through a combination of logging-based soil disturbance and canopy thinning, or gap creation, which introduces more sunlight to the forest floor. Manual planting may be used to increase the desired species composition and density (refer to Chapter 12).

Pre-Commercial Thinning (Stand Age 10 to 20 Years)

The term *pre-commercial thinning* (PCT) refers to the cutting of trees when no trees are sold. Stands that qualify for PCT are typically ten to twenty years old and exceed the optimal density for the dominant species.

The primary objective of pre-commercial thinning is to avoid the competitive exclusion phase of young stand development and maintain optimal tree growth. Secondary objectives may include adjusting species composition to favor trees suitable for the site and improving timber quality if timber production is desired. Thinning can also reduce a stand's susceptibility to natural disturbance events, such as high winds, and pests and diseases that are attracted to stressed trees.

PCT is one of those stand improvement projects that I think is a perfect fit for the do-it-yourself small woodland owner. Some landowners forgo PCT as it's difficult on a short rotation to recover the cost of thinning if the work is contracted out, although you may be able to obtain cost-share funding to offset the cost of hiring a contractor. But if you're managing a small woodland as a hobby and have the time to do the work yourself, PCT can be financially feasible and it definitely improves the growth and value of a stand.

Here are some reasons you might want to carry out PCT on your young stands:

- You want to accelerate the development of the stand to older forest conditions.
- You're seeing signs of competition and drought stress and want to improve the vigor of your stand.
- You're in a high fire risk area and want to reduce fuel buildup.

Pre-commercial thinning reduces competition between trees and improves timber quality by favoring the most dominant and highest quality trees.

Thinning Coastal Forests

Special consideration must be given to thinning forests along the coast given the frequency of strong winds and presence of steep slopes. Most coastal forests are dominated by western hemlock, Sitka spruce, and western redcedar, all of which are very shade tolerant and therefore capable of growing at much higher densities. Allowing coastal stands to self-thin may be a viable option, as thinning younger and smaller-diameter trees is usually not economically viable (especially if hauling long distances or thinning lower-value species such as western hemlock or Sitka spruce). Where thinning is deemed economically viable, or when costs can be offset by external funding, stands should be thinned. However, unlike shade-intolerant species, coastal stands should be thinned to a much higher residual density, as well as to promote an uneven-aged composition. Complex forest canopies tend to be more resilient to windstorms, and uneven-aged stands with ample regeneration tend to recover faster following a storm. Stands can be thinned to lower densities on leeward slopes.

- You want to improve timber quality and growth.

Depending on the original density of the stand, PCT may result in the most number of trees being cut during any thinning entry over the life of a forest. For instance, if a twelve-year-old, naturally regenerated red alder stand has more than 800 trees per acre, some 75 percent of the trees may need to be cut in order to bring the stand down to an optimal density of approximately 200 trees per acre (see Figure 13-1).

When carrying out a PCT, a "best tree selection" approach should be used to determine which trees to cut. This means that the most vigorous and highest-quality trees of each species present in the stand that are suitable for the site should be retained, and most of the suppressed, deformed, or unsuitable species are cut. Leave trees that have the largest live crown, the tallest height, and the straightest stem and show no signs of defect (e.g., broken tops, scars, leaning). For the benefit of wildlife and biodiversity, some defective trees should be retained, as well as underrepresented tree species.

Thinning in this manner typically results in variable spacing between the remaining trees versus the even spacing you would get if you were to thin trees purely based on distance between stems. Trees should be cut within six inches of the ground using either a chainsaw or handheld saw, brought down so they are not leaning on the retained trees, and bucked to the extent necessary to get the majority of the tree on the ground, or at a minimum to get the trunk of the tree less than three feet off the ground. Care should be taken not to damage the bark or trunk of retained trees during thinning. The resulting slash can be managed in any of the following ways:

- Lopped and scattered
- Piled into wildlife habitat piles
- Constructed into habitat logs (see Chapter 17)

800 TPA   ## 180–240 TPA

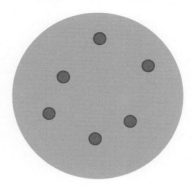

Figure 13-1. You'd have to cut more than two-thirds of the stems in an 800-tree-per-acre stand to bring it down to a density of 180 to 240 trees per acre.

- Cut into firewood and removed
- Chipped
- Converted into biochar

At my family's Oakville forest, which we've had for nearly thirty years, I've been pre-commercial thinning both young alder and Douglas-fir stands for the better part of fifteen years. Alder on highly productive soils responds really well to thinning, and I've found that two light PCT passes spread about five to eight years apart before the trees reach twenty years of age can put alder on a very good trajectory to produce higher value trees. Although the alder naturally regenerated at extremely high densities, exceeding 800 trees per acre in many places, I've thinned the trees down to 180 to 240 trees per acre, and now many of the trees exhibit signs of high-value

veneer-grade timber. For both alder and Douglas-fir, I've simply cut the suppressed and storm-damaged trees, then thinned lightly for optimal crown spacing. By doing this, I've kept the trees in these stands in a robust growing phase, which has resulted in a significant increase in both height and diameter growth as compared to unthinned stands.

IF YOU'VE MANAGED YOUR YOUNG STANDS WELL, your trees should be at an optimal spacing to grow just fine until they're old and large enough to be commercially thinned. From that point forward, most of the density management of your forest can be accomplished through the various commercial thinning strategies that we discuss in the next chapter.

CHAPTER 14

Working with Maturing Forests

BY KIRK HANSON

Most of the stands on my family's three tracts of land are less than forty years old. Although there are individual trees and very small patches that exceed forty years of age, I am primarily working with very young forests. Therefore, most of the work I've performed in my woods falls under the domain of young stand management, the topic of the previous chapter. However, some of the stands on my family's lands have reached an age where the trees are of merchantable size, and their high density warrants thinning. Accordingly, I conducted a commercial thinning of a thirty-year-old Douglas-fir plantation at our Black Diamond forest several years ago, and I am preparing for the first commercial thinning of another thirty-year-old Douglas-fir stand at our Bucoda forest. Having worked in many forests of this age, I've found that this is the time when you can begin tinkering with their structural complexity, start teasing out some of the functions of older forests, and steer the forest onto a very different trajectory than its original fate as an agronomic plantation. I'm assuming that for most readers of this book, the desired future condition for your forest is some semblance of a "natural" forest that includes trees of many different ages and species. This chapter will help you get there.

The pre-commercial thinning and young stand management strategies I discussed in the previous chapter may be applied to any forest regardless of its trajectory. You will take care of your seedlings and conduct pre-commercial thinning whether you're intending to clear-cut

OPPOSITE: *Pine forests east of the Cascades are naturally thinned by frequent, low-intensity fires. This natural thinning process can be replicated by either pre-commercial or commercial thinning.*

your forest at forty years of age or manage for old-growth. Once you get to the point of working with a forest that is at least thirty years old, however, there are many opportunities for doing things differently. Thinning continues to be the primary management tool, even as we work with larger trees that are merchantable and can generate revenue when cut and sold. However, from an ecological forestry standpoint, the central question when designing a thinning project isn't "What can I take?" but "What forest will I leave behind?" Any trees we cut should be a by-product of meeting the biological needs and objectives for the forest.

A thirty- to forty-year-old forest is not an old forest. Given that most tree species in the Northwest can live hundreds and, in some cases, thousands of years, even a sixty- to eighty-year-old forest could be considered young. Regardless of the age of the forest you're currently working with, you still have to keep your desired future condition in mind and continually ask whether your forest is on a path to achieve it. Even an older forest that exhibits characteristics of later seral (a.k.a. old-growth) structure, such as a complex canopy, may benefit from a light thinning to address issues of competition, species composition, and forest health, and to ensure it stays on the desired trajectory.

In this chapter I will take you on a silvicultural journey from a young forest to an older forest. It's in these methods that I think the true art and science of ecological forestry is expressed. First, however, I will share some thoughts on the intrinsic qualities of older forests.

Table 14–1: Forest Age and Average Carbon Storage

FOREST AGE	METRIC TONS OF CARBON (mtC) PER ACRE
>300 years	275
100 years	140
75 years	121
40 years	<70

THE ECOLOGICAL VALUES OF OLDER FORESTS

We are becoming increasingly aware of the valuable ecological functions that intact forest ecosystems provide. As we weigh the logistics and costs of addressing some of the environmental problems our society faces, such as flood mitigation, climate change, endangered species, and wildfire, we are beginning to realize that restoring nature's ability to resolve these problems is not only often less expensive and more effective than engineering solutions but also provides a broader range of co-benefits. When older forests are replaced by younger forests, many of the ecological functions of older forests are compromised or lost. So let's take a moment to look at the ecological significance of older forests, as their performance metrics are outstanding compared to the young plantations that have replaced them.

Carbon. Forests older than three hundred years of age contain approximately four times the amount of carbon as forests younger than forty years of age (see Table 14-1). When forests are clear-cut and converted to wood and paper products, two-thirds of the carbon stored in the trees is immediately lost to the atmosphere through the logging and manufacturing process. Sequestering and maintaining carbon in older forests is a key strategy to mitigating future climate change.

Habitat. Older forests usually contain a higher volume of critical habitat structures than younger forests. These types of structures include large snags and downed logs, as well as habitat features that are important to rare, threatened, and endangered species. Mature forests contain an average of sixteen snags and ninety downed logs per acre, for instance, whereas younger timber plantations may contain none. Some species of wildlife, such as the northern spotted owl, marbled murrelet, and Pacific marten, are highly dependent on the unique habitat and structure of older forests.

Watershed hydrology. Forests that are older than sixty to eighty years of age retain more water higher in the watershed and mitigate the often destructive nature of storm events. Watersheds cloaked in older forests are also capable of supplying up to three times greater summer streamflow than those covered in thirsty, fast-growing, young plantations. They also supply water later into the summer, which is critical for summer-rearing salmonids that depend on clear, cool water for survival.

Biodiversity. Older forests are structurally more complex, meaning they contain multiple species and ages of trees, standing and downed dead wood, varying tree densi-ties, and other features. This heterogeneity provides opportunities for a much broader range of flora and fauna to flourish than younger forests.

Wood production. A forest that is commercially thinned twice and then logged at eighty years of age produces 25 to 40 percent more wood volume than a forest that is clear-cut at age forty then replanted, regrown, and clear-cut when it once again reaches forty years old.

ECOLOGICAL SILVICULTURE

Because of all the benefits just described, restoring old-growth structure, composition, and ecological functions in young, managed forests has become a top priority for many forest owners and managers over the past twenty years. A suite of silvicultural strategies have emerged to help achieve this objective.

Structure–Based Management

In order to restore older forest structure and functions, this book proposes an *uneven-aged and structure-based* approach to management. Structure-based management prescribes a mix of techniques that produce an array of forest stand structures over time, such as areas where new trees are establishing; older trees that have broken tops or large limbs; multilayered canopies; and substantial numbers of rotting logs and large snags. Individual stand types may change through management and natural disturbance, but the objective is to maintain a relatively stable range of stand types across a forest, thereby allowing the forest to provide a steady flow of diverse forest products and highly functioning ecosystem services.

The ability of a particular forest to provide multiple stand types is highly dependent on the size of the forest. A five- to forty-acre forest will have fewer opportunities to provide multiple stand types than a larger forest. Regardless of size, any forest can be managed for older structures and functions.

Using a structure-based approach, stand density is actively managed through a combination of thinning or harvesting techniques such as *variable density thinning*, *variable retention harvesting*, and *individual tree selection*. These are described later in this chapter.

Strategies for Achieving Structural Complexity

A range of silvicultural techniques are available to produce a wide variety of results depending on the objectives for a forest. Some techniques can result in fast-growing, well-stocked stands with higher structural homogeneity that are more suitable for timber production. Other techniques can be used to promote biodiversity and ecosystem services by developing more complex stand structures. The following list summarizes silvicultural strategies that can be used to accelerate the development of younger forests into older and more complex forests:

- Thinning that retains understory conifers and hardwoods: Thinning dominant trees to release nondominant and underrepresented trees in the understory such as western redcedar, western hemlock, grand fir, and bigleaf maple
- Thinning and underplanting: Reducing canopy density to support the growth of planted or naturally regenerating seedlings in the understory
- Thinning to release dominant trees: Releasing dominant trees to spur diameter and branch growth, which are important components of old-growth habitat
- Thinning that is spatially variable: Retaining pairs and clumps of trees and thinning to varying densities
- Retention and recruitment of snags and large dead wood. Retaining and protecting existing dead wood structures, including stumps, downed logs, fire snags, and dead trees of all species and diameters
- Protection of existing understory vegetation: Minimizing disturbance of understory plants—in particular, older and tall shrubs—and leaving areas where understory plants are not disturbed at all
- Creation of gaps or openings: Cutting gaps of at least 0.5 to 1.0 acre in size to support the growth of shade-intolerant tree and shrub species
- Retaining trees on unstable or steep slopes: Avoiding timber harvesting or using equipment on unstable slopes or slopes that exceed 50 percent
- Leaving areas (skips) of varying sizes unharvested: Leaving some ecologically important areas entirely undisturbed such as areas with unique plant communities (e.g., lichens, fungi, and older and taller shrubs), sensitive aquatic areas (e.g., riparian areas, wetlands, and steep

ravines), areas in proximity to old-growth trees or stumps, or habitats that allow for the dispersal of specific wildlife species (e.g., amphibians that thrive in darker, moister habitats)

CUTTING TECHNIQUES

Concerning the management of complex ecological systems, a forest manager can develop principles for management, but we must always adapt these principles to reality. An old teacher once told me, "My job isn't to teach you how to do something; it's to teach you how to think about doing something." What he meant was that it's better to have strategies for problem-solving than literal solutions to problems. The thinning techniques presented in this chapter represent a

thought process, and although examples are provided to illustrate the application of each technique, they should be taken figuratively and in light of the unique circumstances of your forest. In practice, the techniques you decide to use may be a blend of methods, and your forest composition targets may vary from those suggested in this chapter.

The thinning techniques we cover here can be used in most stand types, whether hardwood or conifer dominated or of mixed species. They are adaptable to different stands because they use biological criteria, in tandem with a landowner's objectives, to determine which trees should be cut in a forest and which trees should be retained. In the case of certain forest types, such as east-side pine or juniper forests, or oak or tanoak and madrone forests, these thinning

If Your Neck Doesn't Hurt . . .

One of the best pieces of advice I ever received regarding selecting trees for thinning came from Northwest Natural Resource Group's senior forester Rick Helman. Years ago when I was first learning how to mark trees for thinning, I was working with Rick in a client's forest. Rick taught me to look up into the canopy of the forest and observe the relationship between the crowns of various trees, and the placement of individual crowns in the overall canopy of the forest. To effectively release a tree that you want to retain, he said, you need to ensure its crown has ample room to grow in the canopy. Looking up, I could readily tell which trees had weak crowns and which trees had robust crowns. By imagining what the canopy would look like if certain trees (and their attendant crowns) were removed, Rick further instructed, you can see how much space the remaining crowns would have to grow. If you take too few trees, the canopy remains dense, and the remaining trees may enjoy only a short window of time in which they can grow before the canopy closes in and competition starts again. Gazing up into the canopy also allows you to identify damaged crowns, or other signs of defect along the trunk of a tree, that may cause you to remove that tree.

I spent the rest of that day constantly craning my neck to see what was going on with both individual tree crowns and their placement in the canopy. Later, Rick sagely said, "If your neck doesn't hurt at the end of the day, you're not doing your job right."

techniques need to be interpreted even more generally.

When applied in sequence over many decades, these techniques are designed to move a young stand from a highly simplified, early successional forest type to a complex, late successional forest type. At any point, this sequence of thinning can be interrupted with a *final variable retention harvest* of the dominant trees if a forest owner needs to monetize the value of the trees. The rate of thinning, or number or volume of trees recommended for removal in the following guidelines, is intended to keep the dominant cohort of trees in optimal growth while providing the opportu-

nity for natural understory regeneration and the recruitment of new cohorts of trees into the stand. Cutting intensity can be increased at any thinning stage to either increase revenue or decrease the number of thinnings required to obtain the desired density and composition of trees. However, cutting more trees at any one time can also increase the susceptibility of a forest to windthrow during storm events, as trees that were accustomed to supporting each other at a higher density will be in a vulnerable stage for several years until their root systems firm up. Increasing cutting intensities is typically only advised for stands that are remote or expensive to access, or where

Figure 14-1. Trees within a forest can be classified based on their position within the canopy. These canopy classes include: dominant (D), co-dominant (C), intermediate (I), and suppressed (S).

a high rate of storm damage is tolerable (e.g., forests with a conservation or habitat objective).

Smaller forests (e.g., five to forty acres) that are composed of a single stand type may literally be managed in a successional sequence as described in this chapter. However, larger forests, composed of many different stand types, may employ each of the thinning techniques simultaneously across the landscape, depending on the stand type being treated. This results in a mosaic of diverse stand types and forest habitats that, in total, are more characteristic of forests that develop under natural disturbance events.

Thinning from Below (Stand Age 25 to 40 Years)

The technique of thinning from below, or low thinning, uses a similar "best tree selection" criteria as pre-commercial thinning (discussed in Chapter 13) but is used when a stand is a little older. Most of the trees that are suppressed below the forest's canopy are targeted for removal, hence "thinning from below" (see Figure 14.1). In doing so, this technique further accelerates the natural thinning process of a forest. When working in stands older than thirty to forty years of age, thinning from below will produce merchantable-size trees. Thus, thinning from below is frequently associated with the first commercial thinning of a stand. It may be used in a stand that was previously thinned (e.g., pre-commercially) or as the first thinning in an older stand that has not been previously thinned. As with pre-commercial thinning, the primary biological clue to determine when a stand should be thinned from below is when the average live crown ratio of the dominant trees drops below 40 percent.

If the stand was previously thinned, then typically no more than 30 to 40 percent of the trees (25 to 30 percent of the volume) are removed during this thinning entry. This light thinning is intended to retain sufficient trees and canopy structure to maintain stand integrity during storm events and provide ample opportunities for additional thinning down the road. Thinning too heavily can leave the stand susceptible to windthrow in the first few years after thinning. However, if the stand was not previously thinned and has an extremely high density, such as a naturally regenerated stand of alder, up to 50 percent or more of the trees may be removed, with the majority of these being trees that are suppressed beneath the canopy of the forest. Groups of trees in root rot pockets, trees not suitable for the site, and other nonpreferred species that are competing with preferred trees can be cut at this stage also.

The application of thinning from below is most obviously called for in even-aged stands, such as young Douglas-fir plantations, or dense stands of naturally regenerated alder where there is a clear distinction between dominant and suppressed trees. Although the key at this stage of thinning is to release the most vigorous and dominant trees of each species, some nuance can be applied in order to begin teasing out both species and structural diversity in a young stand. Here are some options to consider:

- If the stand is conifer dominated but hardwoods are present, release and

Table 14-2: Tree Density Before and After Thinning from Below

STAND TYPE	CURRENT TREE DENSITY (TPA)	DENSITY AFTER THINNING FROM BELOW (TPA)
30-year-old Douglas-fir plantation that was pre-commercially thinned	240–280	150–190
30-year-old Douglas-fir plantation that was not pre-commercially thinned	320–360	190–250
25-year-old naturally regenerated red alder stand that was pre-commercially thinned	200–260	120–180
25-year-old naturally regenerated red alder stand that was not pre-commercially thinned	360–420	220–250

retain some of the hardwoods by cutting competing conifers in their proximity.

- If storm damage is evident in the crowns of the dominant trees, some intermediate or suppressed trees can be released by removing the damaged, dominant trees.
- If there are vigorously growing shade-tolerant trees in the understory, they can be released by removing dominant or codominant trees in their proximity.
- Some suppressed trees should be retained in order to maintain vertical heterogeneity in the stand. For example, if one of your objectives is to improve wildlife habitat, retain some trees with defects (in particular, trees with platform tops, forked tops, or cavities); and non-timber trees, such as cherry, willow, cottonwood, or crabapple.

Table 14-2 illustrates how the density of the dominant trees in a stand can be reduced when thinning from below (seedlings and very young shade-tolerant trees are not included in these numbers.)

Variable Density Thinning (Stand Age 40 to 80 Years or More)

Variable density thinning techniques are typically employed during subsequent thinning entries and can be used two to three times over several decades as a stand gradually progresses toward a residual density of dominant trees (a.k.a. legacy trees). The return interval between thinnings may depend on many factors, including the productivity of the soils, the species of trees and their density, and log markets or a forest owner's need for revenue. Forests on highly productive soils (e.g., Site Class I or II) may be thinned as often as every ten to fifteen years, whereas forests on less productive soils (e.g., Site Class III–V) may warrant longer return intervals, such as fifteen to twenty years or more.

There are two primary considerations for when to plan each subsequent thinning entry:

1. The stand should be given ample time for the trees to grow and add volume. Thinning too early or too frequently may shortchange a stand's ability to optimize both timber production and timber quality, as well as damage soils.
2. If the live crown ratios of the dominant trees are close to receding below 40 percent, the stand should be thinned.

Variable density thinning involves varying the thinning intensity to produce a mosaic of unthinned, moderately thinned, and heavily thinned areas of the forest. The use of skips and gaps (unthinned areas and small patch cuts) can also contribute to this mosaic. Variable density thinning helps generate a more complex forest structure by promoting tree growth at different rates. A complex canopy that produces variable light conditions also promotes a biologically diverse understory, as well as natural tree regeneration.

Then there are the benefits to forest resilience. Variable density thinnings do the following:

- Decrease competition and stress and improve vigor
- Increase resistance to disturbance through diversity and complexity

- Increase regeneration and recovery following disturbance
- Improve nutrient cycling, soil health, and water retention

This thinning technique can also be used to produce a wider variety of timber products or grades of timber in two fundamental ways:

1. Trees growing at different densities grow at different rates. Trees growing at a higher density grow slowly and are more prone to self-pruning, which can produce both tighter grain and clear lumber (higher-quality, knot-free timber). Trees growing at a lower density grow quicker and produce more wood volume (although lower-quality timber).
2. By supporting the growth of multiple tree species, the forest owner diversifies their investment.

In contrast to thinning from below, variable density thinning typically occurs "across the diameters," or across canopy classes. This means that trees of all sizes are selected for thinning in order to further enhance canopy complexity. The stand is still primarily thinned from below, removing the most suppressed, least vigorous, and least desirable trees, but dominant and codominant trees may also be selected for removal—in particular, where they will release vigorous understory trees or underrepresented species. Here are some additional nuances to consider when planning a variable density thinning:

In the years following thinning, trees naturally regenerate in the understory, adding new cohorts of trees to the forest.

- Continue to retain and support the growth of hardwoods in conifer-dominated stands. A good target volume would be 25 percent hardwoods, ideally well distributed throughout the stand.
- Continue to retain some number of suppressed trees in the understory that will provide vertical heterogeneity, as well as some trees with defects.
- Small gaps can be introduced to replicate the effects of disease pockets and create opportunities for more diverse shrubs or the reintroduction of shade-intolerant tree species such as Douglas-fir, pines, or alder. If you encounter disease pockets, removing most or all of the susceptible trees within and in proximity to them creates opportunities for planting tree species that are not susceptible to the disease.
- Snags can be created by either girdling trees or using mechanized logging equipment to cut trees as high as the equipment can reach. Selecting trees with defects (e.g., broken or forked tops, spike knots, or curved trunks) minimizes the loss of timber value.
- If natural tree regeneration is not occurring in the understory—or not at the desired rate, distribution, or species type—manual planting can be used to augment natural regener-

ation to ensure new cohorts of trees get established.

Table 14-3 illustrates how the density of the dominant trees in a stand can be further reduced when conducting successive variable density thinnings. Keep in mind that the point of variable density thinning is to vary the density throughout a stand, so there will be areas of higher density and areas of lower density. Therefore, the numbers presented in the table represent an average across a given stand (seedlings and very young shade-tolerant trees are not included in these numbers).

Variable Retention Harvesting

Variable retention harvesting is typically used in older stands during the third or fourth thinning entry, and can represent the final cutting of the original cohort of trees. This technique can also be used in older stands that were not previously thinned, in order to remove trees of low vigor or quality and rehabilitate the stand. For instance, older alder stands that are in

Table 14-3: Tree Density Before and After Variable Density Thinning

STAND AGE (YEARS)*	VARIABLE DENSITY THINNING ENTRY	CURRENT TREE DENSITY (TPA)	POST-THINNING DENSITY (TPA)	NOTES ON THINNING
30–45	First	190–250	120–180	Primarily thin from below. Remove dominant trees only where they will release vigorous understory trees or underrepresented species.
45–65	Second	120–180	80–120	Thin across the diameters (canopy classes) to improve canopy complexity. Introduce gaps. Evaluate stand for planting after thinning to augment natural regeneration.
60–85	Third	80–120	50–80	Thinning will now occur primarily among the dominant trees, selecting trees for removal that will release vigorous understory trees. Consider additional planting as necessary to achieve optimal species and density.

* These ages should be taken figuratively. However, highly productive sites can be thinned more frequently.

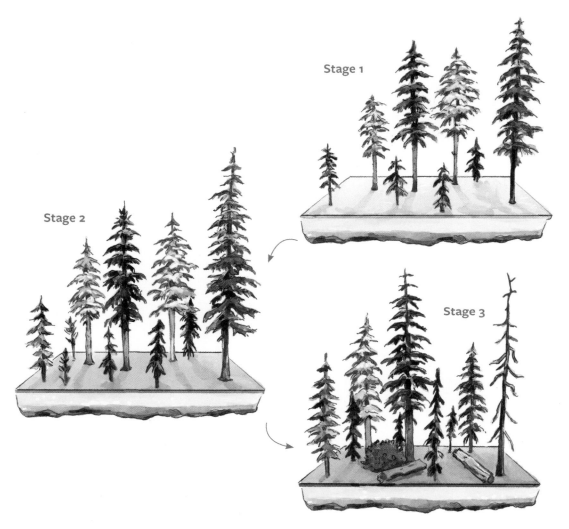

Figure 14-2. As a forest grows older, tree cutting can transition from variable density thinning to a final variable retention harvest that leaves a small number of legacy trees. In the meantime, new cohorts of trees develop in the understory, and thinning can begin again in what is now a forest of varying ages.

a phase of senescence, or decline, can be cut with minimal retention, and the site either replanted or left to naturally regenerate back to alder.

During a variable retention harvest, many of the remaining dominant and codominant trees are removed, with the exception of a predetermined number of legacy trees. These trees will be retained as permanent biological legacies, whether they remain standing or eventually fall down and become decaying logs. The number and species of legacy trees to retain depends entirely on a landowner's objectives. If ongoing timber production is a priority, fewer legacy trees may be retained (e.g., twenty-five trees per acre) in order to minimize their shade effect on the next generation of trees. If wildlife habitat, carbon sequestration, aesthetics, or other objectives are a priority, a landowner may opt to retain more trees. It's useful to keep in mind the concept of carrying capacity, introduced in Chapter 13, and understand the relationship, competitive or otherwise, between the legacy trees and the next generation of trees emerging beneath them.

There are many different ways to conduct a variable retention harvest. For instance, from an operational standpoint, clumping legacy trees may be more efficient. Clumping trees also improves their resilience to windstorms; provides benefits to various wildlife species, such as the pileated woodpecker; and avoids disturbing the soils where the trees are clumped. Dispersing legacy trees may have a greater aesthetic appeal, and may set the stage for better habitat connectivity as the canopy of the next cohort of trees grows and begins to reach the lower canopy of the legacy trees. Ultimately, a combination of clumped and dispersed trees may provide the broadest range of benefits.

Legacy trees should be representative of the stand, meaning that trees of all species suitable for the site should ideally be retained, hardwoods and conifers alike. Most hardwoods do not have the longevity of conifers, but despite their rapid growth and decline, they still provide many ecosystem and wildlife habitat benefits. Although it may be tempting to solely retain poor-quality and unmerchantable trees, doing so

may promote the genetics of trees with low timber value on your land.

A variable retention harvest is a form of regeneration cut (that is, cutting the overstory trees to set the stage for a new cohort of trees to grow on the site), like a clear-cut (see Figure 14-2). But unlike a clear-cut, it will create a more benign and resilient habitat as shade from the legacy trees shelters seedlings from hotter and drier summers, and complex fungal and other biotic communities continue to thrive.

Uneven-Aged Thinning

When working with an older forest that is structurally comparable to a legacy forest, two fundamental options are available to the forester: continue to thin and manage the forest or leave the evolution of the forest to natural stand development processes (storms, disease, etc.).

With the exception of very remote and difficult-to-access areas, and areas where the strictest of conservation measures are essential (rare plant communities or habitats, wetland soils, etc.), I rarely advocate for a do-nothing approach. Given the highly productive soils of the Pacific Northwest, we have a nearly unique opportunity to perpetually thin our forests and, in so doing, glean valuable products and keep enhancing essential ecosystem services.

SLASH MANAGEMENT

Any thinning activity in a forest will yield slash: limbs, treetops, tree trunks, and so on. Call it what you will (woody biomass, forest debris, mushroom fodder), the volume of slash will increase the heavier you thin. There is a strong argument in favor of

Thinning also produces non-merchantable wood that can be left scattered across the forest floor for wildlife habitat and soil nutrients.

using commercial logging as a stand management tool, as opposed to noncommercially thinning the forest and leaving the cut material in place, as the majority of the cut material is removed from the forest during logging, and the forester has complete control over how the remaining slash is distributed throughout the forest. Not all slash is created equal, so let's break it down.

Fine wood. This includes branches, treetops, very small-diameter trees, and any material that is generally less than four inches in diameter. Fine wood is the most flammable of all woody material, and the most responsible for increasing fire risk. As a rule, fine wood should be lopped and scattered in well-dispersed, noncontiguous mats that don't exceed waist height. Lopping and scattering also brings more of the wood in contact with the ground, hastening its decomposition. Fine wood is often best redistributed back onto skid trails, where it can

be incorporated into the soil during future skidder passes. Doing so also reduces soil compaction and minimizes soil disturbance.

Medium wood. This includes large branches and small trees from four to twelve inches in diameter. This material typically does not constitute a high fire risk as it requires a long, sustained heat source to ignite wood much thicker than four inches. Exceptions can include a particular phase of rot when wood is very dry and punky. This material can typically be left scattered throughout a site, keeping as much of it in contact with the ground as possible. If large logs are absent from the stand, small-diameter poles can be stacked in parallel to create constructed habitat logs, as discussed in Chapter 17 on enhancing wildlife habitat.

Coarse wood. This includes logs larger than twelve inches in diameter. These structures are essential to wildlife habitat and nutrient cycling in the forest. Coarse wood presents even less of a fire danger than medium wood and should be conserved and distributed throughout the forest at every opportunity.

Ever since the biomass-rich, old-growth forests of the Pacific Northwest were removed, Northwest soils have been starved for wood. In Chapter 17, I compare the volume of large dead wood in old-growth forests to that of modern-day third-growth forests. The comparative deficit in most managed forests further underscores the need to retain and recruit dead wood. However, overloading forests with dead wood can invite fire and pests. To avoid attracting beetles, recruit new logs into the forest gradually. Aim to reincorporate three to five logs per acre during each thinning entry, in addition to any that are generated naturally.

A conscientious and experienced logging contractor can usually reincorporate all noncommercial wood back into the forest as part of the logging operation. In logging systems that process trees into logs at the landing, skidders can bring woody material from landings back into the forest when they return for their next load of logs, distributing fine material on skid trails and larger pieces of wood throughout the forest. If there is more slash than can be incorporated on-site, consider converting the woody material into wildlife habitat piles, constructed habitat logs, firewood, wood chips, or biochar.

NATURAL REFORESTATION

Two of the biggest arguments against uneven-aged thinning are (1) it pushes forests toward dominance by shade-tolerant trees, and (2) the dense shade of complex forest canopies prevents adequate natural regeneration. As I've described in this chapter, we can address both of these issues through conscientious management—either by creating gaps or by thinning the canopy to allow sufficient light to reach trees in the understory. I'm inclined to push back on advocates of even-aged, plantation-based forestry and argue that one of the biggest challenges to reforestation following clear-cutting is the droughtiness of the soil and excessive brush competition. Seedlings planted into clear-cuts suffer from exposure during increasingly dry summers, as well as browse damage from deer and elk. Replanting plantations that experience high mortality is expensive. Therefore, why not use nature's inherent regenerative qualities and create opportunities where trees will seed themselves?

The protective environment beneath a forest's canopy provides a benign nursery for tree seedlings to get established and flourish. Shade reduces transpiration rates among seedlings, maintaining moisture in the soil longer into the summer. Shade also moderates the growth of understory shrubs that may compete with tree seedlings. Forest canopies interrupt desiccating winds, and the environment beneath a forest canopy is both warmer in winter and cooler in summer with a higher ambient air moisture than that of large clearings. Lastly, older trees can create mycorrhizal associations with seedlings that greatly improve seedling growth and vitality.

The key to successfully using natural regeneration as a reforestation strategy within existing forests lies in the combination of deliberate ground disturbance and thinning the canopy. Creating exposed mineral seedbeds will improve germination of an abundance of tree seedlings of varying species. However, their survival will depend on whether the forest canopy permits sufficient sunlight to foster their growth. Without ground disturbance or canopy thinning, several very shade-tolerant trees are more prone to germinate and slowly colonize a forest's understory—namely, western hemlock, grand fir, western redcedar, Sitka spruce, and bigleaf maple. Shade-intolerant species tend to colonize along forest edges, gaps, or large-scale ground disturbance events, such as landslides, fires, and logging, where soils are exposed. Successfully regenerating these species requires disturbing the ground beneath a forest's canopy *and* thinning the canopy sufficiently to allow adequate light for them to prosper.

It may seem counterintuitive, but low-impact commercial logging can serve as an optimal human-induced disturbance regime that stimulates natural tree regeneration. In most cases, the typical soil disturbance caused by logging (e.g., skid trails) is enough to stimulate tree regeneration, and no additional measures are necessary. Thinning the canopy also increases light availability to the understory. Reducing the density of dominant canopy trees below 100–120 trees across at least an acre will significantly increase sunlight to the forest floor. If a stand is thinned too lightly, and the canopy remains too dense (e.g., more than 70 percent canopy cover), shade-intolerant seedlings may have enough light to get established, but not enough to prosper, or even survive, as the canopy closes back in.

Here are some additional strategies for stimulating natural tree regeneration:

- Thin more heavily along southern edges of a forest, increasing availability of sunlight deeper into the forest.
- Create small canopy gaps (0.5–1.0 acre in size) within fully stocked stands.
- Commercially thin trees within and around disease pockets, creating areas of higher canopy porosity.

Natural regeneration results in a very uneven distribution of tree seedlings throughout a forest's understory and often favors one or two species. Dense groups of seedlings may be found beneath porous areas of the canopy, and very few elsewhere. Manually planting seedlings may be necessary in order to achieve an even distribution and increase desired species. Where seedlings regenerate in dense groups, proactive thinning may be warranted if the objectives are to promote timber growth and quality. However, patches of high seedling density also provide important habitat diversity.

The various options I've described in this chapter for working with mature forests may seem daunting to someone who is new to forest management. Many of these strategies are very technical, and it will behoove you to contract with a professional forester to design and implement them. I'm an advocate for do-it-yourself forestry, though. In the next chapter, I'll turn to one of the most accessible stewardship activities even novice foresters can engage in: pruning your trees.

CHAPTER 15

Pruning and Limbing

BY KIRK HANSON

Pruning trees is truly one of my favorite activities in the woods and is but one way I find my zen moment with my trees. I love going out for an hour or so with my pruning saws and limbing up branches as I stroll along. For me, it's primarily aesthetic. Pruning my trees high enough to actually improve timber quality requires a lot more time than I'm inclined to spend. I just like to lift the lower branches up enough so I can see through the understory of my forest. Pruning is one of those instant-gratification projects. After you've put in an hour or so of work, you can turn around and really appreciate the fruits of your labors. As far as I'm concerned, things just look better.

Pruning can be serious business, however. It requires focus and dedication if your objectives are to reduce fire risk, improve understory habitat, decrease foliar diseases, or increase the value of timber by promoting the production of knot-free wood.

SELF-PRUNING

Density management, particularly when trees are young, is key to promoting self-pruning. Maintaining a high density of trees (see Chapter 12) and a dense canopy is usually necessary to produce sufficient shade to kill off lower limbs. However, maintaining such high densities may come at the cost of tree growth and wood volume production. Highly productive sites (e.g., Site Class I and II) can support continued growth at higher stocking densities. Therefore, maintaining stands at the higher end of the recommended stocking density range for as long as possible before thinning may be a viable option for these very productive sites, as long as the live crown ratio stays at 40 percent or more. Forests on low-productivity sites should be maintained at their recommended densities, which are likely too low to result in self-pruning, and therefore require manual pruning.

Author Kirk Hanson in the middle of his second pruning lift using both manual and mechanical pruning saws.

Shade-intolerant tree species, such as Douglas-fir, pines, and particularly red alder, have a much greater tendency to self-prune, or lose their lower limbs, in the shade of a dense canopy. Although the lower limbs on the coniferous species will die off, given the decay-resistant resins in their wood, the limbs may remain on the tree for years, if not decades, and therefore continue to produce knots as the tree grows in diameter. Eventually, these limbs fall off, and at that point, higher-quality clear wood is produced annually. Alder is much more inclined to truly self-prune, as the brittle wood of its dead branches readily falls off the tree, and does so at a young age.

WHY YOU SHOULD PRUNE

In this section I present a series of rationales for pruning. Taken in total, these reasons for pruning have a beneficial multiplier effect. Therefore, you don't have to rely solely on the hope of financial return, but can rest your justifications on other well-reasoned arguments.

Improve Aesthetics

I list aesthetics first mainly because it's both my primary goal and the most accessible objective to a small woodland owner. By simply pruning trees as high as you can reach with a manual or motorized pruning saw, you will reveal a perspective into the forest that was hidden behind the blur of branches that once obscured your view. With a few caveats (explained later in this chapter), there are no other rules than that. Prune as high and as extensively as looks good to you. I'm six feet tall and can reach up to about eight feet with a regular hand-held pruning saw. That's high enough to cut at least the first two to four whorls, or layers of branches, off the bottom of any tree. Even at that minimum height, the view into my forest is greatly improved. By adding a pole saw into my pruning ensemble, I can reach up to about fourteen feet with ease, and farther if the pole can telescope. Pruning with a pole saw takes a lot more time, however, and is reserved for key areas, such as along roads, near buildings, or at important viewpoints.

Reduce Fire Risk

Now that your aesthetics are taken care of, you should turn your attention to the matter of protecting your forest! This takes pruning to a whole other level. The point of pruning to reduce fire risk is to eliminate fuel ladders, or lower branches that can catch a ground fire and carry it up into the canopy of a forest, where the fire can become very destructive. Branches on conifers tend to be the most fire-prone given the high resin content of the wood. Other trees, such as cedar and juniper, have highly flammable oils in their needles.

The general rule of thumb for pruning trees to reduce fire risk is to remove branches to a minimum of eight to twelve feet high or three times the height of the

Figure 15-1. To reduce fire risk, trees should be pruned to a minimum of either ten to twelve feet, or three times the height of the dominant shrub layer, whichever is greater.

3x

1x

dominant shrub layer (see Figure 15-1). The theory behind the latter is that if the shrub layer were to ignite during a ground fire, flame length typically reaches three times the height of the shrubs. When prioritizing areas to prune, I recommend starting along access roads, along forest edges, and around homes and buildings, then work your way into the interior of the forest. See Chapter 16 for more about wildfires and risk reduction.

Reduce Disease

Certain tree species are susceptible to foliar diseases, and pruning lower branches may improve the trees' resilience. The most common diseases include white pine blister rust, Swiss needle cast in coastal Douglas-fir, dwarf mistletoes in high-elevation and east-side forests, and western gall rust in lodgepole and ponderosa pine. Techniques for mitigating these diseases are addressed in Chapter 7.

Improve Timber Value

There has been much ballyhoo as to the financial benefits of pruning. There's no debate that pruning trees and producing clear timber will result in a higher-quality log. The question remains, however, whether a higher value can be realized for these logs, and if this value is sufficient to provide a reasonable return on investment considering the cost of pruning. If this strategy were to work anywhere, it is where there are markets for short logs: veneer, (also known as peeler logs), hardwoods, and mills east of the Cascades. Conifer veneer logs can be as short as seventeen to twenty feet long. Hardwood peelers begin at ten to twelve feet long. East-side mills purchase conifer

sawlogs as short as seventeen feet long. Mills that manufacture lumber require longer logs (twenty-four to forty feet long), and pruning to these heights is very labor intensive.

On my own land, I have thinned alder to 180–240 trees per acre and pruned it to at least sixteen feet high. Now many of my trees present peeler-grade timber, which can be worth at least twice the value of sawlogs. When pruning my Douglas-fir, I tend to prune everything as high as I can reach for aesthetics, but I only prune the trees that will produce sawlogs to a greater height. There is no added economic value to pruning low-quality trees that will only be sold for pulp or chip-and-saw logs.

Improve Wildlife Forage

Opening the forest canopy will increase light to the understory, thereby stimulating shrub and groundcover plant communities that provide browse, pollen, and mast (fruits and nuts) for a wide range of wildlife. In younger stands, pruning lower branches just before the canopy closes can help maintain canopy porosity for a few more years until the trees are either pre-commercially or commercially thinned. Additionally, pruning along forest edges, around existing gaps or disease pockets in the forest, and in areas of low stocking can help bring more sunlight through the forest canopy.

Improve Access and Safety

Who likes a sharp stick in the eye? Not I. It is undeniably easier to walk through a young forest that has been pruned versus one where branches remain on the trees to ground level. At a minimum, pruning along walking trails and adjacent to forest roads will improve access and the ability to assess your forest from a distance.

Limbs that overhang structures, roads and driveways, trails, fences, and powerlines may pose a safety risk and should be part of annual monitoring and maintenance. Depending on their location and the level of difficulty to remove them, you might consider hiring a contractor.

WHAT TREES CAN BE PRUNED?

Ultimately all hardwood and conifer tree species in the Pacific Northwest can tolerate pruning. The most common trees to prune, and for which there seems to be the least issues, are Douglas-fir, all pines, and red alder. Pruning these species also presents the best opportunity to add marketable value to the tree. Hemlock, true firs, and spruce are more prone to wood-decaying fungi. Therefore, pruning these species may come at a risk. Look for any signs of fungus on trees in your forest, particularly conks (e.g., red ring rot), as these species often spread through wounds on a tree, such as a pruning cut. If you observe conks, save pruning for winter months, when the fungus is less likely to produce spores and the pruning cut will have more time to heal.

HOW AND WHEN TO PRUNE

Pruning is an activity that can be done nearly any time of year. Winter is my preferred time as it's easier to see into the woods when the leaves are off the trees and the brush is down. There are also fewer wasps, or other buzzy insects for that matter. During winter dormancy, I find that

tree branches are more brittle and snap off readily when I prune them. The only time of year I advise avoiding pruning is spring when the sap is running. Tree bark is very sensitive to scarring and then more prone to peel when a cut branch falls. Pruning cuts on conifers also weep large amounts of pitch during the spring, which can attract insects and fungal diseases.

The age at which to prune a tree is determined by your objectives. As mentioned earlier, to reduce disease potential or support forage in the understory, pruning can begin around eight to twelve years of age. To optimize timber quality, the first lift on timber trees should begin when trees average four inches in diameter. If you wait to prune until the forest canopy closes, trees could be fifteen to twenty years old.

Pruning in Lifts

There are many ways to prune your forest in lifts, which involves removing branches successively higher in stages. In my young forests I wait until the canopy closes and shade begins killing off the lower branches of the Douglas-fir and alder (moderately shade tolerant and intolerant, respectively) before I consider pruning. Then, in my first lift, I simply prune as high as I can reach. This accomplishes both aesthetic and access objectives, and reduces ladder fuels. I come back later and prune the most dominant and highest-quality trees (the ones I want to retain for many years) to twelve to sixteen feet. The revealed larger trunks are aesthetically pleasing, and the pruning also produces a higher-quality veneer log.

The basic rule of thumb when pruning in lifts is to never prune more than

Figure 15-2. When pruning in lifts, never prune more than 50 percent of the tree's live crown.

50 percent of the live crown. As shown in Figure 15-2, if my objective were to prune my higher-quality trees to a minimum of 18.5 feet in order to optimize the veneer grade of the first log, I could accomplish this through three pruning lifts, starting when the tree is no more than four inches in diameter at breast height and approximately 16 feet tall.

Making a Pruning Cut

Making a proper pruning cut is as simple as making a perpendicular cut through the branch exactly where it meets the branch collar on the trunk (see Figure 15-3). As easy as this sounds, additional commentary is warranted. Cutting a branch too far away from the trunk and leaving a stub is

undesirable for two reasons: (1) the branch stub can hang on for years and continue to create a knot in the wood, and (2) the decaying branch stub can introduce pathogens and insects into the tree. Conversely, making a pruning cut flush with the surface of the trunk, and therefore through the thickest part of the branch collar, can create an excessively large wound that can take a long time to heal and, in the process, provide an avenue for pathogens and insects. The branch collar tissue belongs to the bole you are leaving behind. It's important to protect it by cutting to it, but not into it. Cutting the branch along the outside surface of the branch collar reduces the size of the pruning cut and provides the quickest opportunity for the tree to heal itself and begin growing clear wood from that point forward.

More often than not, I can get away with starting a pruning cut at the top of a branch and cut until the branch breaks off the tree. Sometimes a branch will break off and leave a splinter of wood emerging from the branch collar. This splinter is easily cut with another stroke of the pruning saw and should be removed. When pruning live branches, especially during the spring, it's not uncommon that the branch will tear a ribbon of bark off the tree below the branch collar when the branch falls. This can be avoided by either pruning the limb off in stages to reduce its weight or first making a shallow undercut beneath the branch, then proceeding with cutting from above.

Some additional recommendations are as follows:

- Cut off epicormic branches (small, bushy branches that emerge from the surface of the trunk) while pruning large branches. Conversely, excessively pruning trees in a manner that exposes a large percentage of their trunks can also stimulate epicormic branching. Epicormic branches can form knots in the wood and therefore decrease timber quality.
- Economize your time. Don't prune trees that you don't intend to grow for timber value unless pruning meets other objectives (e.g., aesthetics).
- Slowly prune branches along the edges of young forests, especially conifer-dominated stands. Pruning too quickly and too high can expose young, tender bark to sunscald, which can weaken the tree by dam-

Figure 15-3. Examples of three pruning cuts: The cut on left sawed into the branch collar, exposing too much surface area. The one in the middle left too long a stub on the branch. The cut on the right was made properly, just outside the swell of the branch collar, where the tree will have the easiest time healing over.

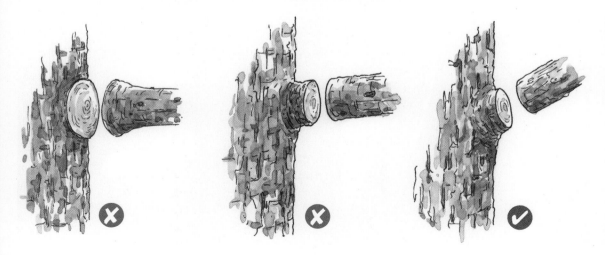

aging the tender tissue beneath the bark.

- Mitigate resulting slash using any of the strategies described in the previous chapter.

RECOMMENDED TOOLS

My two primary go-to tools for pruning are a handheld, fixed-blade sixteen-inch pruning saw and a telescoping pole saw. I prefer pruning with manual tools as they're quiet and allow me to listen to the forest as I work. That's how I achieve my zen while pruning. As I mentioned earlier, I also often carry a folding pruning saw so that I can quickly zip off branches of young trees as I pass by them. Loppers are fine for small branches less than an inch thick, but otherwise have limited utility.

The two tools I strongly dissuade you from using to prune your trees are a machete and an axe. Though they may be sharp, a machete and axe are blunt instruments for pruning as they are inevitably used to strike a branch to break it from a tree's trunk. Breaking branches in such a manner typically leaves a ragged result—either a branch stub or too deep of a wound. I equally urge caution when using a chainsaw, as it can suddenly kick back if used improperly. However, if used with finesse, a chainsaw can make quick work of pruning lower limbs, and newer electric saws are quiet and reduce fumes.

As I described in this chapter, one of the biggest reasons for pruning your trees is to reduce the risk of fire in your forest. This provides a perfect segue to our next chapter on the ecology of wildfire, where we'll discuss the historical role of fire in forest ecosystems on both the east and west sides of the Cascades, as well as how climate change is affecting fire behavior and steps you can take to further reduce fire risk in your forest.

CHAPTER 16

Wildfires and Risk Reduction

BY SETH ZUCKERMAN

Every summer, it seems, wildfires take over the news for at least a month, and a pall of smoke dims the western sun. The media shows a fresh montage of disaster porn as infernos tear through forests and communities across the American West, while an occasional counterpoint of science articles reminds readers that fire is a natural part of the forest ecosystem. Should we be terrified of fire, be resigned to it, or become better masters of it? For forest owners, the question comes into even sharper relief, since you have the opportunity to shape your relationship with wildland fire. This chapter will help you understand the historical role of fire in your forest and think about how to incorporate an awareness of fire—and possibly even the use of fire—in forest stewardship.

The phenomenon we call "wildfire" actually includes a spectrum of fire types that are as different from one another as flurries are from blizzards. Even more crucially, wildfires occur in a diverse range of forest ecosystems that each respond differently to the disturbance. We will tease apart several kinds of forest ecosystems and what fire scientists call their *fire regimes*—the combination of fire severity and fire frequency that has historically characterized that ecosystem and, in turn, has shaped the types of trees and understory plants that can thrive there.

LOW-SEVERITY FIRE REGIMES

We'll begin with the wildfires that have stolen the spotlight lately, which have occurred in forests originally characterized by a frequent, low-severity fire regime, meaning that the typical time between fires was five to thirty-five years, killing less than a quarter of forest. Foresters measure that fraction by basal area, so most of

Not all wildfires are infernos that make the evening news. Some make their way through the forest and consume downed wood and small trees, while leaving the overstory intact.

Some of these low-severity fires were sparked by lightning, while others were set by Indigenous people. American Indians have long used fire for a wide variety of purposes: to maintain grasslands for game to graze on, to control pests that eat the acorns that are a mainstay of their traditional diet, to stimulate the production of camas bulbs and straight shoots for basketry, and more. In fact, these practices (along with lightning fires) were responsible for the very grandeur of the dry forests that greeted the first Euro-American explorers, creating parklike pine groves through which migrants were easily able to drive their covered wagons. Later, Euro-American ranchers took up similar practices, burning rangeland to control the highly invasive Douglas-fir that threatened to take over. These fires weren't anything like what you see on the nightly news: the flames generally stayed close to the ground, and they often moved slowly, creeping around and tidying up by burning off fine woody material that had accumulated on the forest floor since the last fire swept through. They rarely caught the crowns of the dominant trees on fire, much less sparked the firenadoes that we have seen in videos of extreme fire behavior.

the small trees might have succumbed to fire, but larger trees amounting to at least three-quarters of the basal area would have survived. Eastern Oregon and Washington forests follow this pattern, along with those of southwestern Oregon, the drier parts of the Willamette Valley, California's Sierra Nevada, and much of the interior western United States.

Lately, however, the severity of fire in those areas has been anything but low, as a century of fire suppression comes home to roost. Starting around 1910, public resource agencies—from the US Forest Service to state lands departments—aimed to put out every fire by the morning after it was reported. It was largely an achievable undertaking at first, since frequent fires had kept the forest clear of small trees and underbrush. During the twentieth century, fire suppression changed that picture, though. It allowed the open understory to become clogged with smaller trees and shrubs, and it shifted the balance of tree species away from those such as ponderosa pine, whose thicker bark enables it to more easily withstand fire, toward those such as grand fir and white fir that are more susceptible to it. Compounding that, sheep and cattle nibbled the grass to the ground, making it harder for fire to spread across long distances. Without regular burning, the forest developed a fuel ladder of flammable dry branches and smaller trees that could carry a fire from the forest floor into the canopy. Eventually, the forest accumulated so much dry tinder that it became harder to stop fires once they did ignite, and recent fires have been much more destructive than if forest fuels had been scarce.

Out of a combination of ignorance and hubris—thinking they could defeat fire indefinitely and enforce a new fire regime—forest managers tried to exclude fire from the forest, only to realize that it would eventually find a way. This is particularly true because many of the forests in this historical fire regime are located in the drier, hotter parts of the region—east of the Cascade crest and in the Klamath Mountains of southwestern Oregon. Every summer, the

duff, twigs, and dead branches in the forest are dry enough to carry fire. Even if humans (the most common source of wildfire ignition) manage to avoid starting a fire out of carelessness, stupidity, or malice, summer thunderstorms are a regular occurrence, bringing with them lightning that can strike the match.

If your forest is in a place with this kind of historical fire regime (see figure 16-1), the management implications are obvious. Your forest will eventually burn, and probably sooner than later. The more fuel that has accumulated, the hotter the fire and the harder it will be to control. (By fuel, we don't mean gasoline, but rather all the live and dead vegetation, particularly a thick layer of duff, fine branches, and larger wood on the ground; dense concentrations of recently dead trees; flammable shrubs; and dead branches still attached to tree trunks.) If there's a lot of fuel on the ground, the fire will burn so hot that it cooks the cambium layer—the layer of living tissue just inside the bark—and girdles the tree, killing it. Fuel ladders carry the fire from ground level into the canopy, whose torching will also likely kill the tree. The density of trees matters, too, because crowded stands often are less vigorous and stressed for lack of moisture, making it easier for a crown (or canopy) fire to spread from one tree to the next.

To make the forest more resilient to the fires that will inevitably arrive, careful stewards reduce the amount of fuel in the forest by clearing young trees and brush and safely burning the wood produced. (Chipping may be necessary if air-quality concerns prevent pile-burning.) They prune the lower limbs of trees to break up

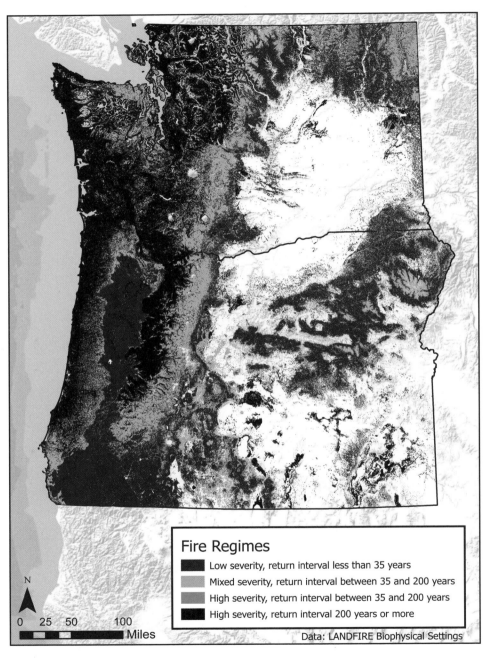

Fire Regimes

■ Low severity, return interval less than 35 years

■ Mixed severity, return interval between 35 and 200 years

■ High severity, return interval between 35 and 200 years

■ High severity, return interval 200 years or more

Data: LANDFIRE Biophysical Settings

Figure 16-1. Fire behaves differently across the region, depending on climate and vegetation. Scientists distinguish fire regimes based on fire's historic return interval and on the fraction of the overstory trees that typically succumbed when the forest burned.

A thinned forest at left, and a pile on the right where slash was burned to make biochar, a soil amendment

the fuel ladder, and toss those limbs on the burn pile as well. They thin the forest, thereby spreading the available soil moisture around to fewer trees. Eventually, the forest can coexist with fire, instead of being destroyed by it.

Making the transition back to a fire regime that can support low-severity fires is an arduous undertaking, but those who have tried it attest to its success. Stoked by high winds and extreme drought, the 2021 Bootleg Fire in southern Oregon was burning so hot that it killed nearly every living tree across thousands of acres. But when it reached tracts of national forest land and Nature Conservancy preserves that had already been thinned and then treated with prescribed (intentional) fire to reduce the remaining fuels, its flame heights shriveled to four feet, and it spared most of the trees—a much better outcome than sur-

rounding, untreated stands, even those that had been thinned but not burned (see Figure 16.2).

It's crucial to note that using prescribed fire isn't a do-it-yourself activity like torching a burn pile. It's one thing to dispose of limbs, brush, and trees that are too small to turn into firewood, taking proper precautions to keep the fire from spreading beyond the pile and refraining from burning when either fire marshals or air-quality considerations tell you to hold off. But laying down a broadcast burn across the landscape is an entirely different matter, requiring coordination with local firefighters, an authorized "burn boss" who can decide if weather conditions are suitable, and an organization to assume liability on the off chance that the fire should escape. In numerous areas across the West, Prescribed Fire Councils have arisen to help one another use fire safely

Figure 16-2. This area in southern Oregon's Black Hills was affected by the 2021 Bootleg Fire. The green area in the center had been thinned and treated with prescribed fire, as part of a cooperative effort by the Klamath Tribes, the US Forest Service, and The Nature Conservancy. To its left is an area that was thinned but not burned; on the right, a blackened area that had not been treated at all.

and effectively—safely so that it doesn't color outside the lines, and effectively so that after going to all that trouble, the fire burns hot enough to accomplish the work that the land stewards have set out to do, consuming the fine fuels and priming the forest to withstand fire when it eventually arrives.

HIGH-SEVERITY FIRE REGIMES

At the other end of the spectrum from the frequent, low-severity historical fire regime are the places that can easily go more than two hundred years between fires. But when the fire does arrive, if it's accompanied by high winds, watch out! These forests will naturally burn so hot during these rare fires that the fire will often kill more than

three-quarters of the trees and lead to the replacement of the entire stand with a new cohort of seedlings.

The infrequent, high-severity fire regime zone stretches along the coastal mountain ranges from southern Oregon all the way to the northwest tip of the Olympic Peninsula, and encompasses much of the western foothills and slopes of the central Oregon to Washington Cascades as well. These are some of the most productive forests in the world, thanks to their abundant supply of moisture, which contributes to their natural fire tendencies in two ways. First, it feeds a rampant tangle of dense trees and shrubs, with biomass loads per acre that are among the highest in the world. But at the same time, the climate is so wet that fire would usually be hard-pressed to take hold—like trying to start a campfire in the rain. These forests developed in a climate where the summer dry season is usually no more than two months long, and even that is usually punctuated by occasional drizzle. But these statistics are just what is average and typical. Every so often, a longer dry spell is followed by strong, hot east winds—winds that come from the dry interior and can push fire ahead of them like a bellows. Add a flash of ignition, from lightning or a trailer in disrepair that throws off sparks as it's driven down the highway, and all that biomass is primed to reunite with oxygen in a cataclysmic fire.

Such fires have occurred within the historical record in the Northwest, including the famous Yacolt (Washington) and Tillamook (Oregon) fires of the early twentieth century. Each of those consumed hundreds of thousands of acres, and in this case, *consumed* is an appropriate verb, with little hyperbole about it. Those fires burned especially hot, because much of the area they reached had recently been logged and was still covered in logging slash. But the arrival of intense fire wasn't simply the result of logging slash. Paleoecologists have reconstructed fire timelines extending back before the industrial logging era, using radiocarbon dating, tree cores, and carbon layers in the soil and lake sediments, and have concluded that many of the old-growth forests we see today had their birth in the aftermath of widespread fire. They've been untouched by catastrophic fire ever since. When it does return, it starts the cycle again, from seedling to old-growth forest.

In areas characterized by this fire regime, fire isn't a concern during most years, and most wildfires can be contained. Even though

fire is a natural phenomenon, our region has a historically low area of older forest, and an unnaturally high proportion of young forest, which is what would grow back after a severe fire restarts the clock of forest development at zero. So from an ecological forestry standpoint, there's a strong case for wildfire suppression in this fire regime. But if a fire does get started in those fire-primed conditions, it's very hard to control. The hot east winds supply two sides of what's known as the fire triangle (heat and oxygen), and

Fires in a low-frequency, high-severity fire regime can kill most of the live trees and set the stage for a new round of forest development, as in Opal Creek after the 2021 Beachie Fire.

the forest is rich in the third (fuel). Once these fires start and grow to several hundred acres, their course is determined more by weather conditions and the steepness of the terrain than by any firefighting tactics. Oregon saw an example of this in the summer of 2020, when the lightning-set Lionshead and Beachie Creek Fires torched nearly 400,000 acres. They burned through old-growth forests such as the Opal Creek Wilderness, which had avoided stand-replacing fire for centuries.

As a landowner in this zone, how do you prepare for the possibility of fire? On the positive side of the ledger, catastrophic fire is inherently unlikely in this fire regime, because it depends on the coincidence of ignition, dry conditions, and east winds. If its return interval is greater than two hundred years, the chance of it happening on a given acre in any given year is less than 0.5 percent—about the chance of being hurt in a car crash if you drove across the country and back. In much of the area covered by this fire regime, the average return interval is longer, on the order of three hundred to five hundred years. Granted, the chance of fire does mount up over the years, but over a decade, it might still not be more than the likelihood of getting injured in a couple of years of average driving.

That said, we take steps to reduce the likelihood of injury in car accidents, wearing seat belts and equipping our cars with airbags and warning signals. What are the equivalent precautions for forest owners

Fighting Wildland Fires

Firefighters speak of the fire triangle, the three factors that enable fire to ignite: oxygen, heat, and fuel. Eliminate any of those three and you can interrupt the fire. Squirting water on a fire ("putting the wet stuff on the red stuff") cools the fuel. Fire retardant can keep the fuel from uniting with the oxygen it needs to burn. But the

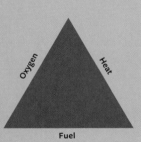

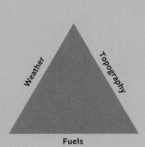

most common techniques of wildland firefighting rely on interrupting the fire's fuel supply by cutting a line around it so that the fire can't spread into the unburned area, or setting a backfire that will scorch the land between some control line and the flame front, thus preventing the fire from reaching new fuel.

Beyond that, wildland firefighters also consider a triangle of fire *behavior*—what makes a fire blow up or calm down. The three elements of that triangle are fuels, weather, and topography. Thinking about these factors helps managers determine where they can safely deploy firefighters. It also guides their decisions about when prescribed fire can safely be used.

Figure 16-3. The structure of a forest edge as it graduates from groundcovers, to shrubs, to low trees, to tall canopy trees. Note the complete absence of combustible material within five feet of the house.

in these wetter locales? Techniques that are effective in frequent, low-severity fire regimes lose their power here; you can't effectively control fuel levels in these productive forests, because it simply grows back so fast. Where fuels reduction *can* make a difference is along roadsides and immediately surrounding cabins and other structures. It also makes sense to harden the building envelope. Metal roofs instead of shake roofs, clean gutters and eaves, and screens to help block embers from blowing through attic vents or under decks and stairs where they could ignite needles and twigs—these are all strategies that can reduce the chance that your forest sanctuary would be lost along with your trees. In addition, creat-

ing a fuel break between structures and the forest can give firefighters a chance to try to stop a fire that starts in a building from reaching the wildlands.

Maybe the best analogy to these infrequent, high-severity fire areas comes from forest ecologist Daniel Donato, who compares major fires to earthquakes: disruptive, unpredictable eventualities whose initiation is beyond our control. The great Cascadia Subduction Zone earthquake will probably occur sometime in the next two hundred years, and we are powerless to stop it. All we can do is prepare for it, minimize the harm that will result, and prepare ourselves to ride it out safely. By the same token, fire-hardening your homestead and ensuring that you and firefighters would have safe access to it are steps you can take to address the fire risk that is an inextricable part of owning forestland (see Figure 16-3). How much attention you dedicate to those steps will be a reflection of your own personal tolerance for risk.

MIXED-SEVERITY FIRE REGIMES

If you look at the map of fire regimes (Figure 16-1), you will see that much of western Washington and Oregon—notably the eastern slopes of the Oregon Coast Range, the northeast side of the Olympic Mountains, and the eastern and southern shores of Puget Sound—fall between these two extremes. There you can expect mixed-severity fire, with some amount of low-severity fire as well, and fire return intervals between thirty-five and two hundred years. That's a huge range! At that rate, you might see fire on your family land twice in your lifetime, or neither you nor your kids and grandkids would be affected by it. The reason is simple: the climatological driving forces fall in between the frequent low-severity regime and the infrequent high-severity regime. Summers are hotter and drier, so the fuels have more opportunity to get crispy. In these areas, the forest still grows more biomass than can be controlled by the use of frequent prescribed fires. Further, many of the common tree species, such as western hemlock, red alder, and bigleaf maple, have bark that is too thin to insulate their tender cambium layer from the heat of a fire passing through.

Nevertheless, as land managers, you still have an opportunity to affect fire behavior through your management of the forest. It's true that if a fire breaks out when the east wind is howling at fifty miles per hour over the Cascade passes, you might not have much chance to stop it. But if that fire starts two weeks before the wind sets to howling, you'll want to be able to contain it and put a robust line around it so that it won't blow up from a hundred-acre burn to a hundred thousand. If you're already mopping it up when the wind shifts, you have a better chance of reining the fire in. Thinning your forest to promote the growth of larger and more fire-resistant trees, reducing the volume of small-diameter standing and downed dead trees, and matting down the slash from pre-commercial thinning so it swiftly decomposes are ways to load the fire dice in your favor. If a fire starts, you and the local fire agency will be more likely able to corral it before it gets out of hand.

In northwestern California where I used to live, rancher Lloyd Roberts set a fire in 1964 to clear his pasture, but the wind changed and carried the fire into the forest, where it burned for seven miles until it reached the mother of all control lines: the Pacific Ocean. That fire came to be known as the Roberts Fire. If you keep your forest more fire-safe, you have a better chance no momentous fires will be named after you.

CHAPTER 17

Improving Wildlife Habitat

BY KIRK HANSON

One of my favorite personal wildlife stories took place a few years ago when "George the Curious Grouse" took up residence on my family's land near Bucoda. George was a fearless grouse with a lot of attitude and was clearly not smitten with my family, nor impressed by our efforts to manage our forest. What George lacked in smarts he made up for in bravery. He routinely attempted to attack the business end of my brush cutter when I began cutting back blackberries. He relentlessly pecked at the cuff of my mother's pants as she planted tree seedlings. He also assaulted my son, although this at least was justified as my son wanted to see what would happen if he poked George with a sharp stick. I considered capturing and relocating George after he attacked a Natural Resources Conservation Service agent upon exiting his truck. Fortunately this event didn't disqualify me for Environmental Quality Incentives Program funding.

For weeks George greeted us nearly every time we entered our land, and we eventually named the small valley he occupied "Grouseland." One day when George made his appearance, we noticed he was missing his right leg. We all wondered what altercation led to this alteration, and whether his opponent fared worse. The missing appendage didn't diminish George's feisty attitude, and he continued to defend his territory with unmitigated zeal.

Eventually George disappeared altogether, and we've often wondered what fate befell him. I'm not sure there's a moral to this story, and I certainly don't want any of you to fear being accosted by wildlife should you improve habitat on your land. Perhaps the message is to walk softly and carry a big stick . . . but not a pointy one.

IN HETEROGENEITY LIES THE KEY

The Northwest is suffering from a Douglas-fir epidemic. We've converted historically heterogeneous forests, in a mosaic of ages from seedlings to ancients, into a landscape of single-species plantations that exist in the competitive exclusion phase—the least diverse and poorest habitat phase—for most of their growing period. We don't need any more of this habitat type in our region. Therefore, extending the age of your forest, increasing the diversity of trees and other plants, and recruiting ever larger snags and downed logs may be the best things you can do to create underrepresented wildlife habitat.

The habitat structures that are most often missing in second- and third-growth forests are snags and downed logs. When these structures are missing, so are the wildlife that depend on them. What's always astonishing to me is the contrast between historical stocking levels of dead wood and what habitat biologists suggest as minimum quantities to sustain wildlife. For instance, forest biologists have recorded 50 to 140 downed logs per acre in undisturbed forests on the west side of the Cascades, and an average of 16 snags per acre. However, studies also reveal that to retain viable populations of cavity nesters, a minimum of four snags greater than ten inches in diameter are needed per acre, with at least

You can use motion-activated cameras to learn how wildlife use your forest.

61F 16C   O   07-10-2022   20:31:

two of these greater than twenty inches in diameter. Habitat biologists also suggest a minimum of six to eight downed logs per acre of similar dimensions.

For those of us who are starting on this pathway from an even-aged and monocultural plantation, achieving these uneven-aged forest conditions and habitat structures may seem both daunting and a distant goal. I think it's important to keep in mind that we *can* get there from here, and time and careful stewardship are our two best tools. The minimum targets that habitat biologists suggest for dead wood can be short-term goals, and the extent to which you want to increase the quantity of habitat structures should be informed by your own personal forest management goals and objectives.

WHAT IS HABITAT?

Wildlife habitat is the arrangement of three essential components: food, cover, and water. These resources need to be available and abundant enough to support the biological needs of one or more species. For mammals and birds, the critical limiting factor is generally the availability of their preferred food. Shelter or escape cover is of secondary importance. For salmon and other aquatic species, the most harmful factors impacting populations include stream sedimentation caused by erosion, the blocking of stream passage by woody debris, human infrastructure, and various forms of water pollution, including warmer water temperatures.

Wildlife habitat is increasingly contracting as human development expands into forested areas; industrial timber management alters food, cover, and water resources; and other land use practices fragment natural areas. As forest managers, it is important to understand how our management activities impact wildlife and the long-term condition and quality of their habitat. For example, using heavy equipment or conducting logging activities in the spring can disrupt the nesting patterns of birds. Leaving forests too dense can limit the diversity of shrubs and groundcovers in the forest understory and therefore limit forage and browse opportunities. Routinely cutting dead or dying trees for firewood limits opportunities for snag-dependent species.

A well-managed forest can harbor a wide range of animals, birds, and amphibians—not to mention hundreds of species of insects, which make up the lower end of the food chain.

All wildlife species are products of their environment, and each species has specific and unique habitat requirements. The purpose of wildlife habitat enhancement is to conserve or increase the diversity and abundance of native wildlife species. Habitat diversity is naturally maintained when disturbance events such as fire, wind and ice storms, insects, and disease affect portions of the forest. Although severe disturbance events can set a particular area of forest back to the early successional phase of development, disturbance events typically increase structural diversity at the landscape level.

Properly functioning habitat at the landscape level includes forests at every successional stage, including shrubs, seedlings, saplings, mature trees, and, finally, old-growth trees. With each successive

Mixed-age forests with multiple canopy layers attract a broader range of bird species than simplified, even-aged forests.

stage, different combinations of wildlife species establish, persist, and then decline. The diversity of wildlife species present depends on habitat diversity associated with these stages. One of the objectives of ecological forestry is to mimic natural disturbance events in a manner that introduces great structural and species diversity into a forest.

EVALUATING WILDLIFE HABITAT ON YOUR LAND

First, I encourage you to keep a journal of the wildlife species you observe on your land. If they're present on your land, then you can be confident that your forest provides at least some of their habitat needs,

right? As the saying goes, "If it ain't broke, don't fix it." Chances are your forest already supports a broad range of wildlife, so the operative question is, "What other species do I want on my land?"

The larger critters are fairly common and easy to identify. Birds, amphibians, and fish can be harder to distinguish. Fortunately, smartphone apps can help you identify various bird species by their calls with a surprising degree of accuracy, such as the Merlin app created by the Cornell Lab of Ornithology. (See Resources for recommended guidebooks.) You can always send a photo to your extension forester, state wildlife biologist, or conservation district, and someone can help you identify what's occupying your land.

Second, given that habitat consists of three basic components—food, water, and shelter—there are some basic observations you can make to determine what kind of habitat you have, its abundance or limitations, and where there may be opportunities for enhancement. When observing your forest, ask yourself the following questions. If you answer no to any of these, you may want to consider if there's anything you can do to enhance that particular habitat feature.

- Is there a wide diversity of trees and shrubs that produce berries and nuts?
- Is there a mix of diverse hardwoods and conifers?
- Are there multiple canopy layers in some parts of the forest?
- Do stocking densities vary through the forest vary, including areas of high density and areas of low density?

- Is there a diversity of browse: grasses, groundcovers, and shrubs?
- Are there flowers, groundcovers, shrubs, and trees that flower during most times of the year?
- Is there an abundance of snags and downed logs of various sizes?
- Is there a source of year-round surface water on or immediately adjacent to the land?
- Are there areas of dense brush?
- Are there old trees with large limbs and complex crowns?
- Is there mature forest cover adjacent to streams and wetlands?
- Do streams appear to be in their natural condition and free flowing, with woody debris, intact streambanks, channel sinuosity, and gravelly substrate?

UPLAND HABITAT MANAGEMENT

No single forest should be expected to provide the entire breadth of habitat functions necessary to support all wildlife species in a particular region. Rather, the forest should be managed within the context of the surrounding landscape. One question I often ask is, "What are the underrepresented forest habitats in an area?" Typically the answers are either older forests or riparian forests, or both. The second question I ask is, "What are the missing or underrepresented habitat structures?" Typically the answer is large snags and downed logs. It's instructive to review your state's list of priority habitats and species to gain an understanding of which ones are diminished in your area.

Forests can be managed to produce habitat features or functions that are missing or limited at a landscape level. In this way, individual forests work in tandem with surrounding properties to provide a mosaic of habitat types that create optimal habitat conditions for all wildlife. Wildlife corridors, especially those surrounding riparian areas and other seasonal migratory routes, should be retained.

The following list includes a variety of common practices to enhance upland wildlife habitat:

- Conserving or recruiting snags, downed coarse logs, and structurally complex trees that have storm damage, rot, multiple stems, large limbs, and so on
- Planting or promoting the growth of more diverse hardwoods and conifers—in particular, underrepresented species
- Creating and maintaining horizontal heterogeneity (e.g., gaps, patches of high density, and a mix of young and old stands)
- Promoting understory shrub and groundcover diversity by thinning the forest canopy
- Promoting the growth of berry- and nut-producing trees and shrubs
- Planting annual and perennial flowers, groundcovers, shrubs, and trees that provide pollen sources throughout the year
- Installing nesting boxes for birds, bats, and small mammals
- Removing invasive plant species and replacing them with native plants

Larger snags provide opportunities for many species of wildlife.

that provide forage for birds and mammals
- Creating wildlife habitat piles and constructed downed logs using material generated during forest management
- Seeding forest roads, log landings, and soils disturbed by logging with a forage or pollinator seed mix
- Planting wildlife hedgerows composed of trees and shrubs that provide berries, nuts, and pollen sources along field borders or forest edges

Let's look at some of these practices in more detail and what you can do if your forest is lacking adequate diversity.

Snags and Downed Logs

Snags (dead trees) and downed logs provide important structures for cavity-dependent bird and small-mammal species, food sources for woodpeckers and other foragers, and slow-release nutrients for the forest in general. West of the Cascade Range, thirty-nine species of birds and fourteen species of mammals depend on tree cavities for their survival. East of the Cascades, thirty-nine bird species and twenty-three mammal species depend on these snags. In total, more than one hundred species of birds, mammals, reptiles, and amphibians need snags for nesting, roosting, shelter, denning, and feeding; nearly forty-five species alone forage for food in them. This high use of snags by a myriad of species underscores the importance of preserving and including them in your landscape.

As trees die, whether they remain standing or become logs on the forest floor, they pass through several stages of decay, which, in total, can last decades or even centuries depending on the species and size of the tree. Snags and downed logs provide different habitat functions based on their stage of decay, becoming more or less valuable to different wildlife species; therefore, it's important to maintain snags and logs across all decay stages in your forest.

Natural recruitment of snags requires forest conditions that allow for a certain percentage of trees to grow old and senesce, succumb to diseases or pests, or be subject to natural disturbance events such as wind and ice storms. Large snags more than twelve inches in diameter and twenty feet tall offer ideal hunting perches for hawks, eagles, and owls. These types

Table 17-1: Minimum Wildlife Habitat Structure Targets

STRUCTURE	NUMBER	MINIMUM DIMENSIONS
Snag	3 per acre	12" × 20'
Downed log	3 per acre	12" × 20'
If naturally occurring structures are deficient:		
Wildlife habitat pile	1 per acre	10' wide × 6' tall
Constructed logs	3 per acre	12" × 20'
Bird nesting boxes	5 per acre	Small
	3 per acre	Large

of snags can remain standing for decades. The larger the diameter of the snag, the longer it will last and the more intricate and inviting the habitat it will provide. Old-growth Douglas-fir and cedars are extreme examples of this, although they are rare on private forest land.

Coarse wood includes fallen trees and large branches, as well as logs and large pieces of wood left from logging operations. This habitat component serves many of the same purposes as snags: nesting, denning, roosting, foraging, and cover and shelter from inclement weather. At least as many vertebrate species use decaying logs as use snags. Some are the same species, such as black bears who use large hollow logs and woodpeckers who forage for insects. Some are seen on the exterior, such as ruffed grouse who use logs for drumming sites as part of their mating ritual. Many small mammals use this habitat type for hiding and food caches. Probably the most unique

life-forms using decaying wood are several salamander species. Standing and down dead trees are host to a huge number (more than four hundred) of insect species and an unknown but large number of non-insect invertebrates—a food source for many vertebrates in the forest.

Although root diseases and windthrow will naturally create snags and logs, you may need to augment those to achieve the desired targets for these habitat structures. During thinning and other forest management activities, existing snags and logs should be conserved, as well as decadent or defective trees with multiple tops or obvious signs of rot and deteriorations. Additionally, snags and downed logs can be created, as necessary, using mechanical logging equipment by reaching up and cutting trees as high as the machine can reach, enlisting the help of tree climbers, or by girdling individual trees with chainsaws. Lastly, nonmerchantable log sections can be redistributed

Wildlife habitat piles can be made by stacking unsellable logs and tree branches in a pile that is roughly ten feet across and six feet tall.

throughout the forest during thinning or logging activities.

Table 17-1, based on Natural Resources Conservation Service guidelines, provides minimum targets for naturally or manually created habitat structures. Additional habitat structures can be created as desired or to meet specific wildlife recruitment objectives.

Wildlife Habitat Piles

Wildlife habitat piles can be created to provide some of the same functions as large downed logs, dense brush thickets, and even toppled tree crowns. Wildlife habitat piles are typically built from either branches or small-diameter trees removed while thinning overstocked stands. Dimensions of the pile should be a minimum of ten feet across the base by six feet tall. Larger poles are placed on the ground in at least two to three layers laid perpendicular to each other, then branches and finer slash are laid on top.

Habitat Logs

In the absence of naturally occurring logs, manually placed habitat logs provide an immediate opportunity to create an important forest habitat structure until natural recruitment can sustain a constant influx of dead wood onto the forest floor. Over time, logs will decay, and additional natural or manual recruitment will be necessary to ensure continued supply. Habitat logs can be constructed in a managed stand by either distributing nonmerchantable logs during the logging process or using smaller-diameter logs obtained during pre-commercial thinning activities and stacking them parallel to each other. Constructed logs should be a minimum of twenty feet long with a minimum diameter of twelve inches. Habitat value is improved when logs retain some limbs and bark.

Bird and Bat Nesting Boxes

The best way to provide nesting opportunities for cavity-dependent bird species is by retaining and recruiting snags and large, old decadent trees. However, if adequate trees do not exist in your forest yet, you can install nesting boxes. Consult your local Audubon Society or conservation district as to the local bird or bat species that will most benefit from artificial nesting boxes and suggested design specifications.

AQUATIC HABITAT MANAGEMENT

Both riparian and upland forests regulate many of the processes that affect watershed hydrology, including water quantity and quality. Riparian forests are often associated with six key ecological functions: shade, bank stabilization, dead wood that adds structure to streams, nutrient input, sediment and nutrient filtration, and streamflow regulation (see Chapter 6). If you have streams or wetlands on your land, the first question you should ask yourself is whether the forests adjacent to them are providing all six riparian functions. If not, then seeking to remedy this in either the short or long term should be your first objective.

As you develop a familiarity and appreciation for aquatic habitat, you will quickly begin to see what influence your forest and your forest management activities have on this kind of habitat, with the biggest influence coming from within approximately two hundred feet of the streambank. For instance, if riparian forests have been cleared, there may be a deficit of wood within the stream channel; the channel may be deeply scoured, or incised; and streamflow during storm events may have an extremely high velocity that can negatively affect the habitat suitability of the stream for aquatic organisms, including fish. Structural complexity, again, is the key to healthy stream habitat. Healthy stream channels tend to have sinuosity, accumulations of wood, pools and riffles, and varying substrates along the stream bottom.

The following list includes key activities forest owners can implement to protect or enhance aquatic wildlife habitat:

- Ensure your road drainage systems are working properly and not delivering sediment to streams or wetlands.
- Ensure all stream crossings are properly sized and annually maintained.
- If forest cover is missing or sparse adjacent to streams and wetlands, plant the riparian area with a diversity of hardwoods and conifers.
- Over the long term, promote mature, conifer-dominated forests adjacent to streams and wetlands.
- Avoid the use of heavy equipment or any ground-disturbing activities close to streams or wetlands.

- If woody material is missing or sparse in stream channels, consider adding it. This should be done in coordination with a natural resource agency to ensure wood placement is done correctly and doesn't cause unintended consequences.

Now that I've laid out multiple strategies for improving wildlife habitat and forage in your forest, what about forage options for humans!? Clearly we're an important mammal in forest ecosystems, and I think it's just as important to identify and/or cultivate edible plants for our own consumption. In the next chapter, I'll take you on a journey exploring many of the edible, medicinal, and other useful plants that grow in abundance in Northwest forests.

CHAPTER 18

Foraging in the Forest: Foods, Ethnobotanicals, and Floral Greens

BY KIRK HANSON

Ever since my early twenties, when I was introduced to the concept of permaculture while taking an ecological agriculture class in college, I've had a passion for agroforestry, or the art and science of managing forests in a manner that yields numerous non-timber forest products such as food, medicine, craft materials, floral greens, and more. As I learned about the diversity of intact forest ecosystems and all the ways Indigenous peoples have used forests for millennia to support every facet of their lives, I became deeply impressed with the capacity of forests to provide for the well-being of human stewards, and I began realizing we can cultivate forests for so much more than just timber.

I consider one of my greatest accomplishments as a father is having raised two kids who can recognize most of the common edible plants in the woods. Not that these young humans necessarily relish eating everything that's edible (and they readily point out which plants are palatable versus just edible), but at least they know what's what. I frequently remind them of a quote from an old friend, Michael Pilarski, who is a professional wildcrafter: "Once you know everything that's edible in the woods, it's really hard to starve to death." My kids may challenge that assumption (as I'm sure they would attest that attempting to survive off thimbleberry shoots, miner's lettuce, and stinging nettle is probably a fate worse than a quick death), but Michael's point is a good one. During a foraging class I hosted many years ago, with Michael's assistance we identified more than eighty native plants in the forest that have either edible or medicinal qualities. I'm constantly fascinated that

Harvesting Douglas-fir tips in the spring for use in making tea

both a grocery store and a pharmacy can be found amid nature's abundance.

Over the years I've familiarized myself with the panoply of edible and medicinal plants in my forest. My family harvests several of them on a regular basis, including nettles, Douglas-fir tips, mushrooms, and of course, lots and lots of berries. There is enough structural diversity in my forest (edges, gaps, areas of thin canopy, etc.) that I feel it's capable of producing far more than we could possibly harvest or use, without any need for additional management. Therefore, I haven't adjusted any of my forest management practices solely for the benefit of any specific plant, other than thinning to maintain good tree growth.

FORAGING

The term *foraging* refers to the process of collecting useful plants wherever they are found. Foraging can be as simple as going for a walk in the woods and collecting berries, medicinal plants, mushrooms, or edible greens, and it's one of the most accessible ways to engage with a forest on a more intimate level. Learning just half a dozen edible plants can create a more interactive experience that will have you nibbling your way along.

Successful foraging necessitates positively identifying native plants in their environment and knowing which parts are usable and when to harvest them. One of my favorite books for identifying Northwest native plants and learning about their habitats and human uses is *Plants of the Pacific Northwest Coast* by Jim Pojar and Andy McKinnon. See Resources for a list of additional guides.

Whether foraging for plants within your own forest or on public lands, you must be mindful of overharvesting, and should be judicious and sparing when collecting plants. A good rule of thumb is to never harvest more than one-third of any particular item (e.g., berries, leaves, roots) from a given area. It is also important to understand how a plant both propagates and regrows after harvesting. There are as many ways to harvest a plant that stimulate future growth as there are that stunt it. Various guidelines for the ethical and sustainable harvesting of wild plants can be found online, but most center around sustaining plant communities so they can thrive, reproduce, and express themselves naturally in their environment.

The following list includes some of the edible plants my family routinely forages from our woods:

- Blackberry
- Blue elderberry
- Conifer tips
- Miner's lettuce
- Mushrooms
- Oregon grape
- Osoberry
- Red huckleberry
- Salal
- Salmonberry
- Stinging nettle
- Thimbleberry
- Oxalis

Along with this bevy of tasty treats, we also harvest many other useful products including firewood to heat our home, cottonwood buds for salve, floral greens and garland and wreath materials, landscaping plants, and our annual scrawny and misshapen solstice tree.

WILDCRAFTING

"Wildcrafting" refers to foraging for plants specifically for medicinal purposes and may include processing the plants after harvesting into their medicinal end product. Dried roots, tinctures, teas, powders, and salves are all products of wildcrafted plants, and a full-time wildcrafter can make a living from collecting, processing, and selling wild herbs and plants. Wildcrafting as a hobby has become so popular that there are now troves of resources online and in print on the practice of wildcrafting. As with foraging, there are also guidelines for ethical wildcrafting online (see Resources).

Devil's club (Oplopanax horridus) *is related to ginseng and provides similar medicinal benefits.*

As you begin to research ethnobotany (discussed later in this chapter), you will soon realize that there is at least one part of nearly every native plant that Indigenous peoples use for medicinal purposes. Pojar and McKinnon reference many of the cultural and medicinal uses of native plants, which include all of the plants I listed above, as well as western redcedar bark, cascara, devil's club, Douglas hawthorn, usnea, camas, and many more.

FOREST FARMING

"Forest farming" refers to the intentional cultivation of the various layers of a forest's canopy in order to produce a variety of products. Practices can range from simply clearing competing vegetation away from preferred plant species, to propagating particular plants to increase their abundance, to designing, planting, and cultivating small groupings of trees or shrubs. Forest farming may also include creating gaps in the canopy to support various sun-preferring shrub species.

Cultural research in British Columbia has shown that Indigenous peoples deliberately planted patches of fruit trees and berry bushes in the forests surrounding their settlements more than 150 years ago. These were some of the first "forest gardens" to be identified outside the tropics, and it shows that people were intentionally cultivating forests, beyond the use of fire, in the Pacific Northwest.

Products of forest farming can include mushrooms, berries, herbs, timber, honey and maple syrup, nursery plants, value-added crafts, and more. The following practices are examples of forest farming:

- Growing mushrooms in stumps, on logs, and in wood chip beds
- Cultivating edible berries along trails and driveways or edges of the forest
- Transplanting or propagating native nursery plants
- Coppicing, or intentionally sprouting stumps for small-diameter wood

Alder into Shiitake

Many years ago I decided to try "high stumping" alder to grow shiitake mushrooms. High stumping is the act of cutting a tree approximately four feet from the ground and leaving the stump intact. The idea is that, by remaining intact, the stump will continue to wick moisture into it, thereby supporting the growth of the introduced mycelium. This is an alternative to cutting and inoculating poles and manually keeping them moist throughout the year. In my case, I cut half a dozen six- to eight-inch-diameter-at-breast-height alder four feet high along the northern edge of a forest (shady environment). I inoculated the alder stumps with a combination of plugs and sawdust spawn. After about twelve months, the stumps began producing flushes of mushrooms twice a year, and continued this production for about seven years! Eventually the stumps became so rotten they could no longer provide a proper medium for continued shiitake production, but I still consider this my most successful and intriguing forest farming project.

- Managing for high-value firewood
- Thinning to produce higher-quality timber products
- Planting groupings of medicinal plants to increase their abundance
- Thinning the forest overstory to promote berry production in the understory
- Harvesting floral greens in a manner that induces reproductive growth
- Tapping bigleaf maple trees for syrup production

Most small woodland owners will have a sufficient volume of non-timber forest products for personal use or to supply a small side business. However, if you own more than fifty acres, you may have enough plant materials (e.g., cascara, floral greens, and mushrooms) to attract the attention of a commercial harvester. Some small woodland owners collaborate (e.g., the Oregon Woodland Cooperative) in order to have the scale of materials of a larger landowner, and to share in the value-added manufacturing and marketing costs.

COMMERCIAL HARVESTING OF NON-TIMBER FOREST PRODUCTS

Non-timber forest products represent a multimillion-dollar industry in the Pacific Northwest, and many native plants are routinely harvested and sold to domestic and international markets. You may or may not have noticed that the floral bouquet you recently bought included salal, sword fern, and beargrass as a backdrop and complement to the flowers that otherwise caught your eye. Evergreen boughs are also

harvested by the semitruck load to make wreaths and garlands during the holiday season. Here is a list of the most commercially sought-after non-timber forest products in Northwest forests:

- Beargrass
- Cascara
- Edible mushrooms
- Evergreen boughs: cedar, noble fir, and silver fir
- Evergreen huckleberry
- Salal
- Sword fern

I'm often asked by small woodland owners what the opportunity is for selling these kinds of products from their own land. In order to attract the attention of a commercial harvester, scale is important. It's hard to estimate precisely the minimum number of acres that are necessary to yield a commercially viable crop of any particular product as it depends on its quality and quantity. However, if pressed to provide a number, I'm inclined to say that you need at least fifty to one hundred acres of high-quality sword fern, salal, or other non-timber forest products to appeal to a commercial harvester.

On my family's land near Bucoda, we have a robust population of cascara, many of which are quite large for the species, with diameters in the six- to eight-inch range and—thirty to forty feet tall. A couple of years ago, I invited a contractor to harvest the cascara bark, which is a natural laxative. A crew of about six fellows worked for several days and harvested a little over five thousand pounds of bark. At $0.05 per pound, I earned a meager $268. Although this wasn't even enough to pay for the annual taxes on my land, I felt good that I provided an alternative forest-based job opportunity, and hoped that the harvesters earned a decent wage for their labors. Cascara coppices when cut, so it will naturally regenerate and be available for harvesting again in the future.

For a client near Ashford, Washington, Northwest Natural Resource Group man-

Cascara bark is stripped from trees in a family forest near Bucoda, Washington.

aged an innovative harvest of evergreen boughs in 2021. After pre-commercially thinning sixty acres of noble and silver fir, we hired a contractor to come in and harvest the boughs from the trees that were cut. This both made optimal use of a resource and made it easier for the bough harvesters to collect the boughs as the material was at ground level. The sale of the boughs generated $17,000—almost enough to pay for the pre-commercial thinning of the trees.

Most non-timber forest products companies are willing to send a representative out to take a look at your woods and let you know if you have both the quantity and quality of products they're interested in. If your forest has a dense understory of sword fern or evergreen huckleberry, or if you are planning to harvest cedar trees, or if you have an abundance of cascara that are competing with other preferable trees, then it may be worthwhile to have a contractor harvest these materials and provide you with a dividend check. If nothing else, the process is fun and provides a view into a side of the forest industry that few people are aware of.

ETHNOBOTANY

The study of human uses of plants is referred to as "ethnobotany." Indigenous peoples have a use for and have relied on nearly every native plant throughout our region. Early settlers learned many skills and uses of the forest from American Indians, and also brought with them their own cultural understandings of plants. Today there are innumerable books and websites dedicated to documenting and disseminating information on ethnobotany. My curiosity about this subject took hold when I was quite young. My family traveled extensively throughout the state I grew up in, Minnesota, home to many American Indian communities. We visited the cultural centers of these communities, and I was always fascinated by the many ways they utilized the products of their environment.

Whether or not you ever harvest cedar bark to make clothing or a hat, slow cook camas bulbs in a pit, or weave baskets from grasses or pine needles, the study of ethnobotany reveals a world of uses for native plants that most of us have never recognized. From this realization can flow a greater appreciation of their conservation value. Cedar, such a staple of life for the Indigenous peoples of the Northwest, has become an underrepresented tree in the forests of our region; including it in your planting mix (if your site will support cedar in the long term) can help restore this iconic and sacred tree. Thinning your forest to allow more light to support berry production, planting paper birch on wet soils or roses on dry soils, and avoiding disturbing patches of devil's club when operating in the woods are mindful stewardship practices that both enhance the biodiversity of your forest and conserve or restore plants that have significant traditional value. Such practices also help ensure the perpetuation of these important plant species while increasing the range of useful

Chanterelle mushrooms (Cantharellus *spp.*) are a common edible mushroom in Northwest forests that are collected commercially and sold at grocery stores and roadside stands.

plants in your forest. In the next section, I describe one such example.

ETHNOBOTANICAL AGROFORESTRY

The federally funded Conservation Stewardship Program (CSP) provides funding to rural landowners across the nation to support a wide range of conservation practices. The program is funded by the Farm Bill and managed by the Natural Resources Conservation Service. One of the more interesting practices the CSP funds is cultural plantings. The US Department of Agriculture defines cultural plantings as "trees and shrubs that are of cultural significance, such as those species utilized by Tribes

Table 18-1: Some Native Plants of Cultural Significance to American Indians

SPECIES	CULTURAL SIGNIFICANCE
Cedar, red	Shelter, clothing, baskets, and tools
Douglas-fir	Shelter, crafts, tools, and medicine
White pine	Food and medicine
Birch, paper	Food, baskets, and fuel
Oak, Oregon	Food and medicine
Currant, red flowering	Food and medicine
Blue elderberry	Food and medicine
Hazelnut, beaked	Food and tools
Evergreen huckleberry	Food
Oregon grape	Food and medicine
Roses, native	Food and medicine
Salal	Food and medicine
Blackberry	Food and medicine
Mock orange	Tools
Thimbleberry	Food
Salmonberry	Food and medicine
Carex	Baskets
Sword fern	Food and medicine

in traditional practices, medicinal plants, species used in basket-making, etc." The guidelines for this conservation practice also include a list of plants known to have cultural significance to American Indians in Washington State.

I decided to apply to CSP in order to convert a one-acre area of marginal field on my land to an ethnobotanical agroforestry plantation. When I first began researching plants to include, it quickly struck me that I would be hard-pressed to identify a native plant that did not have some value to Indigenous peoples of the Northwest. Would I then just be planting a native forest not dissimilar to the one already growing on my land? I wanted to have some kind of creative twist to this project, so here's what I settled on.

The plantation is designed to mimic the structure of the edge of a forest (see Figure 18-1), graduating from tall hardwoods and conifers to low trees, shrubs, and then groundcovers. Each species was planted in groups to aid in both maintenance and future harvest. The following criteria were used to select the plant species:

- Could I propagate existing plants in my forest to increase their abundance?
- Were seedlings already available in my forest that I could transplant?
- Were there species I could introduce that didn't occur on my land?
- Could I find plants that were suitable to the site I had in mind?
- Do the plants produce something that I actually expect to use: food, medicine, wood, or something else?

Figure 18-1. The structure of a forest edge as it graduates from groundcovers, to shrubs, to low trees, to tall canopy trees.

Table 18-1 lists the trees and shrubs I chose to plant, along with their cultural significance to American Indians.

As you consider planting trees and shrubs on your land, I encourage you to think about how to make any planting serve more than one purpose. It's not hard to choose plants that have multiple purposes, as most do once you learn their ecological functions, pharmacological benefits, ethnobotanical uses, and economic values. However, you don't have to go to great effort to design and install an agroforestry plantation in order to enjoy the abundance of nature. As I've revealed in this chapter, your forest is already a cornucopia of foods, medicines, and goods. Simply taking the time to learn more about the plants that thrive out your back door will bring you into a closer relationship with your land and forest.

CHAPTER 19

Harvest Planning and Management

BY SETH ZUCKERMAN

Abasic premise of ecological forestry is that forests aren't just for timber, but that doesn't mean ignoring their timber value entirely. Land ownership and stewardship cost money, and logs can be one of the most financially valuable outputs of your forest. As you have seen in earlier chapters, it is possible and even profitable to remove trees that would die anyway or interfere with the forest's healthy development. If financial return is among your objectives in owning a forest, you're going to want to understand how to plan and execute a timber harvest.

But how? Cutting timber is a specialized activity. Practitioners of forestry are at a disadvantage compared with, say, market gardeners, because the products of timber harvest are heavy to lift and require specialized skill and equipment to cut down and transport safely. What's more, it's highly regulated, because logging done poorly can leave lasting scars on the land and the streams flowing through it.

By the time you finish this chapter, you will know the crucial decisions you need to make to set a timber harvest in motion, and you'll have a good idea of the resources you can turn to for help in doing so. You will likely enlist the help of a professional forester to manage the harvest, but even so, it pays to understand the implications of the key forks in the road that await you.

Chances are that by the time you consider logging, you are relying on a well-thought-out management plan that cues you when to log each stand of timber in your forest and what kind of treatment is appropriate. Here are some examples:

- A thinning from below that is focused on improving the quality of the trees that are not cut

OPPOSITE: *Marking a tree to be cut in a thinning operation*

A consulting forester can make it easier to obtain your logging permit, find a suitable logger, and market the logs from your harvest.

- A variable density thinning across the diameters to allow trees more growing space
- A thinning of dominant or codominant trees to release smaller trees in their shade
- A regeneration harvest that prepares the bulk of the site to establish a new cohort of trees while preserving some older trees as a legacy to the next generation

You may already have a road map for what you are trying to accomplish with the harvest. You may also have a sense of the annual allowable cut level in your forest, giving you a metric for the volume of timber you can cut, on average, per year while still ensuring that you're growing at least as much timber as you harvest.

The first time you undertake a timber harvest, it's especially worthwhile to have a consulting forester manage the process. This person can connect you with timber operators who will do a quality job and will have a sense of the log markets for your timber. If you are working around streams, sensitive areas, or steep slopes within the harvest unit, you will benefit from a forester's eye in steering clear of trouble spots. After you have been through the process once, you can decide whether you want to try your hand at coordinating it, but a close view might convince you to leave it to someone more skilled and experienced.

Scale is another threshold question. If you are thinning your forest, cutting fewer than eight to ten acres likely won't return enough revenue to pay for the operation, unless the timber is large or valuable. For regeneration harvests, which return more revenue per acre and are less complex to lay out, that threshold can be as low as a couple of acres depending on timber value.

SETTING OBJECTIVES AND EXPECTATIONS

First, review the kind of harvest you are planning, how it achieves your management objectives, and how it aims to advance the forest's development. Then take a quick reality check about what it might mean for you financially. If it's a first-entry thinning in a thirty- to thirty-five-year-old stand, your financial return will be modest at best, because the value of the logs will be low and costs will be high. In this scenario, though your immediate financial return will be minimal, you could receive big gains in future timber growth and forest health. This sort of thinning is primarily a stand improvement that will approximately pay for itself and set your forest on a trajectory to achieve the future condition you desire for it. The older and larger the trees you thin, the more return you can anticipate.

To get a rough handle on the volume and value of timber you're considering harvesting, here are a few rules of thumb for forests west of the Cascades:

- A first-entry thinning will probably produce about one truckload of logs per acre, or roughly 4,000 board feet. A third to a half of that will be pulpwood, which you will likely have to trade to the logger simply for the service of removing it, since the price of pulp tends to barely cover the cost of getting the logs from the woods to the chipping yard.
- A second-entry thinning that is still aimed at stand improvement will likely yield about 7,000 to 12,000 board feet per the acre.

With a very rough sense of log volume, next consider the state of log markets. To get a current bearing on log prices, you can browse your way to the Washington Department of Natural Resources monthly log price report, which is broken out by species

and region. Although there are differences between Oregon and Washington and within regions of the Northwest, log prices rise and fall on similar macroeconomic tides, so you can determine whether you would be selling your logs into a hot or cold market (absent a local disruption such as a windstorm or wildfire that affects log availability).

You'll see from those price tables that there is a wide spread between the value of the best and worst logs. Western redcedar is usually the most prized species, while cottonwood is the least sought after. Even within a single species, though, the cheapest grade of log will often fetch 40 or 50 percent less than the most valuable. So you can't get a sense of the actual value of your logs without getting an expert opinion from a forester or a log buyer from a local mill. Some buyers might be willing to visit the site of a prospective timber sale, particularly if invited by a logger or consulting forester with whom they have worked before.

In a first-entry thinning, your primary goal should be forest health, not revenue, so time your harvest to keep the forest from stagnating, not to maximize revenue. Beyond that, for stands forty years and up, timing log markets is just as difficult as timing the stock market. You would do well to avoid logging during a housing bust, when prices will be low, but otherwise let the state of the forest be your guide. Waiting for prices to peak can be a fool's errand, since loggers are hardest to come by during a hot log market.

From crudest to finest, here are the types of markets where your logs can wind up:

Pulp. Chip yards are the least picky about the quality of the logs. They will take

Estimating Potential Harvest

In Chapter 10, we introduced a formula for an extremely rough approximation of standing softwood (conifer) timber volume per acre: the basal area (in square feet per acre) times the average height of the trees (in feet), times 1.5. Basal area is the cross-sectional area of the tree trunks at breast height. You might recognize this formula as a cousin of the one you learned in geometry class for the volume of a cone. Estimating the potential timber takes into account the conversion of cubic feet to board feet, and the volume lost to chips, sawdust, and bark. For example, let's say the basal area of the stand is 220 square feet per acre (equivalent to 160 sixteen-inch-diameter trees per acre). If the average tree height is 100 feet, then the volume estimate would be $220 \times 100 \times 1.5 = 33{,}000$ board feet per acre. Continuing this back-of-the-envelope estimate, a thinning might remove 30 to 40 percent of the volume, so this site would yield 10,000 to 13,000 board feet per acre.

logs whose diameter at the small end is as little as two inches. As you'd expect, these yards pay the least, in a price reckoned by the ton.

Chip-n-saw. The very smallest logs that can be made into lumber, the chip-n-saw sort go to a mill where the outside of the logs is rendered into chips, leaving a core that is sawn into boards. Like pulpwood, this is sold by the ton. This sort is also sometimes referred to as studwood.

Sawlogs. These logs are debarked and then sawn into boards. The value is determined by species and the grade of the log—how straight, the size and number of knots, and the diameter and length of the log. The logs are scaled (a measurement of volume) according to their length and the diameter of the small end, using the Scribner log scale, which has been a regional standard since the nineteenth century. Saw technology has advanced substantially since the Scribner scaling tables were developed, so lumber mills routinely produce one and a

half or even two times the lumber from a log as its Scribner scale. Those bonus board feet, known as "overrun," are factored into log prices.

Veneer. These logs will be steamed to soften them and then spun on a lathe where they are peeled into strips of veneer. Depending on its quality, the veneer can be used in the interior or exterior ply of plywood, in laminated veneer lumber, or in fine cabinetry. Certain high-quality veneers are sliced from chunks of the log, instead of the entire cylindrical log, to achieve a desirable grain pattern.

Export. Some logs, especially larger spruce and Douglas-fir with tight rings, are valued more in Japan and Korea than they are in the United States. At times, China is also an eager buyer. Savvy log sellers can get high prices from log exporters, who then send the logs by cargo ship to East Asia.

Poles. Wooden utility poles also pay some of the highest prices per thousand board feet, in return for meeting some very demanding specifications of length, straightness, and taper. Even though these logs will not be sawn into boards, but rather just debarked and treated with preservatives, they are still scaled by the Scribner board foot to provide a comparable price quote.

Sort yards. These are useful markets for small harvests, which may not produce a full truckload of the highest log grades. A sort yard will buy mixed loads and sell each log for its highest and best use.

Naturally, you won't pocket the entire gross value of the logs when they get to the mill. You'll have to pay a logger to cut them down, limb them, buck them to log lengths, and load them onto a truck. You'll need to pay timber tax, a permitting fee in Washington State, and the consulting forester, if you hire one. Logging and hauling will likely cost 50 to 70 percent of the gross for thinning jobs, depending on the distance to the mill and the size of the trees, and considerably less for a regeneration harvest. Loggers also need to take into account the cost of moving their equipment to your land and then on to the next job. If your job is small, that fixed cost is spread over fewer loads of logs. The amount you have left over after logging and hauling costs is known as the "stumpage," the net value to you as a timber grower. It can also be thought of as the amount a log buyer would pay you for the right to harvest the timber from your land.

The size of the logs will affect the cost too, as will the difficulty of the terrain. If the volume to be logged will be made up primarily of trees ten inches or less in diameter at breast height, that will drive up the cost, since the logger will have to handle more of them to fill a truckload of logs. On slopes steeper than about 40 percent, the need to use tethered or cable-yarding equipment will increase costs, shrink the pool of properly equipped loggers, and reduce profitability.

The extension services in both Oregon and Washington offer terrific resources for small landowners considering a timber harvest (see Resources). In the remainder of this chapter, I offer some additional considerations as you contemplate a timber harvest from your forest.

STAYING WITHIN THE LAW

Timber harvest regulation is handled very differently in Oregon than in Washington. In Oregon, it is your responsibility to notify the state Department of Forestry (ODF) at least fifteen days before you intend to harvest, but no prior review of your plan is required unless ODF decides it wants one. In Washington, you must file a Forest Practices Application with the Department of Natural Resources, which then has thirty days to decide whether to approve it, and may require a visit to verify that you have accurately characterized the conditions on your site, such as slopes, erosion hazard, and the types of streams traversing the land. If you hire a consulting forester, they would take care of filling out the application, but you still need to sign and submit it as the landowner.

If your forest borders residential lots or if you are planning to build on your property after logging, you may need to get an additional permit from your county before harvest. Your county planning department or consulting forester can guide you.

MARKING HARVEST BOUNDARIES AND TREES TO BE CUT

It isn't enough to delineate your harvest plans on a map; they need to appear in the forest itself. The boundaries of the harvest units need to be marked with colored flagging (or paint) that the loggers can easily see. If any of those boundaries are also a property line, you may want to undertake a professional survey to establish the line. Alternatively, you can discuss your plans with your neighbor and reach a *cutting line agreement*, which stipulates that for the purposes of this timber harvest, you have agreed where the property lines are without creating the legal presumption of their exact location. Especially for a thinning, you also might consider leaving a buffer from the property line in cases where the exact

line is not marked but its approximate location is known—this can often be more cost-effective than hiring a surveyor to establish the exact boundary.

Any setbacks from streams and wetlands need to be flagged at this stage as well. Every state's forest practice rules categorize streams by whether fish live in them, or secondarily, whether they flow year-round. Each category of stream and certain other features such as springs and seeps are entitled to a minimum buffer to maintain shade and bank stability. You need to know those rules and flag the edge of the timber harvest boundary so it can be seen by loggers—and by regulators, should they wish to check your work.

Your logging permit will have required you to spell out where landings will be located and which roads will be used for

Table 19-1: Logging Systems and Equipment

	HAND-FALLING	WHOLE-TREE HARVESTING	CUT-TO-LENGTH
Trees are cut by . . .	Handheld chainsaw	Feller buncher	Harvester
Trees are limbed by . . .	Handheld chainsaw in woods for small jobs; by delimber or processor on the landing for larger ones	Processor at the landing	Harvester
Trunks are cut into logs by . . .	Handheld chainsaw in woods for small jobs; by processor or handheld chainsaw at the landing for larger ones	Processor at the landing	Harvester
Timber is hauled to the landing by . . .	Skidder or shovel; cable yarder on steep ground; tractor with log arch in very small-scale operations	Skidder or, on steep ground, a cable yarder	Forwarder (usually) or skidder; on steep ground, a cable yarder

trucking the logs to market. In addition, you may designate corridors for skid trails or, depending on your experience with the logger and the advice of your consulting forester, trust the logger's judgment of where to put them. This is your chance to consider road improvements as well, since loggers will bring heavy equipment to the site. Review your findings from Chapter 9 about culverts that need upgrading or areas that need repair.

Finally, your prescription—the instructions of which trees to cut—needs to be clear on the ground. If you are thinning, it is common to mark the trees to be cut with a slash of paint on at least two sides of the tree and a spot at the base. (That way, after harvest, you can check that all the stumps created were from trees that were meant to be cut.) You have the option of deciding to mark every single tree that you mean to have cut, and that's a good idea in older stands when each tree cut is the product of a careful judgment call. In a first-entry thinning, however, that can become tedious since there are so many stems to remove. In that case, if you trust the logger, you can mark a sample acre or two, and then check the logger's work to make sure they are following your guidelines. If you work with a consulting forester, one way of keeping costs down is to avoid having them perform a full mark. You can either content yourself with a sample mark, or you can ask them to orient you so that you can mark the bulk of the stand yourself.

If, instead, you are planning to create an opening—whether it is a patch cut to eliminate a root rot pocket or a larger variable retention harvest—you need to clearly mark the edge of the area you plan to cut. You can either mark every tree to be removed or mark the perimeter of that gap-to-be with paint or flagging (harder to attach, but easier to remove from any trees you are marking to be left). However you do it, it's essential to have clear communication with the loggers about how the gaps and leave trees are marked.

FINDING AND HIRING A LOGGER

If you are working with a consulting forester, they will be able to connect you with logging contractors whom they collaborate with on a regular basis. Otherwise, as with any other skilled trade, ask neighbors for recommendations and ask potential contractors to provide references from prior customers.

Logging equipment is powerful, and it can do an impressive degree of damage to the land and the forest if not used carefully. That's why you will want to make sure your contract with the logger spells out some key provisions to protect you. (Even if you have hired a forester, the logging contract will be made between you and the logger.)

The logger should carry a robust form of insurance known as a logger's broad form, which covers the full gamut of things that can go wrong in a logging operation. Make sure the logger provides a certificate of insurance that names you as an additional insured, which will make it easier for you to recover any damages directly from their insurer, instead of having to first demand it from the logger.

Discuss with the logger (and your forester, if you have one) the specific equipment they will use. Ask them to bring their

TOP: *Most timber harvesting in the Pacific Northwest is done with the help of mechanized equipment like this harvester, which cuts trees, delimbs them, and cuts them into logs.* BOTTOM: *Skidders haul logs or even whole trees to the landing to be processed and shipped.*

paction than a larger tracked machine that can spread the machine's weight across a bigger footprint.

There are three basic kinds of logging systems (see Table 19-1). The choice for your job will depend on the terrain, the size of the trees, the scale of the operation, and the availability of contractors with that equipment-set in your area. Hybrid systems are also used, such as harvesters or feller bunchers that work on steep ground with the help of a wire-rope tether that steadies them on the slope.

The contract should also include provisions that allow you or your forester to pull the plug on the operation if weather conditions deteriorate (for instance, if the ground gets so wet that driving the logging equipment around will compact the soil and leave big ruts in the ground), or if the loggers are doing too much damage to the leave trees. Small dings in the trees' bark are unavoidable, but if they are too large to cover with a hardhat, that's a more significant wound that can affect the tree's future growth or allow it to become infected.

The logger will want to tour the site to determine how to price their services. (If a

smallest equipment that can do the job. All else being equal, larger equipment will leave a heavier mark. But that mark doesn't entirely correlate with size: a small, rubber-tired skidder may cause more soil com-

logging outfit provides a price without visiting your forest, that's probably an outfit to avoid.) Some loggers prefer to set a price according to the weight of the wood loaded on board the truck (OBT). To evaluate what that is worth to you, make allowance for the cost of trucking, and convert their per-ton cost to an approximate price per MBF by multiplying by 8 for small sawlogs or 7 for larger ones. (So $40 per ton equals $280 to $320 per MBF.) Other loggers will evaluate the mixture of log grades and name a percentage of the gross as their price, sometimes after a deduction for trucking ("with trucking off the top"). The advantage of this system is that it gives the logger the same incentive you have: to manufacture the highest-grade logs out of the trees they cut down, even if it takes more time and thought to set aside a stack of logs for utility poles at the landing, for instance, leading to higher net income for you and the logger.

As a practitioner of ecological forestry, you might want to ask the logger to do some things that aren't aimed at shipping logs. For instance, depending on their equipment, the logger may be able to turn some trees that wouldn't make good timber into snags by cutting off a tree as high as the machine can reach. (That's different from preexisting snags, which become a hazard as they age, so if the logger wants to cut one down for safety, you need to trust their judgment.) If you're lucky enough to have large downed logs or standing legacy trees that are providing important structure for forest habitat, talk to your logger about keeping them intact, and flag buffers around them to make them visible. It's harder to get a good

Using a feller-buncher, a logger can grab onto a tree, cut it off at its base, and lay it down where a skidder can haul it to the landing, branches and all.

360-degree view from the cab of a skidder than you might think.

The logger's site tour would be the time to mention any other constraints of the site—for instance, if you access your forest through a private road that you share with neighbors who use it to commute at specific times. You will also want to make sure the contract specifies how the logging slash will be treated and whether there are seasonal constraints (e.g., to avoid bird-nesting season). The contract should include clauses allowing for cancellation or renegotiation of rates if timber prices fall dramatically as well as an expiration date, and should give you the right to cancel the job if it hasn't started by a certain date. You'd do well to require that the equipment be cleaned before it arrives, so as not to introduce invasive species to your site.

That said, the contract should also provide a reasonable window for the logger to start the project. It would be lovely to live in a world where logging operations proceeded exactly according to their planned

Goods from Your Woods

Harvesting the surplus trees from your forest doesn't necessarily mean selling them to a lumber mill. With some basic tools, you can turn them into useful products yourself. Here are a few possibilities, starting with the simplest options.

FIREWOOD
Cut the wood to a length that will easily fit into your stove, hearth, or fire pit. Stack or pile it to season (dry out) so that the wood burns cleanly and easily—a process that will take from six to eighteen months, depending on your climate and the species. Split larger rounds (over six or eight inches) with a splitting maul or, for larger quantities, a log splitter. A splitting wedge is helpful for knotty pieces or those with curly grain.

CAMP STOOLS
Nothing says "rustic" like sitting on a hefty round of wood. If you're wearing nice pants, beware of the pitch that oozes from most freshly cut conifer rounds.

POLES
You can use these in all manner of artisanal construction, from table legs to garden sheds. The poles will last longer if you peel them—a process that's best done soon after they've been cut as it gets more difficult as the wood dries . You'll need a drawknife to remove the bark cleanly most of the year, but if you cut your poles in the spring when the sap has just started to run, the bark is loose and will peel off by hand or with a little encouragement from a pocket knife.

BOARDS
All manner of jigs are available that can turn a chainsaw into a slow and labor-intensive sawmill. The basic principle is to attach a frame to the log to guide the saw in creating the first flat edge, and then run the saw through the log repeatedly to manufacture one board at a time. If you have the patience, it's a rewarding way to turn your own logs into actual lumber.

For larger quantities, most forested areas have small-scale sawyers who will bring a portable mill to your land and make lumber—typically for an hourly fee, but occasionally by the board-foot or for a share of the product.

You will need mechanical assistance to extricate larger logs from the surrounding forest. Although a truck-mounted winch might suffice for short distances, longer distances require a brilliant invention called a log arch, which suspends one end of the log so that an ATV or tractor can drag it through the woods and out to the portable mill.

schedule. However, harvest equipment is prone to breakdowns, which in turn cause delays even beyond the routine underestimation of how long a job will take. So don't be surprised if your logger has to revise their planned start date because they fell behind on the previous job, or they are repairing a hydraulic hose or computer controller. By the same token, the logger will give you their best estimate of how long your harvest will take, but you would do well to bring some patience if they take a few weeks longer than projected. The key is to establish good communication and a mutually respectful working relationship.

Drone's-eye view of a logger trimming the butt end of a recently felled tree

The season when you schedule your logging will depend first on the site, and then on the availability of operators. Some soils get too mucky and are too easily compacted by heavy equipment to be logged in the wet season; others may be accessible by unsurfaced roads that can only be used when dry. If your site is well drained and relatively flat, then you can consider doing it during the rainy season, which may make it easier to line up a logger, but heightened vigilance will be required (see "Managing the Harvest," later in this chapter) to make sure that they aren't tearing up the ground too much. Be wary of thinning in the spring when the sap is flowing abundantly and the bark is soft—that's a time of year when the remaining trees are most prone to damage from scraping or rubbing.

MARKETING YOUR LOGS

Logs are a perishable product. You don't want to start cutting timber until you have a firm agreement from a mill to purchase them. While you can shop your upcoming harvest around to mills yourself, the logger you've hired and your consulting forester (if you have one) are apt to have better connections with log buyers at local mills and can speak their language confidently and credibly in terms of log quality and quantity. How local of a mill should you choose?

Log hauling is costly, and it rarely makes economic sense to haul logs more than an hour and a half away. On the west side of the Cascades, that will usually encompass at least a couple of sawmills and as many as half a dozen; on the east side, mills are spaced much farther apart, and some forests are too far from any mills or log yards to support a viable commercial harvest, especially of the less valuable species.

Depending on the trees you plan to harvest, you (or your forester or logger) may peddle your logs to several mills. Most mills deal only in hardwood or softwood but not both. Some prefer whitewoods (including western hemlock and true firs), while others are interested only in Douglas-fir. Export yards pay a premium for high-quality logs over twenty inches, while others won't take anything larger than thirty-two inches at the butt end. Because of mill optimization, the largest logs may not fetch the highest prices per thousand board feet from some buyers. For example, at highly automated small-log mills, logs over twenty inches in diameter at the small end can be worth less per thousand board feet than logs that are twelve to nineteen inches in diameter. You'll want to compare the price each mill can offer, along with the cost of hauling to that mill, to determine which is the best option.

Once you settle on a place to ship your logs, you or your forester can request a purchase order from the mill, which will spell out the initial price (which may change in subsequent months) and the quantity they are prepared to accept. The purchase order will also direct the mill to pay some of the proceeds directly to the logger, perhaps some to the trucker, and the rest to you (or possibly to your forester on your behalf). The benefit of directing the timber proceeds to flow through your forester's account is that they can verify that all loads are being paid for at the agreed-upon rates. Some mills will request that you sign a purchase order with payment details listed on it, while others will simply send a price sheet and forgo a purchase order altogether. Either way, you'll want to make sure that you or your forester is clear with the mill when explaining how revenue should be divided and where it should be sent.

Now you are ready to welcome the logger and their crew to your site.

MANAGING THE HARVEST

Your consulting forester (or you, in a do-it-yourself job) should have a pre-work meeting at the site with the timber operators before they start cutting. You'll want to be sure that the loggers understand the prescription and know what the different colors of flagging and paint signify (riparian buffer, unit boundary, edge of gap, etc.). Make sure that the expectations are clear all around.

Then, once the project begins, you'll want an informed observer—either you or your consulting forester—to monitor the operation at least once a week, and possibly more often at the beginning of the job, to make sure the loggers are staying out of marked riparian buffers, following the mark, and generally sticking to the contract. You may have to steel yourself for what your woods will look like in the midst of harvest. There's no way to make a forest look pristine while it's being thinned.

Heavy equipment driving through the forest on skid trails will trample the undergrowth and possibly tear up the ground, but the shrub layer is resilient and will bounce back. Instead, as you monitor the progress of the harvest, keep a close eye on these two particular factors:

Are loggers taking good care of the residual stand? A certain amount of bark scraping is inevitable along the skidding corridors, but ideally most of it is confined to a few rub trees that are designated for that purpose and will be harvested as the operation is winding down. Timber harvest isn't a garden party, so prepare yourself for up to one retained tree in every twenty to have a small amount of bark damage. But don't make this judgment merely from walking along the skid trails. That's where the worst damage will occur, because the cut trees have been dragged along them. Instead, get off the trail and walk into the forest for a more representative sample.

Are roads holding up without significant rutting, and skid trails not getting torn up by the heavy equipment? Be especially vigilant in the case of heavy or prolonged rains, which can turn a decent worksite into a mudpit (that's a technical term). Regardless of conditions, it is helpful to have the loggers distribute the slash onto the skid trails, where it will form a mat that cushions soil from excessive compaction—a phenomenon that skid trails are especially vulnerable to when the ground is wet. Having the skidders or log-hauling equipment driving over the slash will also flatten it so it decomposes more quickly and poses less of a fire hazard.

TRACKING THE PROCEEDS

During harvest, someone has to make sure that all the logs leaving the property are properly paid for. Logs are branded on their ends before they leave the site so it's clear at the mill who should be paid for them. Loggers give each trucker a numbered load ticket that specifies the species, quality, and ownership of the logs; where they are going; and the trucker's name. These tickets are scribbled with ballpoint pens on old-fashioned quadruplicate carbon-copy pads, and serve both as a way to track production from the site and as the basis for payment. At the mill or log yard, the logs are scaled for volume and quality by an impartial, certified third party, and the tallies of the logs of each sort are sent out in batches (between weekly and twice monthly) in a mill receipt.

The forest owner or their representative matches up the mill receipts with the load tickets, to make sure every load is accounted for, and checks to make sure that the agreed-upon prices per thousand board feet were paid and properly split between the logger, the owner, and possibly the trucker as well.

CLOSING OUT THE JOB

The end of a timber harvest is a crucial moment for leaving your forest in good condition. The logger may be eager to move on to their next job, but while you have heavy equipment on-site, make sure the cleanup is done to your satisfaction. The first four items in the following list should be checked off before the logger removes their equipment from the site—a provision that should be required in your contract.

The Firewood Option

Every harvest project creates some logs that fall below the standard for sawlogs. First-entry thinnings have a lot of small-diameter material, but even thinnings in larger stands will produce small logs from treetops, and some pieces are too crooked or scarred to meet quality specifications for sawlogs.

The commercial outlet for these logs is to sell them as pulpwood, and in many logging contracts, the logger gets the full value of the pulp without having to share any of it with the landowner because it can barely pay its way out of the woods.

Instead, consider whether you could sell any of these logs for firewood. You could cut it and split it yourself, or offer it as a work opportunity to someone else. Firewood at $300 a cord translates to over $150 a ton, compared with pulpwood prices that typically range around $35 to $50 per ton. Granted, it takes a lot more work to turn a ton of logs into firewood, but once they are at the landing, the hardest part has already been done. Firewood also can be a good use for the ends of logs that are cut off to avoid butt swell (a phenomenon in logs that is undesirable at the mill) or pistol butt (a sweep in the trunk right where it emerges from the ground).

If you plan to leave significant amounts of pulpwood on the landing to use for firewood, make sure you discuss that with your logger ahead of time, as it might affect their logging price. The logger puts in a lot of work to cut those trees, bring them to the landing, and process them into logs; they will need compensation from you if they divert logs to firewood that they could ordinarily sell for pulp.

- If any rub trees along the skid trails were slated for harvest, make sure they were indeed cut or intentionally left to become snags.
- If the trees were processed at the landing, make sure the slash was hauled back into the forest. If you want to build habitat piles, you might ask the loggers to stockpile some slash for you for that purpose (see Chapter 17). As a last resort, you may want to pile and burn slash that was left behind at the landing when fire danger is past. Check with your local fire agency to obtain the necessary permits.

- If there are logs left over that weren't enough to compose a final truckload, or that aren't designated for firewood production, distribute those in the forest. Almost every forest has a shortage of large, dead wood.
- Make sure the loggers have left the road network's drainage and stream crossings in good shape. Ensure that the water bars and rolling dips across the roads were restored to functionality. If the traffic on the road has worn through the layer of gravel on the all-season roads, the logger can arrange for a delivery (at your cost) and will have the equip-

ment to spread it or at least pack it down.

- Spread non-invasive (or even better, native) grass seed on the landings and on bare spots on the skid trails, to limit erosion, and cover with straw, along with any areas of bare soil that are near streams and could add sediment to the water.

The way you handle slash will depend on your forest's natural fire regime (see Chapter 16). In high-severity, low-frequency fire regimes, the climate is moist enough that simply spreading the slash through the forest is sufficient for it to decay quickly before it poses much of a hazard. In high-frequency, low-severity fire regimes, logging slash can raise fuel loads higher than is comfortable. You might need to treat it more actively, by lopping and scattering the slash to bring it into closer contact with the ground, or by doing some strategic pile burns in the wet season to reduce slash to safe levels. See Chapter 16.

PAYING TAXES

In Washington, a forest excise tax on timber harvests is due quarterly. Nonindustrial forest owners are taxed on the net income from the harvest, after subtracting the cost of hauling, logging, permitting, and sale administration from the selling price of the logs.

In Oregon, a forest products harvest tax is set for each species as a flat rate per thousand board feet, with different rates on either side of the Cascade crest. Small forest owners who don't pay property tax on the value of their timber must pay a severance tax when they harvest it, also reckoned per thousand board feet.

In addition, you may owe other taxes, such as business and occupations tax in Washington, for harvests that exceed a given threshold per year (e.g., $200,000 in 2023). Consult with a tax professional about how to handle the income from logging on your income taxes.

MONITORING THE AFTERMATH AND BEYOND

The first couple of years after a timber harvest, even a thinning, are a bit like the first few days after surgery. It's important to monitor the patient closely to make sure that everything is healing nicely, and to provide extra care if necessary. If you generally visit your forest at least once a year, you'll want to visit at least every season in the first year or two after harvest.

One of the most crucial visits you'll make is at the beginning of the first rainy season after logging (or the first significant rainstorm after logging, if you logged in the winter), which is when road problems will appear. Use the perspectives and techniques from Chapter 9 to address them. If the timber operators did their mop-up work well, any issues that arise should be so minor that they don't require the use of heavy equipment to correct. Still, come prepared to do some shovel work to fine-tune the water bars and rolling dips, and ensure the culverts are open.

Logging inevitably exposes a lot of bare soil, which is a perfect place for invasive species to take root. In the spring and summer following harvest, pay close attention to any new unwanted species. If you catch an infestation when it's small, you stand a better chance of eradicating it entirely. See Chapter 8 for details.

Finally, your harvest may have left you with the opportunity (and possibly the legal requirement) to establish a new generation of trees in your forest. Whether it is replanting a pocket of trees you had to clear because of root rot, reforesting a gap that you created to introduce more age diversity into your forest, or replanting a unit that you logged using variable retention, this is the moment when you set in motion the forest's next decades. Use the practices spelled out in Chapter 12, and take into account the ways a changing climate influences what will thrive there, as described in chapter 22.

The most amazing thing to me about forest thinning is to see how quickly the understory recovers from disturbance. The extra light reaching the forest floor awakens ferns and berry plants, and within a year or two, it should be hard to tell that loggers were ever there, except for the telltale stumps that they leave behind.

CHAPTER 20

We Build the Trail by Walking

BY KIRK HANSON

Two of the three forests my family has acquired over the years had old logging roads, or skid trails, running through them that provided an existing trail network. Most of these skid trails had become overgrown by the time we purchased the land, but I could see their path through the woods, marked by either a conspicuous ribbon of alder, which tends to colonize disturbed soils, or obvious cuts in the slopes of hillsides. Shortly after we acquired our forest near Bucoda, the very first task I set to was reopening these old trails. Days were spent with a brush cutter and chainsaw slowly revealing the paths through the woods. Though arduous, it was tremendously gratifying work, as I could look back on a day's worth of labor in satisfaction and see the winding path I had just liberated from the chaos of shrubs and small trees.

Though they didn't always have an eye for protecting sensitive areas, such as streams and wetlands, the engineers of these old roads had a good eye for the most efficient route between points A and B. Efficiency was paramount, as constructing roads with the equipment they had at the time was very difficult, time consuming, and expensive. Whether it's on my own land or another forest I'm working on, I often find that these old skid trails were laid out in a manner that provides optimal access to all parts of a forest with a minimum footprint. Any impact these roads will have on the soil and hydrology of the forest has already occurred, so in most cases it makes sense to reuse these trails rather than pioneer new ones into the forest. I do occasionally come across old roads that were clearly made by a cowboy who jumped on a dozer and blazed a trail without much creativity or sensitivity to streams, wetlands, or steep slopes; these trails do not lend themselves to long-term use, but they are fairly rare.

A former logging road is reopened by cutting back encroaching brush and trees.

THE VALUE OF TRAILS

A thoughtfully laid-out trail system is an essential asset to any forest that will receive regular attention—whether actively managed, visited for recreational purposes, or both. Before you either begin to reopen an old or existing trail system, or carve a new one into the forest, you should articulate the reasons why you want a trail. Consider the following questions:

- What functions do you need a trail system to perform?
- Will the trails be used for light recreational use, or do you need to get vehicles, such as a tractor or an ATV, into the woods for ongoing maintenance and management activities?
- Will the trail be used occasionally, perhaps just a few times each year, and therefore be of minimal design and maintenance, or will it be routinely used—daily or weekly—and warrant more work to establish and maintain?
- Will a trail aid with monitoring your forest, gain access to points of interest, or support security and surveillance of your property?
- Will a trail improve your ability to harvest non-timber forest products, or give you an opportunity to cultivate special or useful plants along its margins?

Once you have these questions answered, you can start planning.

PLANNING TRAILS

The fun thing about planning trails is that they can go practically anywhere you want. As long as they don't cause erosion or impact sensitive areas, such as wetlands or streams, trails can go anywhere your imagination fancies. That being said, here are some guidelines to help refine your search for optimal trail routes.

Reopen Existing Trails

As I mentioned in the beginning of this chapter, the most obvious way to establish trails through your forest is to reopen existing skid trails or forest access roads that have become overgrown. Depending on the intended use of your trails, you may choose to reopen these old skid trails for vehicular use. If that is the case, then I refer you to Chapter 9 for guidance on road construction and maintenance. If regular vehicular use is not intended, then you may be fine simply cutting back the encroaching vegetation to the degree necessary to allow foot traffic or very light and intermittent small-vehicle use, such as ATVs or tractors.

Use Wildlife Trails

Deer and elk trails can often be widened to serve as walking trails. These animals have a tendency to find the path of least resistance through a forest, and their habitual routes may very well serve as a logical human route as well. Deer and elk can just as well choose to travel directly up a steep slope, which may not be conducive to trail building, so prudence should apply to following the routes of animals. If you do choose to use wildlife trails, cutting back vegetation to the extent necessary to facilitate ease of human passage may be all that you need to do. I wouldn't be too concerned about interrupting the flow of wildlife on their trails, as I often find that wildlife use trails that

I create given that it's easier to pass along them than push through dense understory vegetation.

Mirror the Veins of a Leaf

If you are establishing a new trail system through your woods, another option that may lend optimal access to your woods with a minimum of trail infrastructure is to emulate the pattern of veins of a leaf. Consider an alder leaf. The herringbone pattern of the veins allows nutrients to flow efficiently to all parts of the leaf. A main route leads up through the center of the leaf, and arterial paths extend to its outside margins. The shape of your forestland may not coincide with the shape of a leaf, so take this idea

The veins of an alder leaf provide a possible pattern for designing forest access trails.

figuratively and adapt it to your circumstances. Either way, a main trail (or road) through the center of your forest, combined with a series of side trails (or roads) that connect with a route that runs around the circumference of your land, may provide just the right kind of access for you.

Create Trails While Logging

If you are planning to commercially thin your forest, this is a perfect time to plan for a trail system. Oftentimes the logging contractor will use a similar herringbone system as described previously to lay out a main skid trail through the center of a forest, along with secondary skid trails that are used once or twice to bring trees or logs to the main skid trail and then onward to the log landing. When the logging is completed, you can instruct the logger to clean the debris off some of the skid trails and grade the trails as necessary to leave them in a condition where they can either be driven on or used by light equipment (e.g., a tractor or ATV) or simply as walking trails.

Construct Willy-Nilly Trails

The final system of trail design is what I refer to as willy-nilly trails. This simply means you can build trails anywhere you want. They don't have to follow a particular pattern and can be designed entirely around your whims, fancies, and notions. You may want to identify features of interest on a map first, then play connect the dots and see what a trail looks like. After you've connected all the places you're interested in getting to, you can decide if you want to add additional trails to further connect

these points or to create shortcuts through your forest.

CONSTRUCTING TRAILS

Aside from reopening old skid trails, I don't know too many people who put a lot of effort into actually constructing trails. Most of the trails I experience on small woodlands qualify more as goat tracks—paths that people walk enough to wear a line in the ground. Some folks hang plastic flagging from tree branches or shrubs to mark the path of the trail, but that's about it.

I'm an avid hiker and backpacker, and there is definitely an art and science to constructing a proper hiking trail. Since there is a distinct difference between a goat track and a constructed hiking trail, you need to revisit your objectives for your trails to determine how much effort you need to put into them.

Trails on Slopes

If you need to construct a trail on a slope greater than 30 percent or so, you will want to be mindful of the potential for erosion. A trail that goes directly up a slope has a high potential to channel stormwater along its path, which can result in erosion, sediment delivery to surface water, and degradation of the trail itself. The wider the trail is, and the more cleared its surface, the more potential there is for erosion. A general rule of thumb is to limit the grade of major trails (anything more than a goat track) to less than half the grade of the slope. For instance, if the slope you need to traverse is greater than 30 percent, the grade of the trail should not exceed 15 percent. Switchbacks may be necessary to gradually bring a trail up a narrow and steep slope.

Drainage

Any trail intended for more than infrequent walking should be constructed with proper drainage in mind. You can use similar, though scaled-down techniques as described in Chapter 9 to ensure proper drainage, such as water bars, ditches, cross drains, and outsloping or insloping the surface of the trail.

Trails on Wet Soils

If you have forested wetlands or other low areas on your land that are seasonally wet and want to make a trail through these areas, here are some things you should keep in mind:

- Add a thick layer of wood chips to the trail to prevent soil compaction.
- Add small-diameter logs perpendicular to the trail across the wettest areas to create a corduroy road that minimizes soil compaction and disturbance, and makes it easier to use the trail without sinking into the mud.
- Build up the surface of the trail by laying small-diameter logs parallel to either side of the trail and add wood chips or gravel. If you do this in areas where there is seasonal inundation and surface water, include either small culverts or an occasional break in the trail that allows water to flow through it.
- Avoid use of the trail when soils are saturated. Delineate these trail

Cross-country ski trails are common throughout the woods in winter east of the Cascade Mountains.

segments as seasonal use only, and traverse them only during summer months.

SOME FINAL THOUGHTS ON TRAILS

If you own a larger tract of land, consider partnering with a local recreational group, cross-country skiers, or horseback riding club to use your trails. In exchange for access, these groups may be willing to help maintain your trails, and they can also provide an extra set of eyes in the woods to help monitor for trespass or forest management needs.

Consider naming your trails and placing signs at intersections. This can be a fun exercise for the family, and gives each family member a sense of connection to a particular trail segment. Naming or labeling trails in some manner also helps identify the location of observations during monitoring walks.

Record your trails with a GPS unit or your smartphone, and download the tracks to Google Earth or your mapping software of choice, to aid in creating a map of your land.

With this chapter we bring to a conclusion the majority of our recommendations for how to physically manage your forest. In the remaining chapters, we'll explore some of the less tangible, but no less important, topics of how to conserve your land through the generations, and how climate change may affect your forest in the future.

OPPOSITE: *A trail in the northern foothills of Mount Rainier, Washington*

Carbon markets

Your forest through the generations

Conservation easements

Adapting to tomorrow's climate

Certifying your forest

PART IV

The Bigger Picture

CHAPTER 21

Committing Your Forest to a Higher Purpose: Easements, Offsets, and Certification

BY SETH ZUCKERMAN

We've made no secret of the fact that ecological forestry isn't the most lucrative way to manage a forest, at least not in the short term. Any business school graduate will tell you that turning trees into logs as soon as their growth begins to slow down is the best way to maximize your financial return on investment. What's more, partial harvests are costlier per thousand board feet. Raising older trees, leaving generous riparian buffers, and maintaining diverse forests may be healthy for the forest, but it isn't best for this quarter's bottom line.

If you have read this far, chances are that cash profit is at most one of the reasons you own forestland, and you might be willing to accept a more modest return in exchange for other sources of sylvan satisfaction. It's certainly true that wildlife habitat, water quality, and carbon storage can get in the way of a quick buck. But in this chapter, we will explore some of the ways you can benefit financially by *not* harvesting your timber all at once. It probably won't make up for all of the timber income you forgo by following the path of ecological forestry, but it can reduce the net cost of making that choice.

For the most part, American society and property law have made a somewhat arbitrary choice to value forests primarily for the physical products they yield. But imagine a parallel universe in which landowners are paid for the volume of clean water that flows out of their forested watershed or the

OPPOSITE: *Pine bark*

number of salmon smolts that swim down-stream from beneath its shade—a universe in which landowners are paid for ecosystem services rendered rather than selling a phys-ical product. In some relatively arid regions, economic studies have shown that the water emanating from forested watersheds is more valuable than the timber those forests can sustainably yield. The rights to that water are not traded on an open market in which water users can bid for the forest against log buyers, however, so that comparison remains in the realm of a thought experi-ment. So here we are: in a society where the most valuable product of the forest can only be gained by cutting down its constit-uent trees. Fortunately, forests are not like golden-egg-laying geese—the choice to cut down a single tree doesn't necessarily inter-rupt the flow of ecosystem services. Their continued provision depends on how the forest is treated as a whole system.

CONSERVATION EASEMENTS

You don't have to venture to a parallel uni-verse to find tools that make it possible to value and protect the ecosystem services that a piece of land delivers—and that you can benefit from financially. The chief instrument that can perform this function is the conservation easement, which is founded on our legal system's ancient idea that property ownership can be thought of as a bundle of rights: you can use and enjoy the land, you can exclude people from it, you can control what happens there, and you can convey it to the next owner. An easement is a grant of an interest in the land to some-one who doesn't possess it but can merely

use it in a specific way. Common examples include access easements, where a neighbor has the right to pass across your property to reach theirs, or utility easements, which allow water, electricity, and telecommunica-tions lines to cross your land as part of a local network.

In contrast, a conservation easement doesn't allow someone else to use your property. Rather, it is a commitment that you will restrict your use of the land in order to conserve some environmental aspect of it. That conservation value could be the maintenance of open space in an urban area, wildlife habitat, stream protection, forest cover, or any of a number of other possibilities. You might agree not to build in a particularly prominent spot on the land, thereby protecting the neighborhood's sce-nic values. Or you might forgo your right to subdivide the land into multiple buildable parcels, thus protecting the area's rural char-acter and potentially promoting more clus-tered development that is more efficient in its use of public infrastructure. Some ease-ments codify the terms of carbon offsets, which are discussed later in this chapter.

In deeding a conservation easement, you give up some of your rights in the land for a higher purpose. The commitment isn't made in the abstract, as a promise to the universe. Instead, the easement is held by an entity (usually a nonprofit land trust or a government agency) that thereby acquires a property interest in the parcel. That inter-est is independent of who owns the land, so the commitment to conservation will bind future owners as well as you—just as a drive-way easement you sell to your neighbor is binding on whoever follows you as the next

This forest in Kitsap County, Washington, is protected by a working forest conservation easement that restricts cutting to 10 percent of the timber volume per decade.

owner. If you or a future owner were to violate the terms of the easement, the easement holder's recourse isn't to prosecute, but rather to sue to enforce their property right.

Why do forest owners consider conservation easements? At the core, a fundamental driver is that they have come to care about their forest, and they want some aspect of it to be protected for the long term. Let's say they have set aside some larger trees to provide shade along a fish-bearing stream. A conservation easement means that their forbearance won't simply have set the stage for a less salmon-spirited future owner to reap a windfall of fine western redcedar logs. For some forest owners, as they contemplate the end of their lives, it is a way to feel at peace with the course their forest will follow after they are gone. Conservation easements are usually perpetual, but they can also be drawn for a specific term—usually at least a few decades.

In addition to protecting environmental values, conservation easements can themselves yield financial returns. If the value it would protect is important enough to a funding agency or land trust, they may purchase the easement from you. What is it worth? An easement is appraised as the difference between the value of the land before it was encumbered with the easement and its value afterward. Sometimes, that can be a very straightforward calculation: the value of timber whose harvest is being placed off-limits, for instance, or the potential sale price of the smaller parcels that the land could be carved into. Other restrictions are a little trickier to value, such as ones that limit the rate of harvest but don't permanently dedicate any trees for preservation.

Funding for public-benefit conservation easements is limited, and is usually directed to projects that have been prioritized by planners looking at an entire watershed or landscape. You may see great value in your frog pond or heron rookery, but that doesn't mean it will top the wish list of biodiversity planners who have a limited budget to support the creation of a regional network of protected areas. Other programs are first-come, first-served, but the actual purchase of the easement is limited by the available funding. In Washington, for example, a state program will purchase a fifty-year easement on trees that forest practice rules have required owners to leave standing in riparian areas to protect stream habitat. However, because of limitations on funding, applicants in the mid-2010s had to wait about six years for their applications to be funded.

Given those constraints, many forest owners have chosen to donate an easement to a conservation group. This can achieve the certainty they are looking for in the forest's long-term management, and depending on their financial situation, it can yield a financial windfall as well. If they deed an easement to a nonprofit, that can qualify as a tax-deductible charitable donation, valued at the decrease in the property's value now that its owners are bound to the terms of the easement. Subject to IRS limitations, such a deduction would reduce their taxes by the value of the easement multiplied by their tax bracket.

The easement may bring with it other benefits as well. If the donor's property would be subject to estate or inheritance tax, an easement may reduce its value, potentially below the threshold where it is subject to taxation. Every case is different, so you would do well to consult a tax adviser before assuming that you understand the implications for your own tax situation.

It isn't free money, though. Grantors of easements have to realize that holding an easement comes at a cost. The land trust or public agency must monitor it in perpetuity to make sure the owners abide by it. If they notice a violation, it is incumbent on them to defend the easement—ideally, reminding the owner of their obligation will suffice, but they might need to take legal action and demand damages if appropriate. As a result, they usually require a gift to their endowment to receive and hold an easement. Donors of a conservation easement should be prepared to make a cash gift to the recipient of the easement to ensure that the conservation easement will truly hold up . . . which, after all, is what they want to accomplish. All of this suggests that tax benefits from donating a conservation easement depend on having an income robust enough both to support the initial cash endowment gift and to translate a partial reduction in taxable income into substantial tax savings.

One thing to be wary of, though, is easement language that is too restrictive and doesn't evolve with the state of our knowledge about forest ecosystems. In the past, land trusts often received gifts of forestland with stipulations that it never be harvested commercially. These easements were well meaning, often in reaction to rapid and extensive logging in the area during the time leading up to them. But recently, land trusts are recognizing that such limits are too restrictive and may actually compromise the health of the forest they are meant to protect. Instead, forest easements are more carefully tailored to protect the underlying goals of forest health. While they might set guardrails around the ways that the forest can be harvested, they now steer clear of outright prohibitions on commercial harvest, walking the line between specificity (so the easement is enforceable) and humility (so that future generations can translate their greater wisdom into action).

If you are interested in pursuing this possibility with your own forest, contact a land trust or public agency near you. Washington and Oregon each have statewide land trust organizations (Washington Association of Land Trusts and Coalition of Oregon Land Trusts) whose websites can point you to the nonprofits that work in your area; wildlife agencies and counties also sometimes have funding for conservation easements. If the land trust has multiple staff, typically the conservation director would be a good person to start with. Be aware that conservation easement transactions take months or even years to consummate, and usually have to pass multiple screenings within the organization, as well as an appraisal process to value the land with and without the easement.

CARBON OFFSETS

One very specific way to dedicate your forestland to public benefit is to commit it to a

Riparian forests like this one can be protected with conservation easements.

strategy of climate mitigation. The theory behind this is straightforward: forests, particularly Northwest forests, can suck a lot of carbon dioxide out of the air and turn it into biomass, where its carbon won't be warming the climate. Most forest management in the region falls well short of its potential to store carbon, and the application of ecological forestry tends to boost the forest's value as a carbon sink—a safe place to increase

Carbon offsets can compensate landowners for stewarding groves similar to this one in the Olympic National Forest.

carbon storage. The idea of protecting the carbon stored in forests was originally floated decades ago as a reason to stop tropical deforestation, and has since been generalized to the rest of the world.

In the Pacific Northwest, carbon offset projects fall into two main categories: affor-estation (establishing forest in suitable places where they are not growing at the moment) and improved forest management. Those improvements typically consist of raising older forests that, as they grow bigger, maintain higher levels of carbon storage on the landscape. That increased carbon storage is one of the many environmental advantages of ecological forestry, along with wildlife habitat and clean water, among others. What makes it a carbon *offset* is that you manage your forest in a way that stores more carbon than it otherwise would, and someone relies on that increase in carbon storage to make up for the impact of actual carbon emissions they are causing through, for instance, the use of fossil fuels.

The devil, however, is in the details. The considerations that make a forest carbon project legitimate have been ironed out in global conferences, and require that any project aimed at mitigating climate change meet the following seven criteria:

Additional. You can only claim an offset for carbon stored beyond a plausible baseline of what would have been stored in the project's absence.

Real. The eventual growth and carbon storage of trees you just planted can't be used to permit fossil fuel emissions until the biomass actually materializes in the forest. (A project developer might pay you now for future carbon storage, but its use by emitters is subject to monitoring in the field.)

Verifiable. A third party can ascertain that the project has taken place and is storing carbon.

Not otherwise harmful. For instance, the project doesn't reduce biodiversity (by planting a monoculture of fast-growing trees) or detract from community well-being in the place where it is being implemented. One consideration in dry forests is whether higher tree densities are predisposing the forest to wildfire—which would not only cause many kinds of harm but also

actually combust the carbon right back into the atmosphere.

Permanent. The project must be guaranteed for the long term. Compliance offsets (see below) typically require a one-hundred-year commitment, while forty years is enough for most voluntary programs.

Exclusive. It isn't counted as an offset by anyone else, to avoid double-counting that would enable one project to be reused to justify emissions multiple times over.

Leakproof. The increase in carbon stored in the project isn't simply erased by additional harvesting and emissions elsewhere in the ownership.

Carbon offsets can be sold in two kinds of markets. *Voluntary offsets* are used by companies and individuals who want to achieve a kind of moral equilibrium, socking away as much CO_2 as their activities generate. These offsets are used to achieve a kind of bragging rights for marketing purposes. In a world awash with marketing claims, if a firm wants to pay for a project that extends the rotation age of a forest, or supports an organization or family that has chosen to manage its forest that way, there's no harm done.

The other type of market is for *compliance offsets*. These agreements to store carbon in the forest play a role in various state, provincial, or regional regulatory programs that set a cap on how much total CO_2 can be emitted into the air in aggregate across the economy or the electric power grid. Any company that wants to sell fossil fuels or fossil-fuel-generated electricity has to obtain enough allowances to cover its emissions, usually by buying them at auction. Purchasing a compliance offset relieves the company of the need to buy an allowance. This trade-off puts extra pressure on the quality of the offsets, which had better be rock-solid since that offset authorizes additional carbon dioxide from fossil fuels to be emitted into the air.

Some offset projects, especially if sold into compliance markets, have faced criticism where it's hard to argue for their additionality with a straight face. For instance, imagine a wildlife preserve that has been held by a nonprofit land trust for decades. In theory, they could change course and sell it to a lumber company that would then clearcut it. But it is unlikely that would happen, so it's hard to believe that the carbon stored is truly additional.

It's a different story when a private landowner is facing financial difficulty, or trying to decide what should happen to their forest after they are no longer around to manage it. If a carbon offset commitment can secure the current management trajectory, which is legitimately in danger, then an offset in the compliance or voluntary market can be a good fit. In between those two cases lies a nuanced spectrum of situations, which each landowner has to analyze with their own moral compass.

If you are interested in developing a carbon project on your land, start by finding a project developer or project aggregator. Most developers will bear the considerable costs of project development in return for a percentage of the project income, if the project passes muster through a rough assessment of its potential. In recent years, a few developers have emerged who bundle together smaller forest offsets as one larger project that can be inventoried and verified

as one. If you are interested in carbon offsets and you own less than five hundred acres of forest, this is probably the best route for you to follow.

Carbon offsets can be a bit of a mixed moral bag. Pundits have likened them to medieval papal indulgences that sanctioned sinning as long as the sinner paid a fee to the Church. But the fact that offsets can be traded doesn't take away from the fact that enhanced carbon storage is a major benefit of ecological forestry. Just as you don't have to get paid for the pileated woodpecker habitat you create through your forest management, you can glory in the enhanced carbon storage of your forest whether you get paid extra for it or not.

CERTIFICATION SYSTEMS

Carbon offsets are just one form of third-party recognition that a forest owner can achieve. The forestry ecosystem supports four main certification standards, with a fifth one on the horizon. Each certification confers its blessing on the kind of land management being practiced, and each has slightly different standards and uses in the marketplace. From simplest and easiest to obtain, all the way up to the most rigorous, here are the four that are currently in place and one that is coming soon.

Stewardship Forest. You may have seen these signs, showing the happy coexistence of a conifer and a hardwood tree, on the gates of nearby forests. It signifies that the owner has created a management plan for their land that has met the USDA's standards for completeness and has been approved by their state forestry department as well.

American Tree Farm. This standard descends from the first self-designated tree farm in the United States, the 120,000-acre tract established by Weyerhaeuser Timber Company in 1941. The national tree farm network was originally managed by the National Lumber Manufacturers Association but was eventually turned over to the American Forest Foundation. Open to ownerships between ten and ten thousand acres, certification is based on compliance standards that require a forest management plan, reforestation of harvested areas, compliance with all relevant laws, use of best management practices, reduction of visual impacts, and protection of special sites, although a lot of discretion is given to the system's inspectors to determine whether a forest is meeting those standards. Logs harvested from certified tree farms are eligible to enter the forestry supply chain of the industry-sponsored international Programme for the Endorsement of Forest Certification and its North American affiliate, the Sustainable Forestry Initiative.

Sustainable Forestry Initiative. This certification was spawned by a timber industry coalition in 1995 in response to the 1993 formation of the Forest Stewardship Council (described next). Originally wholly owned by the industry, it now has a broader board of directors but is still mostly led by the big industrial players and their allies, and receives almost all of its financial support from the fees paid by industry partners. While the Sustainable Forest Initiative (SFI) standard has required owners to create plans to describe how they will handle various challenges, certification guidelines do not impose prescriptive standards, so clear-cuts can be as big as the law allows, for instance, and logging can get as close to streams as permitted by state regulations. SFI has a chain-of-custody program that enables lumber or paper produced with SFI logs to be labeled as end products with the SFI logo.

Forest Stewardship Council. Ever since it was founded in 1993, the Forest Stewardship Council (FSC) has been governed by a unique three-chamber structure, representing economic, social, and environmental interests in forestry. The board of directors is drawn equally from all three chambers, and within each chamber, equally from the global North and South. When members vote on policy, motions must attract majority support from each chamber to pass. Within the FSC, each country sets its own forestry standards, which must be approved by the international board to go into effect. As a result, the standards in the Pacific Northwest limit complete clear-cuts to thirty acres, with progressively more tree retention required as regeneration blocks grow toward the absolute maximum of sixty acres, at which point nearly a third of the trees must be retained. The regional standards also require wider riparian buffers, to protect streams from excessive heating or sediment.

We might as well confess a bias toward FSC certification, since Northwest Natural Resource Group administers a group FSC certificate for forest owners, giving more than eighty ownerships—and over 190,000 acres of forestland—the FSC seal of approval. Their logs can then be sold to FSC-certified mills, who can then produce, label, and sell FSC lumber, plywood, and pulp. The Northwest has suffered from a scarcity of FSC-certified mills, however, so more than 90 percent of our members' harvests have been sold to uncertified mills that were either closer or offered a better price for the logs.

Coming Soon: Climate Smart Wood. Thanks to growing interest from architects, builders, and building owners, a coalition has arisen to label and market "climate smart" wood—wood that is grown with consideration for forests' ability to sequester carbon and for forests' to become more resilient to the changing climate. As of 2023, the Climate Smart Wood Group was in the process of defining standards to designate levels of climate smartness in forest management, and procurement guidelines for people who want to use that kind of wood for their building projects. Check out climatesmartwood.net for the details of this emerging program.

How do you manage a forest for greater climate resilience? That is the topic of the next chapter.

CHAPTER 22

Not Your Granddaddy's Climate: Adaptation and Resilience

BY SETH ZUCKERMAN

When I first dug deeply into forestry, I thought about forests through the lens of ecological restoration. I was living in Northern California, where we were grappling with the unintended consequences of a logging boom that had begun after World War II and tapered off in the 1980s as the old-growth Douglas-fir forests were exhausted. Along with them, our watershed's ability to support abundant chinook and coho salmon runs was exhausted as well. Bulldozers were a new technology when the logging boom began, and their power exceeded the discretion and good judgment of their operators. Roads had been built without fully considering their ability to withstand the relentless Humboldt rain. Creek beds had been used as skid trails to haul logs. Forests were clear-cut right down to stream-banks, raising summer water temperatures beyond what coho could withstand—particularly once the roads started to wash out and pour a slurry of sediment into streams, filling in the deep pools where juvenile fish had taken refuge.

So our focus was in the rearview mirror, on how we could help the watershed heal and return to a time when salmon thronged the streams so densely that their splashing in spawning season might keep you up all night and the stink of their spawned-out carcasses spiced the autumn breeze. The route to that healing led partly through reforestation, to weave anew not only the blanket of shade that had cooled the river in the summer but also the network of roots that had anchored the soil to the riverbank. Reforestation, restoration, recovery—all words beginning with re-, from the Latin meaning "again" or "back," arranged around the notion of returning to a better yesterday. *Return*: there's that prefix again.

But now that focus on the past appears quaint. The notion of recapturing a lost paradise was rooted in an assumption of climatic stability, a frame of reference that has been twisted beyond recognition as anthropogenic climate change ramps up. Instead of looking over our shoulders and trying to drive our ecosystems back to where they came from, we now need to make them fit for a changing climate.

For forests, this poses a significant challenge, because the key species in a forest (trees, obviously) are so long-lived. If a new kind of annual grass or cucumber variety proves to be a better fit in a warmer epoch, then you can just plant it next year. But a tree you establish in your forest this year may still be there a century or two from now—a period that will likely see a much different climate than today's even if all our efforts to curb greenhouse gas emissions proceed as planned. There is a delay between emissions and impacts, so even more warming is "baked in" to our future than has already occurred.

That's why it pays to be extra thoughtful about the changing climate when it comes to managing your forest. We're going to offer a few guidelines here for how to do that, and how you might consider fine-tuning your practices in light of the changes that are headed our way.

To begin, we need to take stock of climatologists' predictions for how the climate is apt to change as greenhouse gas concentrations continue to rise. From their work, we know to prepare for the following drivers of change in Northwest forests:

Summer drought. Climate models forecast a longer dry season, and more precipitation arriving during intense atmospheric river events, which lead to higher floods and yet are less effective at recharging soil moisture.

Less snow. As you'd expect in a warmer world, models consistently predict less snow for the region, with snow levels rising so that mid-elevations receive more of their precipitation as rain instead of snow. What snow does accumulate will melt earlier in the summer, leaving a longer season when mid- to high-elevation soils are not moistened by snowmelt. The effect will be particularly profound below four thousand feet.

More intense wildfires. More drought will mean more trees succumbing to thirst, adding more snags to the forest. Drier summers and standing dead trees make the forest more susceptible to fire. The major stand-replacing fires of moist west-side forests are driven by dry east winds in the summertime, which desiccate vegetation and push the fire ahead of them, as we saw in Chapter 16. There's no evidence that those weather conditions will become more frequent. But if fires become more common, there is a greater chance that one will already be burning when one of those east wind events begins, and will be amplified into a full-blown conflagration. More generally, fire seasons will be longer, and vegetation will be drier, causing it to burn hotter and more readily.

Heat waves. Temperature spikes that last for several days will become more common, with two to seven times as many days topping 86°F. Such conditions in the midst of the dry season will stress vulnerable trees, particularly young seedlings and species already near the dry edge of their range.

Insect outbreaks. Warmer, drier summers and winters with fewer freezes are expected to increase the frequency and extent of insect outbreaks in forests. Summer conditions may exacerbate moisture stress, making trees more susceptible to insects. (Trees' main defense mechanism against boring insects is to drown them in pitch, but if the trees are short of water, they can't produce enough pitch to use this tactic effectively.) Warmer winter temperatures may further assist many insect species, such as pine beetles and spruce budworm, to overwinter and increase overall reproduction, which can lead to larger outbreaks.

South-facing branches of conifers suffered from sun scald after the Northwest heat dome in summer 2021.

Armed with this foreknowledge, how can forest managers prepare their forests for what is to come? Managing a forest for an imagined future climate is a tricky proposition, since the actions you take have to work for the short term as well. Before we get to specific suggestions, here are three general principles that will be important as you prepare your forest for climate change:

1. Understand the particulars of your site and the ways it is especially vulnerable to the five climate drivers listed previously. For instance, if your land has gravelly soils that aren't good at retaining water through the summer to begin with, flashier precipitation and hotter summers are going to be especially impactful.

2. Models are no substitute for empirical observation. Events such as the intense fire season of 2020 and the 2021 Northwest heat dome can offer a window into the future, suggesting how climate change might play out on your site. Given the types of disruptions that climate change is apt to bring, such as insect outbreaks and diebacks of thirstier species, it's worth paying close attention to what

is happening in your forest and scrutinizing it for unwelcome changes. You can no longer count on the future remaining within the bounds of past experience.

3. Diversity is your friend. Since modeling is an inexact science, it's hard to be sure what species of tree will fare the best in the climate of the future. In the face of the collection of stressors that will confront your forest, it pays to hedge your bets with a variety of different species and age classes, instead of putting all your chips on one outcome. This is yet another reason to avoid monoculture plantations.

ADAPTATION TECHNIQUES

You can apply these larger principles anywhere in the Northwest, and indeed in almost any ecosystem. Now we will drill down into greater specificity. The rest of this chapter covers a few practices that are worth considering if they meet your objectives for your land and the needs of your site.

Manage for Lower Tree Densities

Increasing heat and summer drought mean that soil moisture won't support the same densities of trees as in the past. You can think of each tree as a straw, tapped into the glass of soil moisture. The more trees there are, the less water is available for each. Consequently, if you are planting trees, space them a little farther apart from each other, or plan on thinning them when the stand is young, in eight to fifteen years.

Later, as the stand ages, maintain it at a somewhat sparser density than would historically have been recommended. Open up the stand too much, and you might bring on a flush of understory growth that would counteract the gains you are seeking in soil moisture. In some of the hotter parts of our region, overdoing it would allow too much sun to the forest floor and change its microclimate, drying it out beyond the tolerance of some of its damp-loving denizens such as salamanders.

If, despite your efforts, the stand still seems stressed by lack of moisture, consider introducing some different tree species. It doesn't take a very large opening—certainly no more than an acre, but likely half of that—to create planting sites for even the most shade-intolerant species, such as ponderosa pine.

Understand, Maintain, and Use Your Site's Heterogeneity

Forests are composed of microsites—zones with different potentials based on their soil, shading, aspect, and position on the hillside. You might have one area in your woods that is perfect for moisture-loving trees such as western redcedar or western hemlock, and a hundred yards away is a site where those trees would struggle. As the climate becomes hotter and drier, the range of sites that can support thirsty species will shrink. That means you will want to use the moistest of them to maintain species diversity in your forest. Some sites will become less hospitable to seedlings; if you plant there, you will want to mulch the seedlings with forest duff, bark, and logging slash to give them a

Planters install Douglas-fir and western redcedar seedlings in a snow gap (pictured from the air later in this chapter) as part of a trial comparing the success of trees grown from different seed zones.

bit of shelter from the heat and desiccation of summer.

Heterogeneity extends to species and age classes too. If you have a monoculture of a single species, you would do well to introduce new species into the mix. If all your trees are the same age, you might improve your forest's odds by establishing a new cohort, possibly with some new genetic material from other regions (discussed next).

Adapt Your Planting Strategies

Planting a forest is a multi-decadal bet on the seedlings' ability to thrive where you put them. Given the range of climate predictions for the twenty-first century, it makes sense to lean toward seedlings that can withstand a warmer climate, and to add more drought-tolerant native species, including broadleaf trees. But you don't have to go overboard. A tree's ability to withstand grazing by camels is probably not

going to factor into its long-term success in the Pacific Northwest.

The considerations here need to be evaluated species by species. For instance, the native range of the coastal subspecies of Douglas-fir extends as far south as Yosemite and Santa Barbara; its Rocky Mountain subspecies is native as far south as Mexico. So it is unlikely the habitat for Douglas-fir would shift away from the Pacific Northwest anytime soon. In contrast, a species such as Alaska yellow-cedar is at much greater risk locally. The Pacific Northwest is at the south end of its range, because it's already nearly too hot for it here, and it will be at greater risk in a warmer climate. As you choose species for your planting palette, best practices for assisted migration call for the use of species that are already native to the area but perhaps had previously grown only in drier microsites. For instance, the western white pine can be mixed in with Douglas-fir in lowland areas to hedge against a much droughtier turn of events.

The choice you make might be dictated, too, by abiotic factors such as aspect and soil type. Anecdotally, western Washington forest owners are finding it increasingly difficult to establish moisture-loving species such as red alder, western hemlock, grand fir, and western redcedar on south-facing, well-drained glacial soils.

Planting decisions extend beyond a choice of species to the selection of seed zone that the seedlings were grown from. State forestry departments have divided Oregon and Washington into seed zones arranged by region and elevation, based on the idea that local genetics are adapted to the conditions of the place. As the climate shifts, traits such as earlier spring bud break that were selected for in warmer locales will become more suitable farther to the north or higher in elevation. The Seedlot Selection Tool (described in Chapter 12) can help you choose seedlings adapted to the future climate. While we don't recommend getting all of your seedlings from a warmer zone, including these migrants in your mix can help introduce those genetic traits to your area, and provide insurance against a complete planting failure caused by harsh conditions that the home team couldn't tolerate.

Control Invasive Species

Because a warmer climate can set the stage for unusually severe pest outbreaks, it's crucial to stay alert to insect activity and be aware of invasive species, either plant or animal, that are becoming more virulent. If you see something, say something to your local noxious weed board. Refer to Chapter 8 for more about invasive species.

Manage Fire Risk

Hotter, drier conditions mean a greater danger of wildfires. But the specific conditions on your site indicate the best way to respond. First, identify the site's fire regime (see Chapter 16). If you're in a high-frequency or mixed-severity fire regime, reduce fuel ladders and maintain defensible space, and consider the possibility of reintroducing prescribed fire. In infrequent, high-severity fire regimes, roadside fuel breaks and defensible space around homes can make it easier to contain fires before they grow beyond controllable dimensions.

Adjust to the New Water Regime

Predicted climate changes mean that forest managers must prepare not just for drought but also for flood. Predictions are for a larger share of rainfall to arrive in big storm events, leading to higher peak flows. At mid-elevations, as more precipitation arrives in the form of rain instead of snow, or in rain-on-snow events, that will increase peak flows as well.

For forest managers, the biggest implication of higher peak flows is that culverts and bridges that were able to withstand peak flows in the past may be inadequate in the future. As you replace stream crossings in your road network, bear this in mind. In the meantime, be aware that good maintenance is all the more important so that the existing crossings can function to their fullest.

On the flip side, to compensate for drier summers you can make sure to maintain robust riparian buffers, which will moderate

These gaps, cut at four thousand feet of elevation on the flanks of Mount Rainier, demonstrate how small openings or even heavy thinning can promote the accumulation and retention of snow cover.

water temperatures and reduce evaporation compared to an exposed stream. Thinning the forest, too, will help reduce the amount of water that trees pull out of the soil to satisfy their evapotranspiration needs, and leave more in the ground to percolate through the soil to the stream channel. Modeling by the Environmental Protection Agency in Oregon and Washington has shown that older forests don't use as much water per acre as younger stands, so letting the forest continue to age (by thinning it instead of clear-cutting) will yield a water dividend that can help compensate for the reduction in summer flows that climate change will tend to cause in our region.

Finally, if your forest is at an elevation where snow typically builds up through the winter and melts off in the spring, consider creating a snow gap to promote the accumulation and retention of snow to help offset the anticipated loss of snowpack and decrease in summer rainfall. Although trees look very beautiful with snow on their boughs, it turns out that a lot of that snow evaporates right off their needles and never gets a chance to become part of the snowpack that will feed streams in spring and summer. A small gap (as little as half an acre), or even a heavy thinning, will allow more snow to accumulate so that streams get a time-release dose of meltwater.

ALTHOUGH THE NOTION OF CLIMATE CHANGE IS disquieting and destabilizing—even enraging when you consider how long fossil fuel companies have known about the harm their products were causing—it falls to us as forest stewards to make our forests as resilient as possible. For the time being, at least, we have some tools at our disposal to do so.

CHAPTER 23

Succession Planning

BY SETH ZUCKERMAN

An inescapable fact of forest ownership is that the forest can outlive its owners. That's true of any piece of real estate, but it's even more compelling when it comes to forests, since it isn't just the landforms and the soil that will persist beyond our time—it's individual trees and the forest community they comprise. In a way, it's not unlike the situation facing the elderly owners of a golden retriever who want to be sure it is well cared for after their passing.

To prepare for the life of your forest after your death, as with any kind of forest planning, you need to start by trying to determine *why* before you ask *how*. Get clear about your objectives and hopes for the land's trajectory after you can no longer take responsibility for it. To understand the scope of possibilities, you will have to discuss your forest with the people who might have a stake in its future, starting with family members and other potential heirs. Depending on the relationship they have built with the forest, they may have their own vision of the forest's future. Or they may be ready to move away from forest ownership altogether. Or maybe they have never thought about the question at all.

As you learn more about their interests and how those interests intersect with yours, it's important to remember the difference between *succession planning* and *estate planning*. Estate planning helps you think about how to distribute all your material assets, including the forest, after you're gone. Succession planning, in contrast, involves preparing for the next generation to take the reins. It involves identifying the potential forest managers and owners and training them for their future roles. It answers questions about who will manage the forest and on whose behalf. You will want to complete at least the broad strokes of the succession plan before creating any

OPPOSITE: *Succession planning requires a long-range perspective.*

legal structures (e.g., an LLC, a will, or a trust) that will put your plan in place. It's possible the succession plan you devise for your forest will result in your beneficiaries being the new forest stewards, but that isn't necessarily the case. People who are not your heirs or beneficiaries may be enlisted to implement a future vision for your forest, while your kin merely reap the financial benefits.

Oregon State University Extension has created a thorough succession planning curriculum that we highly recommend called Ties to the Land (tiestotheland.org). It encourages open conversation between current owners and potential heirs by asking them to place their feelings about the forest on a continuum from purely a financial asset (1) to priceless family heirloom (10). The spectrum of answers can illuminate the best way to divide the responsibility for the forest and how to allocate its benefits. For instance, imagine you wanted to divide your forest between two kids, one of whom cherishes the forest deeply and lives nearby, and the other who lives far away and cares mainly for its financial value. You might craft a succession plan that vests the decision-making authority for the forest's management in the first kid, while stipulating that they share the income from the land with the second.

On the other hand, if neither kid cares much about the forest, you might plan for them to put it up for sale after your death. To guide its long-term management beyond your lifetime, you could craft a working forest conservation easement, as described in Chapter 21, that defines guardrails for how it may be managed. Depending on your fam-ily's assets, a conservation easement may also ease your estate tax burden as mentioned in Chapter 21.

Finally, depending on your family's financial circumstances, you can consider a gift or bargain sale of the forest to a land trust or other nonprofit that would use the sustainable timber revenue to further their charitable purpose. The price of a bargain sale is deliberately set below the market value of the land, with the difference being considered a tax-deductible donation to the nonprofit.

If the transfer of your forestland to the next generation won't be as simple as handing it off to a single individual, we encourage you to consider the benefits of a limited liability company (LLC). Like a corporation, an LLC is a synthetic legal entity in whose name property can be held and transactions consummated. It is simpler to establish and maintain than a corporation, but it offers the same advantage that the ownership of the LLC can be divided fractionally however you decide among its members, analogous to shareholders in a corporation. The LLC's operating agreement spells out how the major decisions (such as distributing or reinvesting profits or selling real property) are made, and may designate one or more members to serve as managers who handle day-to-day operations and sign documents on the LLC's behalf. In the previous example, Kid 1, who was passionate about the forest, would manage it and share the proceeds with Kid 2. Both siblings would be members, but Kid 1 would be the manager.

If you want to explore this model further, we recommend Nolo Press's excellent book

Looking ahead

Saving the Family Cottage. It spells out the benefits of family LLC ownership over "tenancy in common," which is the type of ownership your heirs will have if you do no legal planning at all. Neither that book nor this chapter, however, is a substitute for professional counsel, and we urge you to get the help of an attorney.

Trusts are another legal structure that can help you achieve slightly different goals. A trust would empower a trustee (e.g., you, a family member, or a third party) to manage the forest for specific objectives, such as conservation, carbon storage, or sustainable income, during your life or after you die. The trust could require the trustee to allocate income to designated beneficiaries. This might be useful if none of your heirs is interested in direct involvement with the forest's stewardship but still appreciates the stream of revenue it can provide. The trust can also be designed as a *charitable remainder trust* that will provide beneficiaries with income from the forest's management for a set term or for one or more person's lifetimes, after which ownership of the forest passes to a nonprofit to support its work. A benefit of this arrangement is that a portion of the value of the forestland can be claimed as a charitable deduction while you, the donor, are still alive, reducing your tax obligations.

THERE ARE CERTAIN EXPERIENCES THAT REMIND us humans that we occupy a minor divot in the space-time continuum. Looking up at the Milky Way on a dark night, we can see how tiny we are in the vast cosmos. Walking through a grove whose trees pre-date Benjamin Franklin, Queen Elizabeth I, or the Magna Carta, we can see ourselves as a similarly minor, temporary presence from the perspective of a western conifer. With this outlook, planning for your woodland beyond your lifetime can seem like an essential duty. We wish you luck as you look toward the future of your forest with a combination of humility and hope.

AFTERWORD

BY SETH ZUCKERMAN

Throughout this book, we've shared a lot of specific ideas about caring for your forest and how it can be a source of food and firewood, financial gain, and personal fulfillment. And sure, those details *are* important—they encompass the day-to-day routine of caring for your forest and being nurtured by it in return. Looking after a forest is a practice, and it's important to do it well.

But ecological forestry is more than just a way to grow timber and build a private trail network for you and your friends. When you step back to take in the bigger picture, it is a way to reengage with nature and restore a connection that has been weakened over centuries of modern industrial civilization and postmodern digital distraction.

Through the last half century, this drive has taken many forms. Backyard gardeners have stuck their hands in the soil and turned the compost in an effort to "make the earth say beans instead of grass," in the words of Thoreau. River restorationists have learned about their watersheds and worked to make them hospitable to salmon again. We happen to feel drawn to forests, and that's why we have made them our entry point to this practice of reestablishing a right relationship with nature.

A connection with nature cannot be had in the abstract. Nor can it be had with the totality of nature—or at least, we confess that we are not skilled enough to pull that off. Rather, it occurs in a specific place, through actions of reciprocal caretaking. My mentor in watershed restoration, Freeman House, used to say before partaking of a salmon that its presence on our plates was a sign that we are still welcome on the planet. You could say the same about a chanterelle—the delicious fruiting body of a fungus that grows in partnership with a stand of trees—or even about a two-by-four. These all emerged from the earth, in forests that have been shaped by human management. So they are in some way the fruit of our stewardship, however neglectful, misguided, or careless our efforts have been. Whether through intention or accident, finesse or blunder, we have made the earth say *mushroom* or *lumber* instead of *grass*.

These gifts of the forest are what we draw from that relationship. As in any reciprocal relationship, the question is what we render in return. Ecological forestry offers this answer: mindful stewardship of the forest, taking account of all its parts. That's the principle; all else is commentary. The details will no doubt change and evolve as attentive forest stewards learn more about how the life-forms of the forest interact with one another and their biophysical setting. In a decade or two, some of what we have recommended here may turn out to be mistaken, overgeneralized, or too prescriptive. But we are confident that the fundamental principle will still endure.

And now, its implementation is left as an exercise for the reader. Put your boots on and get outside!

ACKNOWLEDGMENTS

This book is no more the product of its authors alone than a forest is composed just of just one or two trees.

A Forest of Your Own grows out of the work that Northwest Natural Resource Group (NNRG) has done since it began focusing on forestry in 1997. It is enriched by the insights we've developed with current and former colleagues as we have incubated ideas together and tested them in the woods. Big thanks to Rowan Braybrook, Sam Castro, Alex Dolk, Gustavo Segura Flores, Karen Gray, Rick Helman, Lindsay Malone, Jaal Mann, and Marissa Wyrwitske, both for your teamwork and for holding up more than your end of our shared projects while we scribbled away. Our board of directors—Sophia Amberson, John Harrison, Ben Hayes, Brad Hunter, Chris Larson, Sue Long, Marco Lowenstein, Grace Wang and, above all, board chair Christine Johnson—believed in the project and allowed us to carve out the time to do it justice.

Landowners who are members of NNRG's forest program have offered invaluable proving grounds for our approach to ecological forestry, in particular the Nisqually Community Forest, King County Department of Natural Resources and Parks, and Neal and Ann Koblitz.

Financial support from the Ned and Sis Hayes Family Fund of the Oregon Community Foundation and the Bullitt Foundation was instrumental in granting us the time to gather our thoughts. We're also grateful to the Sorensen-Giller family for supplying a writers' retreat at a crucial time.

Once the chapters were in draft form, we were fortunate that a veritable swarm of colleagues, mostly outside of NNRG, helped sharpen and refine our writing. We extend our appreciation to Marty Acker, Marisha Auerbach, Ken Bevis, Derek Churchill, Alex Dolk, Thomas Dunklin, Dylan Fischer, Rolf Gersonde, Josh Halofsky, Ben Hayes, Peter Hayes, John Henrikson, Joe Kane, Glenn Kohler, Ronda Larson Kramer, Jaal Mann, Daniel Omdal, Skye Pelliccia, Kyle Smith, Mike Stenger, Jack Wight, and Michael Yadrick. Thanks also to Edward C. Wolf, the first outsider to read the entire manuscript, who helped us see new forests amid the trees. If any errors of fact or infelicities of language remain, it is despite all these people's best efforts, not because of them.

At Mountaineers Books, Emily White gave our idea a hearing and shepherded it through the development process. The book benefited from the copy-editing craft of Jenn Kepler, the design eye of Jen Grable, the overall editorial oversight of Mary Metz, and all the other staff there who have watered and pruned our seedling of a book.

Finally, our families have graciously withstood numerous deadlines and false summits along the way to the book's completion. To Ellen, Maya, and Anders; and Jen and Nick, many thanks. Now let's get back into the forest.

GLOSSARY

abiotic pertaining to the physical environment, such as geology, climate, aspect, and elevation, as opposed to living organisms

annual allowable harvest the average amount of wood that can be harvested each year from a tract of forestland without depleting its standing volume

aspect the compass direction that a slope faces

basal area the total horizontal surface area of the tree trunks per unit area, if you imagined they were all cut off at four and a half feet above the ground. A proxy for the timber volume in a stand, it is measured in square feet per acre (or square meters per hectare in the metric system)

biotic pertaining to living organisms

board foot a unit by which lumber and logs are measured, equivalent to a board one foot wide, one inch thick, and one foot long. In Canada, logs are measured instead by the cubic meter, which equals approximately 424 board feet

bole the trunk of a tree

carrying capacity the population of a particular species that a site can support

cohort individuals in a population that are all about the same age, such as tree seedlings that sprouted within a few years of each other

clinometer a tool to measure the angle between your line of sight and the horizontal, available either as a phone app or a manual device

competitive exclusion phase the period during a forest's development when trees die off (are excluded) because of competition for resources such as light or moisture

diameter at breast height (DBH) the diameter of a tree when measured at four and a half feet above ground on the uphill side of the tree

duff the layer of dead leaves, needles, and woody debris that accumulates on the forest floor

ecological forestry an approach to forest stewardship that looks at the forest as a whole system, rather than a source of a single crop or other output

epicormic branches short branches that emerge from the trunk of a tree when latent buds that have been in deep shade are newly exposed to higher levels of sunlight

evapotranspiration the evaporation of water through pores in a plant's leaves or needles

fire regime the combination of fire severity and fire frequency that historically characterized an ecosystem

forest management plan a document that describes a forest and lays out a trajectory for its future stewardship

height-to-diameter ratio (HDR) the ratio between a tree's total height and its diameter at breast height (DBH)

increment borer a tool that extracts a pencil-sized cylinder of wood from a tree trunk, revealing its growth rings without cutting it down

inventory plot a circular area of set size within which you collect information on the trees and the condition of the forest

live crown ratio (LCR) the section of the tree's trunk from which live branches emerge

MBF abbreviation for "thousand board feet," a unit by which logs and lumber are sold

pioneer species life forms that thrive immediately after a disturbance event

pre-commercial thinning the removal of some trees from a site before they are large enough to be harvested for sale

recruitment the increase in a population of interest, such as individuals of a given species, or the quantity of downed logs or standing dead trees (snags)

regeneration harvest logging that creates the conditions to establish a new cohort of trees across the stand

riparian alongside or related to a stream or other body of water

rub tree In a forest unit that will be partially logged, a tree along a skidding corridor that is retained during most of the logging operation to protect adjacent trees from bark damage, and then is removed as the operation is winding down.

seedling release the removal of competing vegetation around a desired seedling in a forest

silviculture the intentional cultivation and stewardship of a forest to produce a desired result

site class the quality of a site for growing trees, from I (best) to V.

site index a measure of a site's capacity for growing trees, based on the height that a tree of a given species can attain in a set period of time, usually fifty or one hundred years

skip a patch left uncut in a thinned stand to promote habitat heterogeneity

slash branches and small-diameter tree trunks that remain on-site after a forest management operation

snag a standing dead tree

stand a specific area of the forest that you are considering at the moment

stand release removing competing vegetation from desired saplings when they are between five and fifteen years old

TPA trees per acre per acre, a measure of how crowded trees are on a site. In Canada, described instead as trees per hectare—about two and a half times the size of an acre.

RESOURCES

For selected chapters, we present here a curated list of resources you may find helpful as you dig deeper into the pursuit of ecological forestry.

Chapter 2: The Northwest Forest Landscape

Arno Stephen and Ramona Hammerly. *Northwest Trees: Identifying and Understanding the Region's Native Trees*. Seattle: Mountaineers Books, 2007.

Franklin, Jerry F., and C. T. Dyrness. "Natural Vegetation of Oregon and Washington" [pdf]. Corvallis: Oregon State University Press, 1988. https://bit.ly/naturalvegetation.

Luoma, Jon R. *The Hidden Forest: The Biography of an Ecosystem*. New York: H. Holt, 1999.

MacKinnon, A., and Jim Pojar, and Paul B. Alaback. *Plants of the Pacific Northwest Coast: Washington, Oregon, British Columbia & Alaska*. Richmond, BC: Lone Pine Publishing, 1994.

NatureServe. "Terrestrial Ecological Systems of the United States." A classification system for complexes of plant communities. www.natureserve.org/products/terrestrial-ecological-systems-united-states.

US Department of the Interior and US Forest Service. "Landfire Program Biophysical Settings." Provides maps of historical vegetation. https://bit.ly/landfire-bio.

US Forest Service. "Fire Effects Information System." Provides information about fire effects and fire regimes by species common or scientific name. www.feis-crs.org/feis.

US Forest Service. "Geospatial Data Discovery: Bailey's Ecoregions and Subregions Dataset." Displays an interactive map of ecoregions based on environmental variables. https://bit.ly/baileysecoregions.

Chapter 3: How Did We Get Here?

Clark, Ella E. *Indian Legends of the Pacific Northwest* Berkeley: University of California Press, 1953.

Olympic Peninsula Intertribal Cultural Advisory Committee. *Native Peoples of the Olympic Peninsula: Who We Are*. Edited by Jacilee Wray. Norman: University of Oklahoma Press, 2015.

Chapter 4: Shopping for a Forest

Search by county for assessor websites

Chapter 5: What Lives Here?

iNaturalist. "The Edible and Medicinal Plants of the Pacific Northwest." Photographic guide to plants found in the Pacific Northwest. www.inaturalist.org/guides/10285.

Morin, R. S. "Forest Ecosystem Health Indicators" [pdf]. Washington, DC: United States Department of Agriculture, Forest Service, 2020. https://bit.ly/ecosystemhealth.

Oregon State University. "Common Trees of the Pacific Northwest." A tree identification tool.

Chapter 6: A River Runs Through It

Opperman, Jeff. *Maintaining Wood in Streams: A Vital Action for Fish Conservation*. Davis: University of California, Division of Agriculture and Natural Resources, 2006.

Quinn, Timothy, George F. Wilhere, and Kirk L. Krueger. *Riparian Ecosystems, Volume 1: Science Synthesis and Management Implications* [pdf]. Washington Dept. of Fish & Wildlife, 2020. https://wdfw.wa.gov/publications/01987.

Chapter 7: Forest Health

Center for Invasive Species and Ecosystem Health. Online source for information about invasive species. www.bugwood.org.

4-County Cooperative Weed Management Area. "Integrated Weed Maintenance Calendar." Guide to the best treatment method and timing for noxious weed and invasive species management. https://4countycwma.org/integrated-weed-maintenance-calendar.

Goheen, Ellen Michaels and Elizabeth A Willhite. *Field Guide to the Common Diseases and Insect Pests of Oregon and Washington Conifers* [online]. Vol. no.01–06. USDA Forest Service, Pacific Northwest Region, n.d. doi:10.5962/bhl.title.80321. www.biodiversitylibrary.org/item/152991#page/3/mode/1up.

Pscheidt, J. W., and C. M. Ocamb, C.M., senior editors. *Pacific Northwest Plant Disease Management Handbook* [online]. Corvallis: Oregon State University, 2023. https://pnwhandbooks.org/plantdisease.

Shaw, David Carl, Paul T. Oester, and Gregory M. Filip. *Managing Insects and Diseases of Oregon Conifers.* Corvallis: Oregon State University, Extension Service, 2009.

Tu, Mandy., Callie Hurd, and John M. Randall. *Weed Control Methods Handbook: Tools and Techniques for Use in Natural Areas.* Davis, CA: Wildland Invasive Species Team, the Nature Conservancy, 2001.

US Forest Service Forest. "Insect and Disease Leaflets." Over 180 leaflets that provide information about insects or diseases affecting forest trees in the United States. https://bit.ly/forestinsects.

Zobrist, K. "Assessing Tree Health." [pdf] Pullman: Washington State University Extension, 2011. https://pubs.extension.wsu.edu/assessing-tree-health

Phone apps for identifying (non-native) plants

iNaturalist. A general plant and animals species identification app that includes natural ranges.

Washington Invasives An invasive species and noxious weed reporting tool that lists regional priority invasive plants and animals and provides a mechanism for reporting them.

WildSpotter Allows to you select a "wild area" (often a national forest or national park) near you, then provides a list of invasives/non-natives found in that area, including photos; also a reporting tool.

Chapter 8: Where'd That Come From?

County weed boards in Oregon: https://bit.ly/oregonweedprograms.

County weed boards in Washington: www.nwcb.wa.gov/contact-your-county-weed-boards.

Oregon State Weed Board. Contains resources for helping to protect Oregon from noxious weeds. https://bit.ly/weedmapper.

Peachey, E., editor. *Pacific Northwest Weed Management Handbook* [online]. Corvallis: Oregon State University. https://pnwhandbooks.org/weed.

Washington State Noxious Weed Control Board. Contains resources for helping to protect Washington from noxious weeds. www.nwcb.wa.gov.

Chapter 9: Roads in a Wood

Oregon Department of Fish and Wildlife. "ODFW Fish Screening and Passage Grant Program." Provides funding and resources for forest owners who wish to improve fish passage. https://dfw.state.or.us/fish/passage/grants.asp.

Washington Department of Natural Resources. "Family Forest Fish Passage Program." Provides assistance to private forest owners in removing culverts and other stream crossing structures. www.dnr.wa.gov/fffpp.

Weaver, W., E. Weppner, and D.Hagans. *Handbook for Forest, Ranch, and Rural Roads: A Guide for Planning, Designing, Constructing, Reconstructing, Upgrading, Maintaining and Closing Wildland Roads* [online]. McKinleyville, CA:

Pacific Watershed Associates, 2015. www.pacificwatershed.com/roadshandbook.

Chapter 10: Forest Inventory and Management Planning

"Forest Inventory and Monitoring Guidelines" [pdf]. Seattle: Northwest Natural Resource Group, 2015. https://bit.ly/monitoringguidelines.

"Healthy Woods Start With a Plan: Manage What You Value, With Assistance From NRCS" [pdf]. US Department of Agriculture, Wisconsin Natural Resource Conservation Service, 2022. https://bit.ly/healthywoods.

"How to Measure Woody Biomass in Your Forest" [pdf]. Seattle: Northwest Natural Resource Group, 2020. https://bit.ly/woodybiomassguidebook.

Oregon Department of Forestry. Website that provides information about Oregon forests. www.oregon.gov/odf.

"Oregon Forest Management Planning System Guidelines" [pdf]. US Forest Services, Oregon Department of Forestry, Oregon State University, USDA Natural Resource Conservation Service, Oregon Department of Fish and Wildlife, 2017. https://bit.ly/managementplansoregon.

Oregon State University. "Forestry & Natural Resources Extension." Provides research-based information and programs for managing forest resources. www.forestry.oregonstate.edu/forestry-and-natural-resources.

Oregon Association of Conservation Districts. "Regions and Directory of Districts." Lists links for conservation districts in Oregon. www.oacd.org/regions-and-directory-of-districts.

USDA Natural Resources Conservation Service. "Web Soil Survey." Provides soil data and information produced by the National Cooperative Soil Survey. https://websoilsurvey.nrcs.usda.gov/app.

Washington Department of Natural Resources. Includes link to DNR's landowner assistance tool, along with other helpful information. www.dnr.wa.gov.

Washington State Conservation Commission. "Washington State Conservation District Directory." Lists links for conservation districts in Washington. www.scc.wa.gov/conservation-district-map.

"Washington State Integrated Forest Management Plan Guidelines & Template" [pdf]. Washington State Department of Natural Resources, US Department of Agriculture, Forest Service and Natural Resources Conservation Service, Washington Tree Farm Program, Washington Department of Revenue, 2017. https://bit.ly/managementplanguidelines.

"Washington State University Extension Forestry Program." Classes, workshops, and online resources for forest owners. https://forestry.wsu.edu.

Withrow-Robinson, B., and D. Maguire. "Competition and Density in Woodland Stands" [pdf]. Pullman: Washington State University Extension, 2018. https://catalog.extension.oregonstate.edu/em9206.

Chapter 11: The Economic Benefits of Ecological Forestry

Zuckerman, Seth. "Longer rotations and carbon" [online]. Seattle: Northwest Natural Resource Group, 2021. www.nnrg.org/longer-rotations-and-carbon.

Chapter 12: Stand Establishment

Environmental Quality Incentives Program. A cost-share program offered by the USDA. Oregon and Washington have different rules and deadlines; find the relevant state's site by internet search.

Climate Change Resource Center. "Seedlot Selection Tool." A web-based mapping application designed to help natural resource managers match seedlots with planting sites based on climatic information. US Forest Service, Oregon State University, Conservation Biology Institute, 2016. www.fs.usda.gov/ccrc/tool/seedlot-selection-tool.

Townsend, L. "Forest Stand Density Guide" [pdf]. Spokane, WA: USDA Natural Resource Conservation Service, 1982. bit.ly/standdensity.

Chapter 14: Working with Maturing Forests

Franklin, Jerry F., K. Norman Johnson, and Debora L. Johnson. *Ecological Forest Manage-*

ment. Long Grove, IL: Waveland Press, Inc., 2018.

Grotta, A. *Two-aged to Multi-aged Stand Management in the Coast Range*. Corvallis: Oregon State University Extension, 2018.

Kohm, Kathryn A., and Jerry F. Franklin. *Creating a Forestry for the 21st Century?: the Science of Ecosystem Management*. Washington, DC: Island Press, 1997.

Simard, Suzanne. *Finding the Mother Tree: Discovering the Wisdom of the Forest*. New York: Alfred A. Knopf, 2021.

Chapter 16: Wildfires and Risk Reduction

Agee, James K. "Fire regimes of the Pacific Northwest and Northern California." 2012. http://bit.ly/fire-regimes.

Greenberg, Cathryn H, and Beverly Collins. "Fire Ecology and Management in Pacific Northwest Forests." In *Fire Ecology and Management: Past, Present, and Future of US Forested Ecosystems*, Vol. 39. Cham, Switzerland: Springer International Publishing AG, 2021. doi:10.1007/978-3-030-73267-7_10.

Mathews, Daniel. *Trees in Trouble: Wildfires, Infestations, and Climate Change*. Berkeley: Counterpoint Press, 2020.

Chapter 17: Wildlife Habitat Enhancement

Kozloff, Eugene N. *Plants and Animals of the Pacific Northwest?: An Illustrated Guide to the Natural History of Western Oregon, Washington, and British Columbia*. Seattle: University of Washington Press, 1976.

Shewey, John, Tim Blount, and Hendrik G. Herlyn. *Birds of the Pacific Northwest*. Portland, OR: Timber Press, Inc., 2017.

Phone apps for identifying wildlife:

iNaturalist. A general plant and animals species identification app that includes natural ranges.

Merlin. Cornell Lab of Ornithology's app that allows you to identify bird species using recordings of songs and calls.

Chapter 18: Foraging in the Forest

San Juan National Forest Service. "Guidelines for the Ethical and Sustainable Harvesting of Wild Plants" [pdf]. https://bit.ly/sanjuansharvesting.

Gunther, Erna. *Ethnobotany of Western Washington*. Seattle: University of Washington Press, 1945.

Kimmerer, Robin Wall. *Braiding Sweetgrass*. Minneapolis: Milkweed Editions, 2013.

MacKinnon, A., Jim Pojar, and Paul B. Alaback. *Plants of the Pacific Northwest Coast: Washington, Oregon, British Columbia & Alaska*. Richmond, BC: Lone Pine Publishing, 1994.

Moore, Michael. *Medicinal Plants of the Pacific West*. Santa Fe: Red Crane Books, 1993.

Natural Resource Conservation Service. "Conservation Stewardship Program." A funding and technical assistance program that helps forest landowners implement various conservation activities in their woods, including ethnobotanical plantings. https://bit.ly/conservationstewardshipprogram.

Turner, Nancy J. *Food Plants of Coastal First Peoples*. Victoria: Royal BC Museum, 2006.

California Native Plant Society. "Policy on Ethics and Best Practices for Collecting Native Plants" [pdf]. 2020. https://bit.ly/bestpracticesharvesting.

Chapter 19: Harvest Planning and Management

Belart, F. and S. Bowers, "Small-Scale Harvesting for Woodland Owners" [online]. Corvallis: Oregon State University Extension Service, 2021. https://bit.ly/smallscaleharvesting.

Bowers, S. and J. Punches. "Selling Timber and Logs" [pdf]. Corvallis: Oregon State University Extension Service, 2007. https://catalog.extension.oregonstate.edu/ec1587.

Chapter 20: We Build the Trail by Walking

Birkby, Robert. *Lightly on the Land: The SCA Trail-Building and Maintenance Manual*. Seattle: Mountaineers Books, 1996.

Hesselbarth, Woody and Brian Vachowski. *Trail Construction and Maintenance Notebook*. Missoula: USDA Forest Service, Technology & Development Program, 1996.

International Mountain Biking Association. *Trail Solutions: IMBA's Guide to Building Sweet*

Singletrack. Boulder: International Mountain Bicycling Association, 2004.

Chapter 21: Committing Your Forest to a Higher Purpose

American Tree Farm System. Offers resources and certification for forest owners. https://bit.ly/americantreefarm.

Climate Smart Wood Group. A climate-smart wood sourcing group. www.climatesmartwood.net.

Coalition of Oregon Land Trusts Frequently Asked Questions. Offers information about land trusts and conservation easements. https://oregonlandtrusts.org/resources/faq.

Forest Stewardship Council® certification. Oversees FSC certification. https://us.fsc.org/en-us/certification.

US Forest Service Forest Stewardship Program. Provides information and guidance on forest stewardship. www.fs.usda.gov/managing-land/forest-stewardship/program.

Washington Association of Land Trusts. "Conservation Easements." Supports land trusts in Washington. https://walandtrusts.org/conservation-easements.

Chapter 22: Not Your Granddaddy's Climate

Lynch, Abigail J. et al. "RAD Adaptive Management for Transforming Ecosystems." In *BioScience*, Vol. 72, Issue 1. https://doi.org/10.1093/biosci/biab091.

Bonneville Environmental Foundation. "Treeline: Climate Resilience & Adaptation." A Pacific Northwest network on climate resilience and adaptation. www.b-e-f.org/treeline-climate-resilience-adaption.

Chapter 23: Succession Planning

Hollander, Stuart J., R. Hollander, and A. O'Connell. *Saving the Family Cottage: Creative Ways to Preserve Your Cottage, Cabin, Camp, or Vacation Home for Future Generations*, 6th ed. Berkeley: Nolo Press, 2021.

Oregon State University Extension. "Ties to the Land." Offers succession planning resources and workshops for landowners. https://tiestotheland.org.

PHOTO CREDITS

INDEX

Italics indicate visuals

ABOUT THE AUTHORS

Kirk Hanson is an experienced forest educator and practitioner who has worked on behalf of small woodland owners for more than 25 years. As a consulting forester, he brings a passion for ecological forestry and simplified hands-on management practices that allows forest owners to take a direct role in the stewardship of their own land. He frequently hosts workshops and teaches eco-forestry classes throughout the Northwest. A member of the Northwest Natural Resource Group (NNRG) team since 2006, Kirk serves as NNRG's director of forestry. He is a member of a three-generation family-owned forest and blogs about his own family's experiences managing 200 acres of forestland in western Washington at www.nnrg.org/hansonfamilyforest.

Seth Zuckerman has spent the last 30 years as a practitioner in West Coast forests and watersheds, and as a writer, telling the stories of people's relationships with the rest of the natural world. His writing on forests, salmon, and the human communities that depend on them has appeared in *The Nation, Sierra, Orion, The Christian Science Monitor,* and numerous other publications. His roots are in Northern California, where he directed the Wild and Working Lands program for the Mattole Restoration Council from 2006 to 2011. He came to the Northwest in 2013 in search of steadier precipitation and has served as executive director of NNRG since 2017.

ABOUT SKIPSTONE

Skipstone is an imprint of independent, nonprofit publisher Mountaineers Books. It features thematically related titles that promote a deeper connection to our natural world through sustainable practice and backyard activism. Our readers live smart, play well, and typically engage with the community around them. Skipstone guides explore healthy lifestyles and how an outdoor life relates to the well-being of our planet, as well as of our own neighborhoods. Sustainable foods and gardens; healthful living; realistic and doable conservation at home; modern aspirations for community—Skipstone tries to address such topics in ways that emphasize active living, local and grassroots practices, and a small footprint.

Our hope is that Skipstone books will inspire you to effect change without losing your sense of humor, to celebrate the freedom and generosity of a life outdoors, and to move forward with gentle leaps or breathtaking bounds.

All of our publications, as part of our 501(c)(3) nonprofit program, are made possible through the generosity of donors and through sales of 700 titles on outdoor recreation, sustainable lifestyle, and conservation. To donate, purchase books, or learn more, visit us online:

www.skipstonebooks.org
www.mountaineersbooks.org

SKIPSTONE

LIVE LIFE

MAKE RIPPLES

YOU MAY ALSO LIKE

   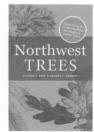